You Can Be A Hero Alone

Survival Stories for the Courageous Isolated Christian

With Easy Survey of Bible For Personal Worship & Meditation

Katheryn Maddox Haddad

You Can Be A Hero Alone

OTHER BOOKS BY THIS AUTHOR

HISTORICAL NOVELS & STORY BOOKS
Series of 8: They Met Jesus
Ongoing Series of 8: Intrepid Men of God
Mysteries of the Empire with Klaudius & Hektor
Series of 10: A Child's Life of Christ
Series of 10: A Child's Bible Heroes
Series of 8: A Child's Bible Kids

WORLDWIDE HISTORICAL RESEARCH FOR
DOCUMENTARY, THESIS, NOVEL & SCREENPLAY WRITERS

TOPICAL
Applied Christianity: Handbook 500 Good Works
Christianity or Islam? The Contrast
The Holy Spirit: 592 Verses Examined
Inside the Hearts of Bible Women-Reader+Audio+Leader
Revelation: A Love Letter From God
Worship Changes Since 1st Century + Worship 1sr Century Way
Was Jesus God? (Why Evil)
365 Life-Changing Scriptures Day by Date
The Road to Heaven
The Lord's Supper: 52 Readings with Prayers

RESTORATION REPRINT LIBRARY
Instrumental Music in the Public Worship of the [Presbyterian] Church, 1880
Best of Alexander Campbell's Millennial Harbinger, 1830-1839
Writings of and About Churches of Christ 14th to 17th Centuries England

FUN BOOKS
Bible Puzzles, Bible Song Book, Bible Numbers

TOUCHING GOD SERIES
365 Golden Bible Thoughts: God's Heart to Yours
365 Pearls of Wisdom: God's Soul to Yours
365 Silver-Winged Prayers: Your Spirit to God's

SURVEY SERIES: EASY BIBLE WORKBOOKS
→Old Testament & New Testament Surveys, →Questions You Have
Asked

GENEALOGY: CLIMB YOUR FAMILY TREE WITHOUT FALLING OUT
Volume I & 2: Beginner-Intermediate & Colonial-Medieval

My Dear Friend,

When you were younger, did you dream of being someone's hero? Did you dream of making a difference in the world?

Instead, do you feel like you are at a dead end and your dream will never happen? Has everything gone wrong (well, nearly everything)? Have you been stopped by barriers not your fault?

Do you feel ALL ALONE in this world with your faded dream?

COME ALONG WITH ME

In these pages are heroes who seemed like failures to the world and deserted by the world, perhaps forgotten, and left ALL ALONE. But, to God, they were heroes.

YOU, TOO, CAN BE A
HERO ALONE

It is natural during self-reflection and reaching a whole new appreciation for God that you will want to know him better, worship him, and meditate on him.

Therefore, at the back of the book is an easy survey of the Bible beginning with the birth, life, and death of Jesus, the misunderstood and...

Greatest
HERO ALONE
the world has ever seen.

OTHER BOOKS BY THIS AUTHOR 2
DEAR FRIEND....

YOU CAN BE A HERO ALONE....

LIKE NOAH 11
  Noah Is Different 12
  God Can Only Dwell With Good 13
  God Takes Care Of Noah's Heart Loneliness 13
  God Takes Care Of Noah's Physical Loneliness 14
  How Was Noah Able To Endure This Alone?............15

LIKE JOB 17
  He Looked Like a Monster 17
  A Form of Leprosy 18
  Deserted and Betrayed 18
  Depressed Beyond Endurance..................................19
  Job's Assignment 20
  Enduring to the End...21

LIKE ABRAHAM 23
  Legal Religion 24
  Stubborn Community..25
  Stubborn Family 25
  Breaking With The Family 27
  Leap Of Faith 28

LIKE JACOB..29
  Selfish Demands 29
  A Cheater..30
  A Family is Broken 31
  The Cheater Is Cheated 32
  He Demands Yet Another Blessing..........................32
  A Surprise Reunion 33
  His Descendants 34

LIKE JOSEPH..35

You Can Be A Hero Alone.................................5
From Rags To Riches And Back To Rags.................36
From Prisoner Or Warden 37
Forgotten By People, But Not By God 37
From Prison Or Palace.................38
Joseph's Own Dream Comes True 39
At Last: Family Reunion.................39

LIKE MOSES.................41
A Failed Prince 41
A Fugitive.................42
A Lost Cause.................43
Un-Convinced 44
THE RELUCTANT LEADER.................45

LIKE JOSHUA & CALEB.................47
Ready to Conquer.................47
But Giants? 48
We Can't Do It!.................49
Yes, We Can!.................50
A General.................50
A City for the King.................50

LIKE SAMUEL.................52
Boy Prophet 52
Defender Of The Holy Ark.................53
Defender Of The Faith 54
Rejected & Alone In A Crowd.................56

LIKE NAOMI.................57
Life In A Foreign Land 57
Marriage In A Foreign Land.................58
Death In A Foreign Land 59
Leaving The Foreign Land.................59
Bitterness 61

LIKE DAVID 63
Strong In Weakness 63
Writing His Thoughts And Prayers.................64
A Good But Hard Life 66

Eyes Only On God 67

LIKE MEPHIBOSHETH 70
  Boy King in Hiding 70
  A Promise Kept 71
  The Unexpected 71
  Betrayal 72
  Content, Even With Nothing 73

LIKE ELIJAH 74
  The King Didn't Like Him 74
  The Widow He Helped Didn't Like Him....................75
  The Prophets Didn't Like Him 75
  The Queen Didn't Like Him 77
  All alone? No! 77
  Ups And Downs...78
  One final "up"..78

LIKE JONAH 80
  He Refused to Forgive Mean People.........................81
  He Refused to Forgive Himself 81
  The Sailors Did Not Want Him 82
  The Great Fish Did Not Want Him 83
  God Forgave Jonah 83
  Jonah Obeyed With His Actions...............................84
  He Did Not Obey With His Heart..............................84
  God Used an Imperfect Man 85

LIKE JEREMIAH 86
  At Long Last, The Day Arrives.................................87
  Death Threats 88
  Prophecies Of Hope 88
  Ears That Would Not Hear.......................................89
  Doom And Rebirth...90

LIKE DANIEL & THREE FRIENDS 92
  Resentment Over Food 92
  Resentment Over A Statue.......................................93
  Resentment Over A Prayer.......................................94

LIKE ESTHER 97
  Beauty Queen 97
  Fearful Queen 99
  Triumphant Queen...101

LIKE MORDECAI..103
  The Slave Who Pulled Himself Up........................103
  He Stood Alone for what was Right.....................104
  When His Life was Threatened, He Stood Alone 105
  Respect Stood Where Hatred Failed.....................106

LIKE ANNA..108
  Age 23, Widowed And Moved To The Temple..........108
  Age 52 And Still At The Temple 110
  Age 84, And Finally The Savior Comes.................111

LIKE JOHN THE BAPTIST 113
  In Prison For His Beliefs.................................113
  Always Different...114
  Outspoken Challenger......................................115
  Reassurance 116
  Waiting And Praying.......................................116
  Dying For His Beliefs......................................117

LIKE EPANET...119
  The First And Only Christian............................119
  God's Assignment: Wait..................................120
  On Wings As An Eagle.....................................121
  The Dream At Last Fulfilled.............................122
  Not Weary In Well Doing..................................124

LIKE PAUL - I..125
  House Arrest..125
  What is that in your hand?...............................126
  Letter To Friends In Turkey 126
  Letter To Friends In Greece 127
  Letter To More Friends In Turkey 129
  Good Out Of Bad...130

LIKE LYDIA 131
  Hated For Being A Jew 131
  Clandestine Worship 132
  Then A Hated Christian..133
  True Amidst Persecution 135

LIKE AQUILA AND PRISCILLA 137
  The Turmoil Begins In Italy 137
  They Move To Greece..138
  They Move To Turkey 139
  They Move Back To Italy...141
  Peace Amid Turmoil 142

LIKE PAUL - II...143
  Released From Prison...143
  Goes Back To His Old Ways....................................144
  When He Was Weak, He Was Strong......................145
  Loyal To The Death 146
  Troublemaker And Hero 147

LIKE LUKE..149
  Slave & Physician...149
  Freedman...150
  Personal Physician of Paul.....................................150
  Historian..151
  Loyal to the End...152

LIKE JOHN 155
  Alone...155
  Prayer 156
  Song 157
  Words Of God...158
  Lord's Supper..159
  Alone But Not Alone 160

EASY SURVEY OF BIBLE FOR PERSONAL WORSHIP &
MEDITATION

Week 1   Birth & Adult Baptism of Jesus 164
Week 2   Famous Sermon On the Mountain) 167
Week 3   Selects 12 Apostles, Then Warns Them 171
Week 4   Farmers & a Judge 174
Week 5   John is Beheaded & a Storm is Stopped 177
Week 6   Children, Backsliders, Forgiveness 180
Week 7   How to Treat Your Family 183
Week 8   Enemies Try to Trap Jesus 186
Week 9   A Wedding, a Rich Man & a Judge 189
Week 10   John Baptist & Miracles 192
Week 11   Terrorist, Demon, Farmer, Light 196
Week 12   A Woman, a Little Girl & Rejection 200
Week 13   Legalists, Deafness, Demons 203
Week 14   Feeds 5000, Heals, Escapes Death 206
Week 15   Glowing, Voice from Heaven, Epileptic, ...210
Week 16   Miracle Baby John the Baptist) 214
Week 17   Agels, Shepherds, Miracle Baby Jesus 217
Week 18   Farming, Lamps, Woman & Dead Girl 221
Week 19   Training His 12, & a Hated Foreigner 225
Week 20   Fear, Wealth, Sudden End of World 228
Week 21   A Lost Sheep, Lost Coin, Lost Son 232
Week 22   A Dead Good Man & a Dead Bad Man 235
Week 23   Children, Bad Examples, End of World 238
Week 24   Self-righteous, Humble, & Blind 241
Week 25   A Tax Collector, the King, & Cheaters 245
Week 26   Words Become Flesh, God Arrives 249
Week 27   Reborn in Water & Spirit, Lamb of God 253
Week 28   Loved by Outcasts, Saves a Dying Boy 257
Week 29   1 with God, 2 Resurrections, 4 Proofs 261
Week 30   Walks on Water, is Bread of Life 264
Week 31   Guilty Person Trapped & Light of World 268
Week 32   A Man Born Blind &"Kill Jesus!" 272
Week 33   Bad Shepherd & Good Shepherd 275
Week 34   Returns Man to Life, ...278
Week 35   The Church Begins & 3000 Baptized 282
Week 36   5000 More Baptized, Apostles Arrested 286
Week 37   Church Grows, Apostles Imprisoned 289
Week 38   An Ethiopian & a Terrorist are Baptized ...292
Week 39   Christians are Beloved Children of God 295

Week 40   Love All & Obey Even Bad Rulers............. 298
Week 41   Love & Bodies Changed in Heaven............301
Week 42   How to Get Into Jesus & List of Sins.........305
Week 43   Saved from Hell, Alive in Jesus.................308
Week 44   In Prison for Jesus, Peace, Dying Now 311
Week 45   All are Saints, Jesus Emptied into Body ...315
Week 46   Chirstian Death & End of the World 318
Week 47   Only Church Officers & Warnings.............321
Week 48   God Changes Last Will & Testament 325
Week 49   The "Royal Law" & Treating Others...........329
Week 50   Persecution & The World Will Burn Up 332
Week 51   Loving & Not Loving. 336
Week 52   Visions of Heaven Seen by old John..........340

THANK YOU 345
CONNECT WITH THE AUTHOR 346
ABOUT THE AUTHOR 347

1

YOU CAN BE A HERO ALONE

LIKE NOAH

*And **ONLY** Noah was left,*
and those with him in the ark.
(Genesis 7:21c)

It seemed that Noah was a failure. By human standards he was. But by God's standards he was a hero.

Noah was the only one among his family members who believed in and followed Jehovah God. He was especially disappointed in his father, Lamech, and grandfather, Methuselah (Genesis 5:25-26).

It was a very lonely life for him in many ways. His relatives and even his friends and neighbors were always thinking of ways to give themselves power over other people, or make them feel good, or make them look richer than anyone else. Noah wasn't like that.

The Bible in Genesis chapter six, verse eight (6:8) says, *The Lord saw that people thought only about evil things all the time.* Remember, these were Noah's friends and relatives.

Not only were Noah's friends and relatives sinning all the time, but they liked doing it. Satan leads us to believe that, if we're having a good time when we do something, it cannot possibly be evil. Satan has always deceived people; he is like a dangerous wolf disguised as a gentle sheep (Matthew 7:15).

Noah Is Different

In Noah's time, people did know who God was, and good people were supposed to pray to him, worship him, and try to be like him. But Noah was the only one who even tried to be good.

While Noah's friends and relatives were bragging to each other how important they were, Noah was at home humbly praying to God, asking forgiveness for his sins, and promising to try to do better. While Noah's friends and relatives were pursuing sexual conquests, eating all the time, or making their bodies wonderful to look upon, Noah was quietly teaching his children to love and honor God, take care of the sick, and work for an honest living. While Noah's friends and relatives were building bigger and better houses, riding on faster animals than anyone else, and making fine clothing and jewelry, Noah was offering sacrifices of whatever he had in loving adoration for his Maker.

Genesis 6:11 explains, *God looked at the earth, and he saw that people had ruined it. Violence was everywhere—{people had become evil and cruel} and had ruined their life on earth.*

Noah's lifestyle and moral standards were definitely different than those around him. It wasn't any fun being different than other people. Those other people must have taunted Noah with sarcasm, calling him names and saying things to him like, "You think you're better than the rest of us!".

God Can Only Dwell With Good

All the bad things going on among people made God very sad and very angry. God is all goodness. Therefore, God cannot dwell with bad and still be God.

The Bible says God is Love. He created the world because Love must have someone to love. It is the same when people marry and have children. Parents do not have children so the children will admire them, but so the parents can have someone special to love. Parents have children knowing those children may turn against them some day. But parents long so much to love, that they have the children anyway. God is the same way. Love requires free will. God did not create people to be robots. If robots did good all the time and said they loved someone all the time, it wouldn't be true goodness and true love.

It broke God's heart to see everyone turn to evil all the time.   But there was a hero in this true story.

The Bible says in Genesis 6:8-9, *But there was one man on earth that pleased the Lord—Noah. Noah* *was a good man all his life. Noah always followed God.*

God decided to protect Noah and get him away from the evil people. How was that possible? By destroying everyone who purposely did evil all the time and enjoyed doing it. God decided to give the world a "bath", to flood the world and wash away its sins.

God Takes Care Of Noah's Heart Loneliness

Noah must have been very lonely with very few friends. Imagine what it is like to be the only one standing up for right while everyone else is mad at you for not being sinful like them.

Whenever Noah was around his relatives and friends talking about things they shouldn't, or doing things they shouldn't, or planning things that never should have entered their mind, Noah had two choices: (1) He could remain silent and feel left out. (2) He could speak out against what they were doing and be mocked.

As long as Noah remained silent, he remained lonely. So God took care of his loneliness by the only alternative: Talking. Heroes don't become heroes by doing nothing. They do not become heroes running from challenges.

Noah, a plain farmer and carpenter (Genesis 6:14-16 and Genesis 9:20) became a preacher, an imam, a rabbi, a priest, a monk, a prophet. II Peter 2:5 in the Bible explains, *Noah was a man who told people about living right.* Apparently, every spare moment Noah had, he preached. Did his friends and relatives like it? No. They didn't want to change their way of living. But Noah kept on preaching.

God Takes Care Of Noah's Physical Loneliness

God gave Noah a second thing to do to take care of his loneliness. He told Noah to build a very large boat, sometimes called an ark. It is all explained in Genesis 6:12-13, 14-17, 18:

So God said to Noah, "All people have filled the earth with anger and violence. So I will destroy all living things. I will remove them from the earth. Use cypress wood and build a boat for yourself. Make rooms in the boat, and cover the boat with tar.

"This is the size I want you to make the boat: 300 cubits long, 50 cubits* wide, and 30 cubits* high. Make a window for the boat about 18 inches* below the roof.* Put a door in the side of the boat. Make three floors in the boat; a top deck, a middle deck, and a lower deck.*

"Understand what I am telling you. I will bring a great flood of water on the earth. I will destroy all living things that live under heaven. Everything on the earth will die. I will make a special agreement with you. And you, your sons, your wife, and your sons' wives will all go into the boat.

Can you imagine how much Noah's neighbors must have made fun of Noah building a huge boat far away from any large body of water? His sons must have been made fun of at school. His wife must have been made fun of at the market. But they stayed physically busy and it helped get their minds off the bad way people treated them.

How Was Noah Able To Endure This Alone?

God did not give Noah time to brood and feel sorry for himself. He put him to work preaching and building, preaching and building, preaching and building. It took Noah 100 years to build his big boat, and during that time he preached to his neighbors, his friends, his relatives.

Did they like someone preaching to them all the time? Of course not. Did Noah like it when they insulted him in order to get him to stop? No. He must have gone to bed many a night week after week, month after month, year after year feeling like a failure.

But he couldn't stop. Why? Because God loved everyone in the world and did not want to see any of them perish. Noah loved whoever God loved ~ Noah's neighbors, friends and relatives. His love was so strong, nothing could stop him from going to them over and over begging them to change their ways. Their insults hurt, of course, but he kept going back to them. Oh, how God loved these evil people and wanted them to change; God did not want to destroy them. Oh, how Noah loved these people and wanted them to change; Noah did not want God to destroy them.

Eventually, after giving everyone chance after chance after chance to escape death, the cleansing had to come. For righteous Noah's good, the cleansing had to come. After all, Noah was just human. God needed to protect him and help him. So, he sent the flood to destroy everyone who was not on the boat. Only Noah and his family went into the boat.

Noah endured because of love: Love for God and love for others. His heart never centered on himself and the rejection he felt. Because of this, after the flood, Noah's family went out and repopulated the earth. Because of Noah's faith, mankind got another chance. Rejected Noah was a hero.

2

YOU CAN BE A HERO ALONE

LIKE JOB

I despise my life; I would not live forever.
*Let me **ALONE**; my days have no meaning.*
(Job 7:16)

It seemed that Job was a failure. By human standards he was. But by God's standards he was a hero.

Never in Job's wildest dreams did he think he would ever have to face seemingly unlimited calamities. He lost his income, then his children died in an accident, and finally he was stricken with a terrible illness. He could not leave his home. Day after day, month after month, he was confined to his home as he became sicker and sicker, and increasingly depressed.

He Looked Like a Monster

The Bible says he was full of boils from head to foot. Just one boil is enough to make a person sick. But boils everywhere must have taxed Job's endurance to the limit. Probably he was even unable to wear clothes. He sat on the ground with a piece of pottery scraping the boils, but since they were coming from within his body, he could not stop them from growing. He was so sick that, when his old friends came to see him on his sick bed, they didn't recognize him. (See Job 2:7, 8, 12).

   Job had become so thin, his bones stuck out and he said "My bones are pierced in me in the night." He complained that his body is covered with scabs and worms and his skin broken and festering. (Job 7:4,5; 30:17). And yet parts of him were swelled so much that his garments bound him if he tried to wear them. His skin was black, his bones burned, and his digestive system boiled. (See Job 30:17, 18, 27-30.)

   His breath tasted terrible and his voice was changed to similar to that of an owl, and he claimed he looked like a dragon. (See Job 17:1; 30:30-31).

A Form of Leprosy

   It is believed that Job had a form of leprosy called elephantiasis, the most terrible form of leprosy. He felt intense heat within and burning and ulcerous swelling. His body was covered with knotty, cancerous bark like the hide of an elephant (perhaps what he was referring to when he called himself a dragon).

   Although the ulcers (boils) normally attack the limbs, the worst forms attack the entire body. The ulcers are very inflamed and sometimes discharge a white fluid which burns, irritates and has a terrible odor. They attract maggots. The deep burning sensations are worse at night and can even lead to nightmares.

Deserted and Betrayed

He looked and smelled so bad, even his relatives and friends didn't come see him. He'd send for a servant, but none would come help him. Even his wife and brothers found his breath loathsome. And little children made fun of him.

Three friends came to see him from other kingdoms and when they saw him he didn't recognize him (Job 2:12). Then, when they began to talk to him, they continually accused him of offending God, resulting in God punishing him.

Job replied to them sarcastically, "Doubtless you are the people, and wisdom will die with you! But I have a mind as well as you; I am not inferior to you" (Job 12:1-2). When another spoke, trying to get him to admit whatever sin he was committing that was making God so mad, he replied, "Miserable comforters are you all! Will your long-[winded speeches never end? What ails you that you keep on arguing?" (Job 16:1-2).

After another friend gave another "long-winded speech", Job replied, "How long will you torment me and crush me with words? Ten times now you have reproached me; shamelessly you attack me. Have pity on me, many friends, have pity, for the hand of God has struck me." (Job 19:1-3).

Depressed Beyond Endurance

All Job wanted to do is die. "Why did I not perish at birth, and die as I came from the womb? If only my anguish could be weighed. What strength do I have that I should still hope? Therefore I will not keep silent, I will speak out in the anguish of my spirit. I will complain in the bitterness of my soul. I loathe my very life. If only I had never come into being, or had been carried straight from the womb to the grave. My face is red with weeping, deep shadows ring my eyes. Even today my complaint is bitter, his hand is heavy in spite of my groaning" (Job 3:11; 6:2,11; 7:11; 10:1,19; 16:18; 23:2).

He even had a love-hate relationship with God. "If I have sinned, what have I done to you, O watcher of men? Why have you made me your target? Have I become a burden to you? I will say to God: do not condemn me, but tell me what charges you have against me. Does it please you to oppress me, to spurn the work of your hands, while you smile on the schemes of the wicked? Remember that you molded me like clay. Will you now turn me to dust again? Though he slay me, yet will I hope in him; I will surely defend my ways to his face" (Job 7:20; 10:2-3,8; 13:15).

"I know that my Redeemer lives, and that in the end he will stand upon the earth. And after my skin has been destroyed, yet in my flesh I will see God; I myself will see him with my own eyes – I, and not another. How my heart yearns within me!" (Job 19:25-27).

Job's Assignment

Unbeknown to Job, this was Job's assignment. God did not consult Job first. It was up to Job to maintain faith in God when he was physically and mentally at a breaking point.

One day, Satan was in heaven confronting God. Remember, Satan wants to be God, and so is God's arch enemy. With the angels gathered around, Satan once again confronted God. God bragged on Job, but Satan is the Great Accuser (Revelation 12:10). Satan said Job would blame God if things went bad in his life. God said he would step back and let Satan do whatever he wanted to Job except take his life, but Job's faith in God would never waiver. (See Job, chapter 1).

Were God and Satan playing games with each other, using Job as a pawn in their game? No. Job was a good man, but God knew he would come out of his ordeal stronger than ever.

When Job lost his income and his children, Job replied, "Naked I came from my mother's womb, and naked I will depart. The Lord gave and the Lord has taken away. May the name of the Lord be praised" (Job 1:21). The Bible says that Job never charged God with any wrong doing. When Satan attacked Job with his terrible disease, he said Job would curse God (Job 2:4). But it didn't happen.

Job may have come close, but just as he would start blaming God for something, he would turn right around and praise God. Throughout his ordeal, he just wanted to talk to God. He wanted God to explain what was going on and why God was "picking on him". Finally God did speak to Job. He never explained what was happening, but he did ask Job many scientific questions that Job could not answer.

Enduring to the End

In the end, Job became a better person. "Surely I spoke of things I did not understand, things too wonderful for me to know. My ears had heard of you, but now my eyes have seen you" (Job 42:3b, 5). Because of what Job suffered, he now saw and understood God with new spiritual eyes.

Eventually, Job did recover. But he had learned a big lesson. It is explained in Ephesians 6:12, "For our struggle is not against flesh and blood, but against the rulers, against the authorities, against the powers of this dark world and against the spiritual forces of evil in the heavenly realms."

To Job's family and friends, he was a man who was being punished by God. In fact, his friends occasionally considered themselves God's spokesmen. They believed Job deserved to be punished, and his illness would go away if he admitted his sin and repented. To them, Job was suffering justly. But Job never spoke for God. He observed things about God and questioned God and asked to state his case before God, but he never spoke for God. Far from being the great sinner his friends considered him, to be, n God's eyes and in the eyes of us today, Job was a hero.

3

YOU CAN BE A HERO ALONE

LIKE ABRAHAM

*Leave your country, your people and your father's household
and go [**ALONE**] to the land I will show you.
(Genesis 12:1)*

It seemed that Abraham was a failure. By human standards he was. But by God's standards he was a hero.

Abraham started out in life with everything in his favor. He came from a powerful and well-known family led by his father, Terah. A city was named after one of Terah's sons, Haran, who died as a fairly young family man.

Outsiders intermarrying with Terah's family could possibly weaken them. By making sure family members married each other, Terah, the father of Haran, Nahor and Abraham, could maintain strong control over his family.   Also, the family ties would remain strong.

Apparently Terah wanted to make sure his family remained strong. Terah's son, Nahor, married Terah's grand daughter. Also, Terah's son, Abraham, married his other wife's daughter, Abraham's half-sister. (Read Genesis 11: 26-30). Such close family marriages were not illegal or immoral thousands of years ago when these things happened.

Abraham grew up in the city of Ur in today's Iraq. In Abraham's time, the Persian Gulf went further north than it does today, and Ur was a seaport on that gulf. Ur was a very important and powerful place in which Terah's important and powerful family lived.

Legal Religion

Abraham's family was also very religious. Abraham's father, Terah, worshipped as he had been taught and which had always been accepted in his homeland (Joshua 24:2).

History books tell us that the ruler of their land told everyone what to believe. People had to obey their ruler. Therefore, it was illegal to believe in any other religion than that which the government endorsed. If people did not believe in the chosen religion, they could be imprisoned and even executed as apostates, infidels and traitors.

There was a famous place of worship in Ur. Everyone went to it. Just because all the citizens of a nation follow the same religion, that does not make the religion true. Just because a religion is selected by a government, that does not make the religion true.

Even today, people growing up in one part of the

world are told one religion is true, and people growing up in a different part of the world are told a different religion is true. Just because someone is told all his life a certain religion is true, and everyone in his homeland believes it, that does not make it true.

Stubborn Community

We do not know how long Abraham followed the religion of his homeland and his family. All we know is that, while living in Ur, he learned about the one God who had created the world, and apparently believed in him and tried to worship him.

Did Abraham try to worship in secret at first so his neighbors wouldn't pressure him to worship the same way they did? Did he later get up his courage and begin to explain the one true God to his friends and neighbors? How did they treat him? Did they laugh at him, scorn him, call him an apostate? Did they report him to their religious leaders?

Worse still, did his friends and relatives threatened to report him to the government and have him arrested for not worshiping the legal way?

What a life of turmoil! It would have been much easier for Abraham to give up his new religion and conform to his friends, his family, and his government.

But how could he? How could Abraham give up his faith in and love for the one true God? What turmoil and emotional agony he must have gone through.

Stubborn Family

Then, when Abraham's nieces and nephews were grown and married, God came to Abraham and told him to leave Ur and go to a land he would show him. (See Acts 7:3-4a.) Perhaps Abraham was around 50 years old by this time. He must have been so relieved. The one true God had actually appeared to him and reassured him that he would guide him to an easier life.

Father Terah did not believe in the one true God. Abraham tried to convince his father, but his father was stubborn and would not change his beliefs. Terah had been taught all his life to believe something different. Terah would not shame the family by leaving the religion of the kingdom.

What about the move? Would Terah at least agree to leave Ur? Father and son must have discussed this day after day, week after week, perhaps month after month. Finally, to his great relief, Abraham apparently convinced his father to leave Ur.

Next Abraham tried to convince his father to go west to the land God promised him. But his father decided to go to a city of his own choosing instead of the land Abraham told him about. He wanted to go north to Haran, the city named after Terah's deceased son, Abraham's brother.

What choice did Abraham have? Should Abraham stay behind in Ur to get away from his father's strong influence? In that case, he'd still be around all his neighbors and the government that insisted he worship the way all good citizens were ordered to worship.   Besides, God had told him to leave Ur.

Terah, who was head of his powerful family, insisted that Abraham obey him. Perhaps, out of loyalty to his father, Abraham finally gave in with a compromise. They would leave Ur, but they wouldn't go to the land in the west. They would go north. So, Abraham followed God's command to leave Ur. He obeyed half of what God told him to.

Breaking With The Family

At first, Abraham, along with his father, Terah, and the entire family, left Ur and went to Haran in today's northern Iraq.

We do not know how long Abraham lived in Haran. He and his family must have been very important in this city named after Abraham's deceased brother. Perhaps they were part of the ruling family. While in Haran, Abraham had accumulated many possessions and servants (Genesis 12:5). He had become rich.

But surely Abraham's heart was full of turmoil. Was compromise enough? He continued to secretly worship the one true God. He did not want the wrath of his father.

One night, God appeared to Abraham again, and once more told him to go west to a land he would show him, a land that his descendants would inherit some day. The Lord said to Abram, *Leave your country and your people. Leave your father's family and go to the country I will show you.* (Genesis 12:1).

Abraham continued to be torn. He had to make a choice. He had to choose between obligations to his family and city named after a family member, or a new land somewhere to the west. God had promised he would make a new nation from his descendants, even though Abraham was old and didn't have any children (Genesis 17).

Still, he didn't have anyone to worship with other than is wife. His nephew, Lot, seemed to be coming along and believing in the one true God. But he longed to be with others who believed as he did. How lonely it was without others.

Leap Of Faith

Abraham finally made his decision. The people he left behind in Haran must have thought he was out of his mind, crazy. After all, he was leaving behind his influential name, probably a big fancy house, and his important place in society. When asked where he was going, Abraham couldn't tell them. All he knew is that he was headed west, and somehow God would bless his efforts.

He took his wife, his deceased brother's son, Lot, and all his possessions, and left Haran. He wanted to establish a place where he could openly worship the one true God, and where he could teach and convince others to do the same. He longed for the day when not only his family, but his community and eventually an entire nation would worship God. Could he, just one man, accomplish so much?

Abraham walked into the unknown. His friends and family considered him an apostate, a traitor, and a deserter. Hundreds of years later, we consider him a hero.

4

YOU CAN BE A HERO ALONE
LIKE JACOB

*So, Jacob was left **ALONE.***
(Genesis 32:24a)

It seemed that Jacob was a failure. By human standards he was. But by God's standards he was a hero.

He had always been a trouble maker. He was the second born of twins and hated the idea. He wanted to be first. In everything he had to be first, even if he didn't deserve to be first. It was just the idea of being first that appealed to Jacob. It was the thrill of being first, on top, the best, the greatest, the richest, the most important.

What Jacob resented most about his twin brother was the few minutes between his brother's birth and his own. That few minutes cost Jacob everything. Everything!

Selfish Demands

Picked fights with his twin brother all the time.
His brother had brawn – a mighty hunter prowling the

forest for meat. But Jacob – the spindly guy who settled for farming - was the one with the brains. And he knew how to use them. The key was patience and staying alert like a panther waiting for its prey. Finally, he got his chance.

His brother had been out in the forest hunting game, stayed longer than he should, came back home exhausted and spotted Jacob. Jacob had just finished cooking up a big batch of stew. Esau smelled the aroma and asked his brother to share some of his stew with him. Jacob refused. "All I want is one spoon full." Jacob refused. "But I'm about to die of starvation!"

Ah-ha!. Jacob knew how to spot someone's weak point and he saw his chance to be better than his brother. "Well, I won't let you have any of my stew, but I will sell it to you."

"Name your price. I'm about to die!"

"Give me your rights as first born, and the stew is yours," Jacob said. "No!" Esau said. "Well, it won't do you any good dead. You yourself said you were about to die," Jacob said.

His brother relented, but that wasn't enough for shrewd Jacob. "Swear it!" In desperation, Esau swore it. Then Jacob not only gave him all the stew he wanted, but he threw in bread to sop in it

He is so dumb, Jacob must have thought. Now with his brother's rights as first born, Jacob was a rich man. When their father died, Jacob would get all the family wealth. (Genesis 25:21-34)

A Cheater

How he hated anyone who was bigger, better,

faster than him – and that described his twin brother.
And more popular. That's the thing that got to him the
most. His brother was the favorite of their father, Isaac.
He would do anything to change that. Anything.
Always he watched for his chance. And one day it came.

It may be that Jacob and his brother kept the
birthright thing a secret between them. Jacob's mother
did not seem to know about it. She wanted to even
things out between her twin sins. On that fateful day,
their mother overheard their father telling Jacob's twin
to go out and hunt some fresh game and cook like he
loved it. Then, as soon as he was done eating it, he
would give Jacob's twin his final blessing, kind of like
an oral last will and testament.

Jacob's mother rushed to Jacob, told him about
it, and urged him to pretend he was Esau so he would
get the blessing instead of his twin brother. All he had
to do is dress like his brother and their blind father
would not know the difference. And their mother said
she would cook a young goat the way Jacob's brother
always cooked his meat.

A Family is Broken

Jacob was shrewd, but not stupid. He objected to
the whole thing, but their mother insisted it would
work. Finally, she said, "If your father curses you
instead of blesses you, I will take the curse onto myself.
(Genesis 27:13). Little did she know.

So Jacob carried out their mother's plan and got
the special blessing intended for the firstborn. (Genesis
27:30-40)

"I'm going to kill that Jacob!" Esau shouted when
he found out. "I'm going to kill him!" The family rift had
finally come. Their mother told Jacob to go up to

Turkey and hide there with her brother. Jacob did.
He was alone away from his family for twenty years.
When he finally took a chance and returned home, he
went to see his father, but not his mother. She had
apparently died, and so the curse meant for Jacob was
carried out by his mother.

The Cheater Is Cheated

While with his uncle up in Turkey, Jacob fell in
love, and her father agreed to let Jacob marry her by
working 7 years for him free. But on the wedding night,
the father switched things and Jacob married the
bride's sister instead. Jacob demanded justice. So his
uncle said he could marry his daughter who Jacob
really loved by working for him another 7 years – 14
years total. (Genesis 29:16-29 & 21-27).

Still the cheating did not stop – this time Jacob
being the victim. Over a total of 20 years, his uncle
reduced his wages ten times. In addition to serving his
uncle 14 years for his two wives, he had to serve him
another six years to become the owner of the flocks
Jacob had taken care of. So his uncle grew richer and
richer. He knew his uncle would never let him leave.
(Genesis 31:38-42) But God appeared to him in a
dream. Jacob had apparently learned his lesson, for
God told him to go back home. (Genesis 31:3)

He Demands Yet Another Blessing

Jacob feared his brother, remembering his
promise twenty years earlier to kill him. Jacob knew he
deserved it, for he had gotten his brother's birthright
and blessing. But he could no longer suffer abuse under
the hand of his uncle. So he took God's advice and
headed for home anyway. As soon as he got out of
Turkey and Syria, he saw something no one else did.
He saw angels everywhere as though they were camping

there.

Then he sent messengers to his brother saying he had all the flocks and herds he needed. In other words, he didn't need his brother's birthright and blessing anymore. But, when the messengers returned and said Esau was coming to him with 400 men, Jacob feared his brother even more.

So Jacob sent his brother 200 female goats, 20 male goats, 200 ewes, 20 rams, 30 camels, 40 cows, 10 bulls, 20 female donkeys 10 male donkeys as a peace offering. Then he sent his own herds, his servants, and finally also his family on ahead.

Now, Jacob was all alone in the place where he had seen the angels. And he waited. Who would come to him first? The Lord or his feared brother? The Lord came and knocked Jacob over. Jacob got up and a wrestling match began that lasted all night. Why? Why would Jacob wrestle with God who had apparently materialized as a man?

Jacob no longer needed or wanted the blessing of a man. He needed a blessing from God. And that is when God changed Jacob's name to Isra-el – Prince of God. (Genesis 32)

A Surprise Reunion

As much as Jacob – er, uh, Israel, feared his brother, he continued on praying that God's blessing would prevail. Then the brothers who had once hated each other spotted each other in the distance. Immediately, Israel began bowing himself to the ground as he drew closer to his twin brother. Seven times he bowed to the ground. And how did Esau respond? With a sword? No, he ran to meet his younger brother and they embraced in love. Stubborn love that always seems to have been there, but hidden until it was almost too late.

His Descendants

   This man, Israel, had 12 sons who ended up in slavery. But his sons had such large families, people called them tribes. Four centuries later, they are freed and become a nation – the nation of Israel. (Exodus) And about 1500 years after this twin had been born, a man (the one he had wrestled?) came to earth as one of his descendants. His name was Jesus. (Matthew 1:1-2)

   The man, Israel, had deserved to be punished and he knew he deserved it. For a long time, Jacob was a loser in every sense of the word. But he was not a quitter. God saw a stubborn determination in him, once used for the wrong things, and used him for the right things. And today, when we think of Israel, we think of him as a hero.

5

YOU CAN BE A HERO ALONE
LIKE JOSEPH

However, he did not remember Joseph.
*He forgot him [all **ALONE**].*
(Genesis 40:23b)

It seemed that Joseph was a failure. By human standards he was. But by God's standards he was a hero.

He was a teenager and his father's favorite son and very spoiled. His older brothers resented him for it and were jealous of him. Joseph's father gave him a richly ornamented coat which made his brothers even more jealous; so much so, that the Bible says *they hated him and could not speak a kind word to him* (Genesis 37:4). But he was so guileless, when they spoke mean to him, he would think they were just having a bad day or were just joking. He always spoke well of his brothers, and because of his guileless nature, sometimes he talked to his father about something they had done, not realizing their father had told him older brothers not to do it. He never purposely hurt his brothers.

He was so guileless that, when he reported to his brothers that he had dreamed twice that they and even his father and mother bowed down to him, he thought it was just a silly dream. But it just made them madder. So, when Joseph was 17, his brothers decided to kill him. But they changed their mind and sold him to a slave trader in a caravan headed for Egypt. They kept his ornamental robe, dipped it in animal blood, and told their father a wild animal had killed Joseph. (Read about all this in Genesis 37). Meanwhile, in the caravan, teenaged Joseph was all alone with no more family, and no more friends. All alone.

From Rags To Riches And Back To Rags

When the caravan finally got to Egypt, Joseph was sold as a slave to the commander of Pharaoh's army. Did Joseph become bitter? No, Joseph continued to be guileless and to do whatever he could for his new master. So God blessed everything he did. Finally, his master put Joseph in charge of his entire household, not withholding anything from him but his wife.

But there was one problem. The commander's wife fell in love with Joseph. One day she sent all the slaves out of the house and tried to entice Joseph to her bed. He was young and handsome. She grabbed hold of his cloak and tried to pull it off of him. But Joseph ran out of the house away from temptation.

This made the commander's wife so angry that she screamed and claimed he had tried to molest her, using as proof his cloak he had left in her hands when he fled. Of course, she also told her husband, and her husband had Joseph stripped of all privileges and put in prison. With his feet shackled and his neck in irons (Psalm 105:17-22). Joseph by now was in his twenties.

From Prisoner Or Warden

Once again, Joseph could have become bitter and resentful. He could have sat in a corner of his cell and destroyed himself with hatred for how unfair life was being to him. Years of wondering if he would ever get out alive. Years of eating prison food and sitting in a smelly, dark cell behind bars.

But, being guileless, Joseph tried once again to turn a bad situation into a good one. He began speaking decently to the prison guards and asking about their families. He began passing on to the guards some of the concerns of the other prisoners, explaining that, if they were helped, they would probably be more cooperative and less trouble to the guards.

Pretty soon the warden handed over some responsibilities to Joseph. Eventually, the warden let Joseph pretty much take over the control of the prison. He never usurped his authority. He just wanted everyone to try to be content with their present situation It seems impossible in a prison situation where there is so much hatred, but God was with Joseph and gave him wisdom, and this helped the others want to be Joseph's friend. (See Genesis 40.)

Forgotten By People, But Not By God

One day Pharaoh's cup bearer arrived as a prisoner. The cup bearer is the one who guards royalty from being poisoned, always taking a sip of whatever was in their cup first. One day the cup bearer had a strange dream. Joseph understood it to mean that, in three days, he would be restored to his former position.

Joseph asked the man to remember him to Pharaoh and tell Pharaoh he was innocent of all charges. Sure enough, in three days, the cup bearer

was restored to his former position. But he forgot.
Did Joseph become bitter? No.

Another official of Pharaoh was also in the prison:
Pharaoh's baker. They obviously knew someone was
trying to kill Pharaoh, but could not find out who.
Soon, the baker had a strange dream. God was with
Joseph and helped him interpret it. He predicted that
in three days, the baker would be hung, and this is
what happened. But Joseph remained in prison. Did
he become bitter? No. God blessed everything he did
and kept his courage up. Joseph was now 28 years old.
(See Genesis 40, especially 40:23; 41:1,46.)

From Prison Or Palace

Pharaoh's birthday arrived, and he had two
strange dreams. Pharaoh sent for every wise man in his
kingdom he thought could interpret his dreams, but no
one could. Then his cup bearer remembered his
promise to Joseph. Desperately, Pharaoh sent for
Joseph. Of course, he was washed good, deodorized,
shaved and given decent clothes to wear.

When Pharaoh told Joseph he heard he could
interpret dreams, he said he could not., but God could.
He explained that there would be seven years when
crops would flourish throughout Egypt. But they would
be followed by seven years of famine everywhere.

Notice, when Joseph met Pharaoh, he did not
complain. He didn't say anything about being sold
unfairly as a slave., or being falsely accused of
molesting the commander's wife, or being forgotten by
the cupbearer for two whole years while Joseph
languished in prison.

Because of his positive attitude, Pharaoh put
Joseph *in charge of the whole land of Egypt.* He even

put his signet ring on Joseph's finger and dressed
him in royal robes and a gold chain. And, whenever
Pharaoh went out among his people, Joseph was in the
second chariot right behind Pharaoh. Joseph settled in
a place called On, but today is called Cairo. He was
now thirty years old. (See Genesis 41.)

Joseph's Own Dream Comes True

The famine finally hit, and it covered the whole
world. Joseph was now 40 years old (Genesis 41:53-54;
42:3,8). When Joseph's father, Israel, heard that Egypt
had food for sale, he sent his ten oldest sons to Egypt to
buy enough for his family. As soon as Joseph saw
them, he recognized them. But they didn't recognize
him because he had changed so much.

His brothers returned to their father, Israel, but
finally ran out of food again, and had to return to Egypt.
This time they came with their youngest brother,
Benjamin, even younger than Joseph. They were taken
to Joseph's house. When they were presented to Joseph
this time, they brought gifts and they all bowed down to
their brother, just as Joseph's own dreams had
predicted would happen so long ago in his youth. (See
Genesis 43 and 44.)

At Last: Family Reunion

Joseph was now 32 years old. (Genesis 45:6).
Once again, when Joseph's brothers arrived, he ordered
that they meet him at his house. But this time it was
different. He planned for them to eat with them. To
their surprise, he had them seated in order of age.

They ate their meal while Joseph pretended he
was just an Egyptian prince. But eventually he could
control himself no longer. He ordered all his servants to
leave. Then, there alone with his eleven brothers,

Joseph announced, "I am Joseph, your brother! Is father still alive? Come to me! Come! Don't be afraid of me! It was to save your life that God sent me into Egypt ahead of you! It was not you who sent me into Egypt, but God!"

Then Joseph sent his brothers back to get their father, and wives and children. When they returned, beloved Israel, who had thought for fifteen years that his son, Joseph, was dead, was reunited with his beloved son, whom he bowed down to as predicted in the dream, and then embraced.

Pharaoh gave the section of Egypt called Goshen to Joseph's family. Seventy family members entered Egypt. Many years later they will leave, and there will be over three million of them. And they will be ready to begin the great nation of Israel.

Joseph endured all the loneliness and betrayals and lies about him because he refused to be bitter. He refused to destroy himself in order to punish others. He endured the unendurable. And so, today, we consider Joseph our hero.

6

YOU CAN BE A HERO ALONE
LIKE MOSES

*What if they do not believe me [**ALONE**]*
*or listen to me [**ALONE**]?*
(Exodus 4:1b)

It seemed that Moses was a failure. By human standards he was. But by God's standards he was a hero....

A Failed Prince

The one thing he always knew is that he was a born leader. Raised in Pharaoh's palace, he had the best education and the best opportunities to lead his country to greater things. Acts 7:22 says, *The Egyptians taught Moses about all the things they knew. He was powerful in the things he said and did.*

When he was grown, his half-brother became Pharaoh. Moses was a prince. He was royalty. He was a born leader and intended to do just that ~ lead. But it did not last. His life was about to take a down turn.

One day Prince Moses went out among the slaves because they were his own nationality. He wanted them treated fairly, but found they were being badly mistreated. He defended them by killing the worst of their cruel task masters (Exodus 1:12). For some reason, Pharaoh did not like Prince Moses. Perhaps he was afraid Moses would take the throne from him some day. So, when Pharaoh heard what Moses had done to the cruel task master, it was his excuse to kill him. Moses fled Egypt (Exodus 1:15).

All of this confused Moses. He thought he had been doing the will of God. He thought God was using him to help the slaves.   (Read Acts 7:23-25).   Why were things going so wrong? He was just trying to be a good leader. Now he was no leader at all. In fact, he was no longer a prince.

A Fugitive

Moses was now a commoner. He was also a fugitive, someone the authorities back in Egypt were looking for so they could execute him. He went to a country called Media, an arid and hilly wilderness. Surely he wouldn't be found there.

But, being a born leader, Moses could not be held down long. He still could not resist taking the lead to help others whenever he saw the need. One day he saw some maidens at a well trying to water their sheep, and some male shepherds scaring them off. Single handedly, strong Moses drove away all the shepherds. Then he watered the maidens' sheep for them.

In gratitude, their father gave Moses one of his daughters to marry. They had a son. Exodus 2:22 says *Moses named him Gershom. Moses gave his son this name because Moses was a stranger in a land that was not his own.*

His heart ached. He was exiled from his birth

home, his family, his countrymen, everyone and everything he had known.

Then he became a shepherd. For forty long years, Moses wandered the wilderness of Media, his only followers being dumb sheep. He knew he could lead, but there was no one to lead. His father-in-law was a local priest and did not believe in the one God ~ Yahweh (Exodus 2:16; 18:11) and it seems Moses was never able to convince his wife to be a believer either (Exodus 4:25-26). Moses spent forty long years with no one to lead, whether politically, socially, or religiously. Further, he had no one to worship with. What a failure!

A Lost Cause

As time slowly passed during those forty years, Moses gradually lost all his self-confidence. He must have decided he had misunderstood God. God could not possibly use someone like him to lead his people out of slavery. But one day something strange happened. God actually spoke to him out of a burning bush. How did Moses react? He began to argue with God. Surely God was wrong. Moses could not lead his people. Let's listen in as they speak to each other in Exodus 3:10-14 ~

10So now I am sending you to Pharaoh. Go! Lead my people, the people of Israel, out of Egypt!"
*11***BUT** *Moses said to God, "I am not a great man! How can I be the person to go to Pharaoh and lead the people of Israel out of Egypt?"*
12God said, "You can do it because I will be with you! This will be the proof that I am sending you: After you lead the people out of Egypt, you will come and worship me on this mountain!"
*13Then Moses said to God, "***BUT** *if I go to the people of Israel and say to them, 'The God of your ancestors* sent me,' then the people will ask, 'What is his name?' What*

should I tell them?"
14*Then God said to Moses, "{Tell them,} 'I AM WHO I AM.'*
{YAHWEH} When you go to the people of Israel, tell them,
'I AM' {YAHWEH} sent me to you."

Still Moses argued, still convinced he could no longer lead his people. Moses continues to say **BUT** this won't work. **BUT** that won't work. Exodus 4:1 says, *Then Moses said to God, "***BUT*** the people of Israel will not believe me when I tell them that you sent me. They will say, 'The Lord did not appear to you.'"* So God showed him how to perform two miracles.

Moses continued to argue with God, no longer convinced God could use him. Let's listen in on some more of their discussion in Exodus 4:10-13 ~

10**BUT** *Moses said to the Lord, "***BUT*** Lord, I am telling you the truth, I am not a skilled speaker. I have never been able to speak well. And now, even after talking to you, I am still not a good speaker. You know that I talk slowly and don't use the best words."*
11*Then the Lord said to him, "Who made a person's mouth? And who can make a person deaf or not able to speak? Who can make a person blind? Who can make a person able to see? {I am the One who can do all these things—} I am YAHWEH.*
12*So go. I will be with you when you speak. I will give you the words to say."*
13**BUT** *Moses said, "My Lord, I beg you to send another person—not me."*

Eventually God was able to convince Moses. How? By sending him an encourager ~ his younger brother whom he hadn't seen in forty years ~ Aaron.

Un-Convinced

Moses' brother, Aaron, sneaked out of Egypt and met him on a wilderness mountain in Midian. Aaron had been a slave all his life. But it was now the slave who had to encourage the prince. Together they turned and walked in the direction of Egypt. (Read about it in Exodus 4:27-31.)

When they got to Egypt, they demanded that Pharaoh free the slaves. Of course he didn't. This was a new Pharaoh who probably had never even met Moses. Pharaoh did not obey fugitives and slaves. Instead, Pharaoh doubled the hard work the slaves already had on them and made their lives harder than ever.

What had happened forty years earlier had just happened again. Forty years earlier Moses had tried to help the slaves by killing the evil task master; but both the Egyptians and slaves turned against him. Now, once again, the Egyptians turned against Moses, and the slaves blamed him for making their lives harder, not easier.

Why had Moses listened to God? How could God use a loser like him? He went back to God and said this in Exodus 5:22-23 ~

Then Moses prayed to the Lord and said, "Master, why have you done this terrible thing to your people? Why did you send me here? I went to Pharaoh and said the things you told me to say. **BUT** *since that time he has been mean to the people. And you have done nothing to help them!"*

THE RELUCTANT LEADER

Once again Moses felt like a failure. Born leader? Never! Everything he had ever tried had failed.

However, as it turned out, God did have a leadership place for Moses. God performed so many great miracles that hurt Egypt, that Pharaoh and the people finally let the slaves go. Moses led them out of their slavery.

Perhaps Moses wasn't ready for it when he was younger. Perhaps he had needed to be humbled so he could understand that it was God working through him that saved his people from slavery, not Moses working on his own. Moses had to get to the point that he was saying, "But I can't" before God was ready to tell him, "Now you can."

For decades, Moses had been a leader with no one to lead. But, when he was ready, a multitude followed him. When the time was right, this reluctant leader became a hero.

7

YOU CAN BE A HERO ALONE
LIKE JOSHUA & CALEB

*Leave these men **ALONE**…it will fail.*
But if it is from God, you will not be able to stop these
men.
You will only find yourselves fighting against God."
Acts 5:38-39

It seemed that Joshua and Caleb were failures. By human standards they were. But by God's standards they were heroes.

Ready to Conquer

They were two among twelve men sent out to spy out the land God had promised to give the new nation of nomadic Israelites – not because the Israelites were so good but because the Amorites and Canaanites were so bad. They worshiped gods that either demanded or at least allowed throwing their children into fire as a sacrifice, pornography, and temple prostitutes.

God used the Israelites to punish them. So, after Moses led over three million Israelite slaves out of Egypt, he led them to the edge of their promised land,

and appointed twelve spies – one from each tribe of Israel - to help him with his first attack strategy. Joshua was from Joseph's tribe of Ephraim, and Caleb was from Judah. Numbers 13 tells about it.

They were gone 40 days and covered about 400 miles up to somewhere around today's Lebanon, and back down to somewhere south of the Dead Sea – a total of around 800 miles. So, they traveled around 20 miles a day which was fairly fast.

When they got back, here are a few things they did not say: They were not attacked by anyone even though they would have had to go to the market sometimes to get food and they probably slept outside under tents. What they did say it that it would be a wonderful place for anyone to live in and they had several strong, walled cities. All that was true.

But Giants?

Then they brought up the giants. The descendants of Anak were there and they definitely were giants. Abraham, Isaac, and Jacob had lived in the territories the spies covered and they weren't afraid of the local people. If anything, the local people were afraid of rich and powerful Abraham, Isaac, And Jacob.

Well, these former slaves still with a slave's mentality of complaining about everything people began the mutter and mumble. So, Caleb jumped in an tried to calm the Israelites. "We can take the land!" he shouted. "Let's do it!"

But ten of the spies countered Caleb. "No! We can't! They are too strong for us! The land devours its inhabitants!" Huh? But they just got through saying the inhabitants were strong. Scared people usually do not make sense.

Then, for good measure, the ten kept emphasizing, "But the giants! We saw the Neph-ilim (that word just means giants) and the Anak-ites are Neph-ilim!" So, the former slaves cried and wept and complained all night. The next morning, they declared, "We wish we would have died in this wilderness! We want to go back to Egypt!"

We Can't Do It!

But Joshua and Caleb cried out, "No! No! Don't do this! The Lord promised to deliver the land to us, so do not rebel against him!" But, it was 10 against 2. They had no chance against the majority.

So, the very same people who were afraid of dying in their promised land decided to stone Joshua an Caleb until they died (Numbers 14:2-10).

Joshua and Caleb tried their best, but they were failures. Did they hide somewhere to escape being executed? Probably. They must have gone through the whole scene over and over in their minds. What could they have said differently? What could they have done differently?

Their shame. Their humiliation. They were all but cast out from their people. Rejected.   When they were younger, they never thought about being failures. But here they were. Outcasts. Nobodies. All alone.

But God had not forgotten them. They were not failures to God. Numbers 14:20-35 says that God told them, "Turn around. Tomorrow you get your wish, You will go back into the wilderness and die there. You will be nomads for 40 years – one year for each day they spied out the land I had promised you. Everyone who saw my miracles performed to get you out of Egypt –

from age 20 and over - will die.

Yes, We Can!

        "But Caleb and Joshua will be the exceptions. They will struggle with you in your punishment for the next forty years. You don't like them, but you are doomed to travel with them anyway until the day you die. They will survive but you will not. They will enter the land I promise. You will not."

But, is that all? Failures, Caleb and Joshua just got to survive? Not at all. There's more. They were only 40 years old when they were appointed to be spies. Since a lot of people lied to be around 120 at that time, they were pretty young.

A General

Just before Moses died, he commissioned Joshua to take his place (Numbers 27:15-23 and Deuteronomy 31:23) as leader and to have some of the Holy Spirit that was on Moses. One book of the Bible is even named after failure Joshua who the people started to stone.

And failure Caleb? What happened to him? After Joshua finally conquered the evil people living in Canaan, he assigned land to each tribe. Caleb was of the tribe of Judah. Joshua 14 says that, on Caleb's 85th birthday, he reminded Joshua that Moses determined he could have whatever land he wanted. He reassured Joshua he was a strong now as he had been when he was forty and he was up to the challenge. Guess where Caleb chose.

A City for the King

Hebron, headquarters of Arba, "the greatest man

among the Anakim" and therefore, the strongest
fortified city in the land! Joshua 15:14 says Caleb, the
"failure" drove out the three sons of Anak.

When Caleb's first wife died, he married Ephrath, and
then they had a son, Hur. Genesis 35:16 says Ephrath
was the early name of the town later named Bethlehem.
Micah 5:2 said that the eternal ruler was going to be
born in "Bethlehem Ephrathah."

So, even though these two men had to run for their lives
for being in the minority and having a positive attitude,
and even though they were considered failures by their
countrymen, to God and to us today, they are heroes.

8

YOU CAN BE A HERO ALONE
LIKE SAMUEL

*No one is near to comfort me [while **ALONE**],*
No one to restore my spirit.
(Lamentations 1:16b)

It seemed that Samuel was a failure. By human standards he was. But by God's standards he was a hero.

Boy Prophet

Samuel was born to lead, not because he was a "born leader", but because he was raised from the time he was about three years old by the highest-ranking person in the nation who was both high priest and the supreme judge (1st Samuel 1:24-28; 1st Samuel 4:18). In fact, when Samuel was still a little boy, God spoke to him and told him to pass this prophecy on to the high priest, which he did. (See 1st Samuel 3.)

The most important and sacred object in Israel

was guarded by the high priest. The Ark of the Covenant was the chest in which Moses had placed the two stone tablets of the Ten Commandments, a bowl of manna, and Aaron's rod that budded to prove he was to remain the high priest. The chest had two carved angels facing each other on the lid with their wings touching tip to tip. Everything was covered with gold and was sacred. When Moses spoke with God, it was at the "mercy seat" of the Ark of the Covenant. In Samuel's day, it was in the tabernacle, a tent of worship, which was set up at Shiloh half way between Jerusalem toward the south, and Shechem in the middle of the country.

When Samuel was grown, he was made supreme judge over the entire nation of the Israelites, (1st Samuel 7:15-17), and it was expected that he would continue to the day of his death, since this was a life-time position.

The Lord was with Samuel as he grew up, and he let none of his words fall to the ground. And all Israel from Dan [in the far north] to Beersheba [in the far south] recognized that Samuel was attested as a prophet of the Lord. The Lord continued to appear at Shiloh, and there he revealed himself to Samuel through his word (1st Samuel 3:19-21).

Defender Of The Holy Ark

During the time Israel had been led by Samson and by Eli (the one who raised Samuel), the land was pretty much controlled by the a neighboring nation. But, when they tried to show their muscles during the time of Samuel, he put a stop to it. After all, Samuel was born to lead, and he did it well.

During the centuries of supreme judges, the priests kept watch over the Ark and sometimes even took it to war in hopes that God would protect their soldiers more with the Ark nearby. There was a battle between the Israelites and their enemy, and the enemy killed some 4,000 Israelites. So, they sent for the Ark of the Covenant. When it arrived, there was a great shouting in the camp of the Israelite soldiers.

The cheers were so loud, the enemy in their camp heard them and became afraid. They referred to the gods of the Israelites being in the enemy camp, so probably thought the two angels carved on the lid were the gods. They recalled that the "gods of the Israelites" struck Egypt with all kinds of plagues.

There was so much fear, that the enemy leaders ordered the soldiers to be strong lest they become slaves of the Israelites, just like the Israelites had been slaves to them. They took heart and killed 30,000 Israelite soldiers, and captured the Ark of the Covenant. (See 1st Samuel 4.)

The enemy took the Ark to the temple of their god, Dagon. But every night, the statue of the god fell over. This frightened the enemy, so they moved it to another town. Once there, the people in the town began to break out in deadly tumors. So they sent it to yet another town and the same thing happened there. (See 1st Samuel 5.)

Eventually, the deadly tumors hit everywhere in the enemy territory. So, after seven months, they sent it back to the Israelites in a cart drawn by two cows. (See 1st Samuel 6.) They sacrificed the cows to God, and placed the Ark of the Covenant in a different town where it stayed twenty years.

Defender Of The Faith

At that time, there was no capital city in Israel. So Samuel set up regular court sessions at Bethel,

Gilgal and Mizpah, though his home was in Ramah (1st Samuel 7:15-17.) When the Ark was returned, Samuel ordered all the men of Israel to come to Mizpah. There he ordered them to get rid of their pagan idols, and worship only the God of heaven. The people obeyed Samuel because they respected him and he had been born to lead. They got rid of their idols and repented.

But, when their enemies heard the Israelites were all at Mizpah, they decided to attack them there. When the Israelites found out, they begged Samuel to keep praying for them. He offered a special sacrifice and did continue to pray for them.

Suddenly there was a thunderstorm and threw the enemy into such a panic that they ran away. The Israelites pursued them and won the war. After that the enemy stayed away from the Israelites and, during Samuel's lifetime, never went to war against them again. (See 1st Samuel 7.)

Eventually Samuel grew old, but still was the supreme judge of the nation of Israel. He had two sons who served as priests also, but they were not wise. They were so unpopular that the people went to Samuel at his home in Ramah, and what they said hit him like a lightening bolt: *Give us a king to lead us!* Samuel was so upset, he prayed to God about it. This was God's reply:

"Listen to all that the people are saying to you; it is not you they have rejected, but they have rejected me as their king. As they have done from the day I brought them up out of Egypt until this day, forsaking me and serving other gods, so they are doing to you."

Samuel warned the people, trying to change their mind. "A king will take your sons to serve in his armies. He will take your daughters to serve in the palace. He will take the best of your fields and vineyards and orchards. He'll take a tenth of your grain and the best of your animals for his own use."

"When that day comes, you will cry out for relief from the king you have chosen, and the Lord will not answer you in that day."

The people swore none of that would ever happen. Samuel prayed again, and sadly God answered that he was to go ahead and give them a king. (See 1st Samuel 8.)

Rejected & Alone In A Crowd

Nothing was ever the same for Samuel after his being rejected. Besides being deserted and left alone, he had nothing but trouble from the king ~ King Saul. He continued to judge until the day he died, but the new king had the real authority. And, with a new leader that their enemies saw as weak, they rose up against the Israelites and were a plague to them the rest of Samuel's life.

Samuel had been rejected and deserted and replaced by a tall, handsome man who was inferior to Samuel in integrity, morality, intelligence, wisdom, and spirituality. Samuel could still serve as priest, but his authority was overshadowed by this new king. He had lost his position, if not in name, but in reality in deed. The whole nation was going down hill, and all he could do was warn people things would only get worse.

When Samuel died, he must have felt like a failure. But when we view what he accomplished to keep his nation protected from their enemies as long as he did, and the dignity with which he anointed (crowned) the new king who was to be his replacement, we see that he was truly a hero.

9

YOU CAN BE A HERO ALONE
LIKE NAOMI

Naomi's husband died....After they had lived there about ten years, both [sons] died.
*Naomi was **left [ALONE] without** her two sons and her husband.*
(Ruth 1:5)

It seemed that Naomi was a failure. By human standards she was. But by God's standards she was a hero.

Life In A Foreign Land

There was a drought in her land, so she and her husband and their two young sons went to a nearby country across the river where the economic situation was better and people had plenty to eat. Things were better there. (See Ruth 1:1-2.)

But one day, her husband died and left her all alone to finish raising their sons. How lonely she was. She had no other family there. Sure, she had friends, but that's different from family. Family knows all about you ~ the good and the bad ~ and accept you anyway.

You know all about them too and accept them too. That's the way families are. But Naomi did not have that. She felt so alone. (See Ruth 1:3.)

Marriage In A Foreign Land

Luckily her sons were old enough to support their mother, so they got by. Eventually she realized they needed wives. How she wished she was back in Bethlehem where she could select good Jewish girls for them, but it was not to be. But her sons were beginning to pressure her. They wanted to be married. They had already selected the girls they wanted. She, of course, had final say on who they married. She would have to select wives for her sons among the pagans. The selection process was hard. How she dreaded selecting future daughters-in-law who didn't worship the same God that she did.

Sometimes she would cry. "Why did you have to die? Our boys need their father, but you're not here. I need you to help make repairs on things. I need your advice. I need your touch. Oh, why did you have to die, my husband? Things weren't supposed to turn out like this. I'm so lonely. So alone...."

Finally, Naomi made her choices. She gave in to her sons who were sweet on Orpah and Ruth. They were nice enough girls. They did come from good, moral families. Solid families. Perhaps she could teach them the Law of Moses so they will want to become Jews after they are married. (See Ruth 1:4.)

There are two weddings, one year apart from each other. The wedding guests are unbalanced because there are so many from the bride's family in attendance, but only Naomi and her other son from the groom's family.

Death In A Foreign Land

Then the unthinkable happened. After Naomi had been in this foreign land for ten years, both her sons suddenly died. Suddenly she had nobody. There were four who came to this land a decade earlier; now there is only one.

Naomi worshiped alone the best she could. She got out her scripture scrolls and read about Jacob who fled his home and was gone some twenty years away from his family before returning at last to see his father and brother. She read about Joseph living in a foreign land for 23 years before being reunited with his family. How lonely Joseph must have been all those years. She read about Moses leading her ancestors all over the desert for 40 years as nomads with no country at all. How displaced everyone felt. Naomi understood.

And she prayed. Only now her prayer was different. Almost hollow. "Jehovah God," she was begin, "I'm all alone here. What am I doing here? I have no one except my two daughters-in-law. Oh, God, why couldn't they have been Jewish girls?" Worshiping all alone was so hard. She had no one to encourage her. No one in her entire town kept the Sabbath holy except her.

Then there were the pagan religious holidays. She was expected to participate, but she just couldn't. It was no secret she was a Jewess, but people didn't usually talk about it. They did, however, leave her out of certain activities because she was both a foreigner and not of their religion. She felt more and more isolated. "Oh, God, what am I going to do?"

Leaving The Foreign Land

Then she heard about a caravan forming that

would cross the river and go to her homeland. They were even going near Bethlehem. Word was that the drought was over and there were abundant crops everywhere.

She needed to go home. Maybe they had forgotten her, but she had never forgotten them.

That night she had a long talk with her daughters-in-law who were still living in Naomi's home. They didn't have to go with her, of course. But, to her surprise, they had grown to love her and did want to go with her. So they began to pack, selling things they could not carry with them on the trip, and giving away what they could not sell. (See Ruth 1:6.)

Naomi wondered how they would handle being foreigners in her homeland. How would people treat her pagan daughters-in-law? She warned them that it would not be easy for them, but they wanted to go with her anyway.

Finally, the day came and they went out on the road toward the caravan heading back to Naomi's home. But, the more she thought about her loneliness living in a foreign land, the more she thought she did not want Ruth and Orpah to go through the same thing.

"Go back to your mothers' homes."

"What? We don't want to. We want to stay with you. You are our mother now."

"May the Lord show kindness to you, as you have shown to your dead and to me. May the Lord grant that each of you will find rest in the home of another husband."

"No, don't say that! We want to stay with you."

But Naomi kissed them and they wept aloud. "Return home, my daughters. Why would you come with me? Am I going to have any more sons who could become your husbands? Return home, my daughters. I am too old to have another husband." (See Ruth 1:8-13.)

Still they wept and refused to turn back. "Go back, my daughters. You're still young and pretty. Marry again and have children and a family for yourself."

Finally Orpah was convinced, and left.

"Now you must go, Ruth." But Ruth refused.

"Look," said Naomi, "your sister-in-law is going back to her people and her gods. Go back with her." How hard it was for Naomi to send them away. But it was only fair to them.

"Don't urge me to leave you or to turn back from you," Ruth replied. "Where you go I will go, and where you stay I will stay. Your people will be my people and your God my God. Where you die, I will die, and there I will be buried. May the Lord deal with me, be it ever so severely if anything but death separates you and me." (See Ruth 1:14-17.)

Bitterness

So Naomi consented. Reluctantly. But she consented. Days later, they walked together into Bethlehem, the town Naomi had left ten years earlier. The whole town was astir. "Can this be Naomi?"

She had aged a lot over the past ten years. Aged because of time. But also aged because of the strain of living in a pagan land where no one believed in the God of the Bible except her little family. Aged because of the strain of losing her beloved husband. Aged because of the strain of losing both of her children. Almost completely gray haired now. The former vivacious Naomi was now an old woman.

"Don't call me Naomi," she said to them, "Call me Mara because the Almighty has made my life very bitter. I went away full, but the Lord had brought me back empty. Why call me Naomi? The Lord has afflicted me; the Almighty has brought misfortune upon me." (See Ruth 1:19-21.)

Naomi returned home feeling like a failure. But what she didn't know is that one day Ruth will marry, have a little boy, and eventually become the great grandmother of King David, the sweet psalmist of Israel. Naomi endured her bitterness, but she knew when it was time to give up her bitterness and live once again for the future. In doing this, Naomi became a hero.

10

YOU CAN BE A HERO ALONE
LIKE DAVID

I am lonely like an owl living in the desert.
*I am **ALONE** like an owl living in old ruined buildings.*
I can't sleep.
I am like a lonely bird on a roof.
(Psalm 102:7)

It seemed that David was a failure. By human standards he was. But by God's standards he was a hero.

Strong In Weakness

David spent much of his life in hiding. Was it because he was weak? No, it was because he was strong. Did things that pleased the people. The present leader of their nation, Saul, had become a bad leader. King Saul almost had his own son killed (I Samuel 14:24-45). He took over parts of their religion that was illegal for him to do (I Samuel 15:10-29).

David was a strong but kind person and the people loved him. Saul was jealous and got so he hated him more and more. He was also smart enough to realize that some day David could lead the people in his downfall if he wanted to. Finally he decided to have David killed. Read about this in I Samuel 18:1-11.

Writing His Thoughts And Prayers

David was not only a strong man, he was a gentle poet. His habit of writing his thoughts helped him through many difficult times. He wrote much of one of the books in the Bible called the Psalms. Many of his poems were written while he was running from Saul. Most of David's poems were prayers.

Sometimes David was afraid, and sometimes he felt courageous. He wrote Psalm 34 during one of his courageous times:

> 4 I went to God for help.
> And he listened.
> He saved me from all the things I fear.
> 5 Look to God for help.
> You will be accepted.
> Don't be ashamed.
> 7 The Lord's angel builds a camp
> around the people that follow him.
> The Lord's angel protects those people.
> 19 Good people might have many problems,
> but the Lord will save them
> from every one of their problems.

David knew that God could set up circumstances to deliver him. Such was Psalm 54 where he acknowledged God's direction in saving him. Here it is in part:

> 1 God, use your power and save me.
> Use your great power to set me free.
> 2 God, listen to my prayer.
> Listen to the things I say.

3 Strangers that don't even worship God
have turned against me.
Those powerful men are trying to kill me.
4 Look, my God will help me.
My Master will support me.

He constantly moved so he would not be
discovered. He wrote Psalm 56 to ask God for courage.
Here is some of it:

3 When I am afraid,
I put my trust in you.
4 I trust God, so I am not afraid
of what people can do to me!
I praise God for his promise to me.

At other times, he was angry at the thoughts and
ways of people hunting for him who believed they were
doing what was right, but was wrong in God's eyes.
Such was Psalm 57. Here it is in part:

4 My life is in danger.
My enemies are all around me.
5 God, you are high above the heavens.
Your glory covers the earth.
6 My enemies set a trap for me.
They are trying to trap me.
They dug a deep pit for me to fall into.
7 But God will keep me safe.
He will keep me brave.
I will sing praises to him.

David could never thank God enough times for
God's love and protection. He reflected this in Psalm
63. Here it is in part:

1 God, you are my God.
And I want you so much.
My soul and my body thirst for you,

You Can Be A Hero Alone
like a dry, weary land with no water.
6 I will remember you
while lying on my bed.
I will remember you
in the middle of the night.
7 You really have helped me!
I am happy that you protected me!
8 My soul clings to you.
And you hold my hand.

A Good But Hard Life

David's original enemies finally died out. You would think that David would have had a peaceful life after that. But Satan is always out there. (Most of David's life is found in the 2nd book of Samuel in the Bible.) Godly people are always being attacked by someone.

Life is like that, especially for people who spend their life trying to stand up for goodness and godliness. How can a person keep a proper balance in life? David lived to be an old man, but he never forsook God, no matter what happened around him or to him.

Did he sometimes have doubts? Of course, he did! He was human and Satan attacks everyone. He reflected his struggle in Psalm 42 where he had a talk with himself:

1 A deer gets thirsty
for water from a stream.
In the same way, my soul is thirsty
for you, God.
2 My soul is thirsty for the Living God.
When can I go to meet with him?
3 My enemy constantly {makes fun of me}.
He says, "Where is your God?
{ Has he come to save you yet?}"

{I am so sad} that my only food
is the tears {that fall from my eyes}.

Twice in this poem (verses 5 and 11) he told himself

5 Why should I be so sad?
Why should I be so upset?
I should wait for God's help.
I will get the chance to praise him yet.

Another time, David committed a sin that he was
later very ashamed of. He wrote this prayer poem to
God. Here is part of that prayer in Psalm 51:

1 God, be merciful to me,
because of your great loving kindness,
because of your great mercy,
erase all my sins.
2 God, scrub away my guilt.
Wash away my sins,
Make me clean again!
3 I know I sinned.
I always see those sins.
4 I did the things you say are wrong.
God, you are the One I sinned against.
I confess these things so people will know
I am wrong, and you are right.
Your decisions are fair.
10 God, create a pure heart in me!
Make my spirit strong again!

Eyes Only On God

No matter what David did in his life, his eyes were
always on God. Even though he was human and
sometimes sinned like all humans do, he loved God with
his whole heart. Twice in the Bible, David is called "a
man after God's own heart" (I Samuel 13:14 in the Old
Testament, and Acts of the Apostles 13:22 in the New

Testament).

One of the most beautiful poems of praise in the Bible was written by David. It is Psalm 19. Here it is in part:

1 The heavens speak about God's glory.
The skies tell about the good things
his hands have made.
2 Each new day tells more of the story.
And each night reveals more and more
about God's power.
3 You can't really hear any speech or words.
They don't make any sound we can hear.
4 But their "voice" goes throughout the world.
Their "words" go to the ends of the earth.
The sky is like a home for the sun.
9 Worshiping the Lord is like a light
that will shine bright forever.

UNTIL THE DAY HE DIED

David remained faithful to God until the day he died. Here is one of the most famous of David's poems. It is often recited at the funeral of Christians. It is part of Psalm 23:

1 The Lord is my shepherd.
I will always have everything I need.
2 He lets me lie down in green pastures.
He leads me by calm pools of water.
3 He gives new strength to my soul
for the good of his name.
He leads me on paths of goodness,
to show he is truly good.
4 Even if I walk through a valley
as dark as the grave,
I will not be afraid of any danger.
Why? Because you are with me, Lord.

Your rod and staff comfort me.

David had enemies all his life. To many it would seem that David didn't know how to be happy and didn't know how to keep his friends.   But he kept his most important friend ~ God. That made him a hero.

11

YOU CAN BE A HERO ALONE
LIKE MEFIBOSHETH

*No one is near to comfort me [while **ALONE**],*
No one to restore my spirit.
(Lamentations 1:16b)

Was it his fault when his nurse dropped him when he was 5 years old? The fall resulted in deformed, atrophied, paralyzed feet with no feeling At the end of each day, he had to examine his feet because sometimes they were cut or bruised when he was not looking. (2nd Samuel 4:4 & 19:24). People just called him "the cripple".

Boy King in Hiding

Me-fib-o-sheth was supposed to be king. He was the grandson of King Saul and the first-born and only son of Jonathan, the crown prince. But before he was old enough to understand, it was too late. His grandfather, King Saul, was killed in battle. His father, Crown Prince Jonathan was killed in battle. And he never got his chance to be king. He was bypassed because of many things. Instead he became a royal failure in exile – and a runaway just trying to survive assassination.

Somehow the family was able to slip the boy out of David's territory and hide him because, some believed Mephibosheth was the rightful king instead of David. They were afraid David's allies might be after Mephibosheth's life.

A Promise Kept

Many people did not know about David's close friendship with Jonathan who loved and respected David, his father's competitor to the throne. Jonathan had conceded that David was a better fit to be king than him. But he also knew he would have to continue to go to war against all the neighboring countries who were also trying to take the land of Israel away from Israel. So, Jonathan asked David, if he died in battle, would David be kind to his descendants. Of course, David kept his promise.

He even kept Saul's entire remaining family in custody in the palace rather than have them killed as was the custom of all other usurping kings.   So later when some complicated circumstances arose, David handed over the seven still-living grandsons of King Saul – two sons of Saul's concubine and 5 sons of Saul's - to be hung They were all first-cousins of Mephibosheth. However, he would not hand over Jonathan's son because of his vow to Jonathan. (2nd Samuel 21:1-14). But, despite everything, Mephibosheth's whole family were failure. He never had a chance.

The Unexpected

Some time later, though, he married. Married? Who would want to marry a cripple? Remember, his grandfather, Saul, was the tallest (probably nearly 7 feet tall) and most handsome man in the land (1st Samuel 9:2). He was a little hard to get along with, but his son,

Jonathan was the opposite. Jonathan seemed to get along with everyone. Certainly Mephibosheth inherited at least some of his grandfather's good looks and height and his father's easy-going personality. So, he was married and had a son named Micah at the time David first met him (2nd Samuel 9:11-12).

Betrayal

Now let's meet crafty Ziba. Ziba was a servant to Saul's household (2nd Samuel 9:2-4) and had 20 of his own servants. So apparently he just stayed in Saul's palace. It is interesting that no one knew where Jonathan's son was but Ziba. And it is even more interesting that Ziba voluntarily gave the city and exact house ten miles south of the Sea of Galilee Mephibosheth was apparently hiding in. Was he being like the servants in one of Jesus' parables who beat up all a king's servants, then killed his son so they could claim the land for themselves (Matthew 21:33-46)?

Well, it must have backfired because, rather than kill the grandson of the conquered king, he gave all the land and his palace to Mephibosheth. But revenge takers are patient and wait until time for their vengeance arrives. So, when King David fled from his usurping son, Ziba met David and said Mephibosheth had stayed back in so he could become king in David's plate. Thar did the trick. David immediately declared everything that Mephibosheth owned now belonged to Ziba.

When David returned to Jerusalem, Mephibosheth rode out to meet him. Now, if he was planning to usurp David's throne, why would be go meet him with no army? Further, why would he go meet the king unshaven, wearing the same clothes he had been wearing when David left. So distraught he was that he hadn't even checked his feet. The truth came out. Ziba had told him he would go meet King David on his behalf because of his lame feet. David realizes he has been caught up in a personal feud and just tells Mephibosheth and Ziba do divide the Saul's possessions between them.

Content, Even With Nothing

And what did Mephibosheth say in response?   Ziba can have it all. My reward is that my king has returned safely. Yes, even though he probably took after his grandfather's height and good looks, it seems he took after his father in wanting what is best for someone else. Mephibosheth, who had spent most of his life in hiding, would now spend the rest of his life owning nothing. Yet he was content.

Yes, in the eyes of the world, this man who would be king had failed at everything But to God and to those of us today, he was a hero.

12

YOU CAN BE A HERO ALONE
LIKE ELIJAH

*"I am the **ONLY** prophet still living. And the people are trying to kill me now....*
But God said, "I have kept for myself ___ men that still worship me".
(Romans 11:3-4)

It seemed that Elijah was a failure. By human standards he was. But by God's standards he was a hero.

The King Didn't Like Him

Elijah was a prophet of God who lived during the time of one of the most evil kings of Israel ~ Ahab. Ahab established such evil "religions" that they required both male and female prostitutes to be their priests and priestesses. (Read I Kings 16:29-33.)

God certainly picked Elijah to do a hard job. The first thing he did was tell Elijah to go to the king and tell him God was going to send a drought to last several years. Then God told Elijah to hide. No one likes someone who brings bad news. So Elijah went into hiding. (Read I Kings 17:1-6.)

Eventually the brook where Elijah was hiding went dry, so God sent him to Sidon, a town in today's Lebanon.

The Widow He Helped Didn't Like Him

While in Sidon, Elijah met a widow with just enough food left for her and her son for a last meal before they died. Elijah performed a miracle so that her food supply never ran out. Then she was not only able to feed herself and her son, but also Elijah.

But some time later, the son got very sick. The ungrateful widow really surprised Elijah when she went to him. *And the woman said to Elijah, "You are a man of God. Can you help me? Or did you come here only to cause me to remember all of my sins? Did you come here only to cause my son to die?"* (Read this in I Kings 17:18.)

But Elijah was patient, begged God to heal the boy, and the boy became well again. (See I Kings 17:19-24.) Elijah had been falsely accused, but he was humble and handled a bad situation well.

The Prophets Didn't Like Him

After three years of drought, it was time to meet the real enemy. Elijah sent word for 450 prophets of the false religion to meet him on a mountain for a spiritual challenge. *Elijah said, "I am the only prophet of the Lord here. I am alone. But there are 450 prophets of Baal"* (I Kings 18:22).

He told the false prophets to build an alter and put a bull on it. Then he told them to pray for their god to bring fire down on it. They agreed, and prayed and danced around the alter from morning to noon for Baal to send fire down from heaven onto their sacrifice.

Even though it was one prophet against 450, Elijah began making fun of them. Let's read about it in I Kings 18:27-29 ~

27At noon Elijah began to make fun of them. Elijah said, "If Baal is really a god, then maybe you should pray louder! Maybe he is thinking! Or maybe he is busy! Or maybe he is traveling! He could be sleeping! Maybe you should pray louder and wake him!"
28So the prophets prayed louder. They cut themselves with swords and spears. (This was the way they worshiped.) They cut themselves until the blood flowed over them.
29The afternoon passed but the fire still had not started. The prophets continued to act wild until the time came for the evening sacrifice. But nothing happened—there was no answer from Baal. There was no sound. There was no one listening!

Then it was Elijah's turn. He built his alter and put a bull on it. Then, of all things, he had the observers pour four buckets of water over the sacrificial bull. There was so much water, it even filled the trench around the altar. Then Elijah prayed a simple prayer, and God sent fire down from heaven that not only burned up the sacrificial animal, but also the stones and water.

That morning Elijah had told the observers and the prophets, *"When will you people decide who to follow? If the Lord is the true God, then you should follow him. But if Baal is the true God, then you should follow him!"* (I Kings 18:21). When the people saw Elijah's sacrifice to Yahweh God burned up, they fell down to the ground and called out, "Yahweh is God" (I Kings

18:39).

The Queen Didn't Like Him

But Elijah did not have much time to enjoy his victory. When Queen Jezebel heard what happened, she sent soldiers out to find and kill Elijah. So Elijah ran for his life. This time he escaped to the southern-most part of Israel out in the desert near Egypt. There he gave up and prayed to die.

Then Elijah walked for a whole day into the desert. Elijah sat down under a bush. He asked to die. Elijah said, "I have had enough, Lord! Let me die (I Kings 19:4).

An angel fed him. Then Elijah traveled farther and finally went into a cave for the night. His depression had actually deepened. Why? I Kings 19:10 explains it ~

"Lord God All-Powerful, I have always served you the best I can. But the people of Israel have broken their agreement with you. They destroyed your altars. They killed your prophets. I am the only prophet that is still living. And now they are trying to kill me!"

All alone? No!

Much to Elijah's surprise, he found out he was not alone. He was not the only one who worshipped Yahweh, God of heaven and earth. There were others who secretly worshipped too. Ten others? No. Fifty others? No. One hundred others? No. Never in Elijah's imagination did he think there were so many others just like him. This is what God told him:

Elijah, you are not the only faithful person in Israel. Those men will kill many people. But, even after that, there will still be 7,000 people living in Israel that never bowed down to Baal! I will let those 7,000 people live—and none of those people ever kissed a Baal idol (I Kings 19:17-18).

Ups And Downs

Perhaps Elijah needed this reassurance. For the next three things Elijah did were more dangerous than ever. He sent word to Queen Jezebel that she would die, later he sent word to King Ahab he would die, and finally, he sent word to Ahab's successor son, King Ahaziah, that he would die. Of course, they didn't all die at the same time, so Elijah had to keep running and hiding after each announcement.

Elijah had work to do for God. But it was dangerous work. He loved God and just wanted to do what was necessary to get people to stop worshiping false gods and to worship the one true God ~ Yahweh. Obviously, Elijah wanted people to love him. That is just human nature. But he was sent to the leaders more than the common people. Leaders can be dangerous. They don't want to lose their power.

Why did God choose Elijah to do such dangerous work? Yes, Elijah complained a lot and got depressed a lot. But God knew that inside, Elijah had what it would take to get up and make prophecy after prophecy that would, each time, put his life in danger. Was it all for nothing? Defending God alone like that all the time?

One Final "up"

Elijah spent most of his religious life with people angry at him, and running for his life. People may have wondered why. But Elijah believed in God so much that he would do anything for him. He finally received an amazing reward. Moments before his death, he didn't die!

The Bible itself explains this exciting event best in
II Kings 2:11 ~

*Suddenly, some horses and a chariot came and
separated Elijah from Elisha. The horses and the chariot
were like fire! Then Elijah was carried up into heaven in
a whirlwind.*

Elijah's life had been a hard one. Most people
didn't like him. The leaders certainly didn't like him.
He spent most of his adult life in hiding and depressed.
Most people didn't even want to associate with him. But
God was able to use a man like that. We today now
understand that Elijah was a hero.

13

YOU CAN BE A HERO ALONE
LIKE JONAH

*That person should sit **ALONE***
and be quiet when the Lord puts his yoke on him.
(Lamentations 3:28)

It seemed that Jonah was a failure. By human standards he was. But by God's standards he was a hero.
rebel

Jonah was a prophet who believed people should get what they deserve.   If things were going bad for people, he thought they deserved it. If things were going good, it means they must deserve that. He thought it was just fair.

He had a powerful personality and people often did what he said. He could easily tell people to start doing good and they actually would. But there were just some people in life that were so bad, he looked forward to the day they got what they deserved. People knew not to cross Jonah.

And that is exactly what he felt about people who crossed God. In the powerful city of Nineveh way over in As-Syria, people were mean and always would be mean. They would go to war, capture the enemy and torture them. He knew God would punish them for all the terrible things they had done and looked forward to that day. It was just a matter of time. Well, he heard they had a new king, but he would be like all the rest. He knew that much.

Vengeance was part of Jonah's nature. But God used him anyway.

He Refused to Forgive Mean People

God gave him a new assignment. It was to travel to Nineveh, capital of a great As-Syrian empire east of Palestine and preach against their wicked ways. God knew they could repent. Jonah knew they could not. In fact, Jonah did not want them to repent. Jonah wanted them to get what they deserved for all the terrible things they had done to his people in the past.

So, Jonah took off in the opposite direction. Perhaps he had heard God wrong. Or perhaps he was afraid of what the people of Nineveh would do to him if he preached against them. One thing was for sure, he wanted them to get what they deserved.

So he got on board a ship heading far from where God told him to go. The ship was headed west to Spain, not east to As-Syria. But you cannot flee from God. God caused a violent storm to toss their ship around. The sailors saw their ship begin to break up, so threw all their cargo into the sea to lighten it. An each sailor was ordered to pray to whatever god he believed in.

He Refused to Forgive Himself

But no one could find the stranger on board - Jonah. They needed all the gods they could muster up to save the ship. The captain found Jonah in the hold of the ship in a deep sleep. He woke Jonah up and ordered him to pray to his God.

But the storm became even more fierce, so they decided it was the fault of the stranger on board - Jonah. The sailors demanded to know where Jonah was from and what God he worshipped. Jonah said he worshipped the God of heaven who made the sea and the land. They were terrified that Jonah would have made such a powerful God so angry.

They asked what he had done that was so bad he would punish all of them. They begged him to tell them what would appease Jonah's God.

Of course, Jonah knew what was happening. Jehovah was thwarting his plans to run away from his responsibilities. Jonah knew he was supposed to do what God told him, even if he did not agree with God.

The ship was still breaking up. Jonah knew the sailors had not done anything wrong. But he was getting punished for what he deserved. Rather than pray for Go to forgive him, Jonah announced, "Throw me overboard, and the storm will cease. I know it is my fault that this great storm has come upon you" (Jonah 1:12).

The Sailors Did Not Want Him

The sailors could not bring themselves to do this. They were afraid of making Jonah's God even more angry and they would all perish in the sea after all. So they tried to row the ship to shore. But it was no use. Finally they cried out to Jehovah, "Oh Lord! Please do not make us die for taking this man's life. Do not hold us accountable for killing an innocent man."

Then they threw Jonah overboard, and instantly

the sea became calm. The still-terrified sailors offered sacrifices to this powerful God, and vowed they would always worship him and would spread news about him everywhere. In fact, they could hardly wait until they landed their ship so they could start spreading the word about this powerful Jehovah God of Jonah's who made both sea and land, and control them both. And those they told spread the word even farther. The news of Jehovah God spread like wildfire.

The Great Fish Did Not Want Him

In the mean time, God prepared a great fish that immediately swallowed Jonah where he seems to have died for three days. He wrote later about his experience, just before his death. "From the depths of the grave I called for help.... Seaweed was wrapped around my head....When my life was ebbing away, I remembered you, Lord" (Jonah 2:2, 5b, 7).

Apparently Jonah's body did not go as far as the fish's stomach were it would have been eroded with gastric acid. Instead, three days later, the fish vomited Jonah up onto dry land. (See Jonah 2:10; also Matthew 12:39-41).

God Forgave Jonah

Did Jonah learn his lesson? God ordered him a second time to go to Nineveh in As-Syria and preach. Jonah was sorry he had disobeyed God, so he proved it by obeying God.

Nineveh was so large, it took three days to walk from one end of the city to the other. Nineveh was the capital city of an evil and ferocious empire that had its eyes on destroying Palestine. Jesus said centuries later that the best way to get rid of an enemy is to make him a friend, but Jesus had not been born yet and Jonah did not understand the concept. He did not want these mean people to become God's friend.

Jonah Obeyed With His Actions

"Forty more days and Nineveh will be destroyed!" he shouted to the people as he crisscrossed the city. Alone he walked through that pagan city that he become so evil. Alone he preached, not know what they would do to him out of vengeance for accusing them of doing wrong. Woe to anyone taken captive by them. Some of their enemies they even skinned alive. He was confident that they were so bad, they could not and would not repent. Therefore, they would be punished after all. Vengeance after all.

Much to his surprise, they began to believe him. We do not know how long it took Jonah to get to Nineveh, but perhaps by then the story of the God who controls the seas had been told that far away. If this was the same God and Jonah survived, they knew they had better be terrified.

In fact, when the news reached the king of Nineveh, he took off his royal robes and covered himself with itchy cloth and poured ashes over his head, the common sign of mourning and repentance in those days. Then he put out a decree that everyone, including animals, were to refrain from eating, and were to cover themselves with sackcloth and ashes as a form of repenting of their sins of violence.

He Did Not Obey With His Heart.

Jonah didn't think they were sincere. He thought they were just pretending to repent. So he set up a shelter for himself on a hill outside of the great city and waited for God to punish it. It seems that Jonah had already forgotten that God had forgiven him for running away.

God was happy when they repented Jonah was not. He wanted them to be punished for all the mean things the As-Syrians had done to his people. God explained to Jonah that all people are like children to God and he wanted to show his children the right way to act so he could save his children in Nineveh.

God Used an Imperfect Man

Jonah had done a better job all by himself than he ever thought possible. Jonah spoke and God moved their hearts.

There were two things Jonah did not understand, and even most people did not understand until Jesus came many centuries later. The first thing he did not understand was loving one's enemies. Jesus taught that in his famous Sermon on the Mount on how to live a godly life, and he taught it by example when he forgave those who were crucifying him. (See Matthew 5:43-48 and Luke 23:34).

The second thing Jonah did not understand is that his sacrificing himself to save the sailors was repeated by Jesus when he sacrificed to save mankind. And Jonah's [near]death and resurrection three days later was going to be repeated by Jesus centuries later. But, instead of a great fierce fish, it would be on a cruel cross. (See Matthew 12:39-41.)

Little did Jonah realize that the bitterness he experienced would be turned into glory by the Son of God later on.   He fought and fought God, but despite his arguing, he did what God wanted him to do. That's what heroes do ~ the hard stuff, even when they do not understand. The stuff that requires courage. The stuff that heroes are made of.

14

YOU CAN BE A HERO ALONE
LIKE JEREMIAH

I never sat with the crowd as they laughed and had fun.
*I sat [**ALONE**] by myself because of your influence on*
me.
(Jeremiah 15:17)

It seemed that Jeremiah was a failure. By human standards he was. But by God's standards he was a hero.

God told Jeremiah, "Before I formed you in the womb, I knew you; before you were born, I set you apart; I appointed you as a prophet to the nations" Jeremiah replied that he was just a child, a word used at that time to say he wasn't quite an adult. (See Jeremiah 1:4-6.)

But he had a lot of time to think about it. For it was nearly twenty years before God used him as a prophet. During those quiet years, what did Jeremiah think about? Perhaps that he had been mistaken and God really hadn't called him?

God prepared him for his wait. He told Jeremiah, "Get yourself ready! Stand up and say to them whatever

I command you;. Do not be terrified by them...Today I have made you a fortified city, an iron pillar and a bronze wall to stand against the whole land ~ against the kings...officials...priests and the people of the land. They will fight against you, but will not overcome you, for I am with you and will rescue you" (Jeremiah 1:17-19).

At Long Last, The Day Arrives

When the time finally came, Jeremiah pleaded with the people on God's behalf. "Return, faithless [people]...I will frown on you no longer, for I am merciful...I will not be angry forever. Only acknowledge your guilt." Things were so bad in Jerusalem that God announced through Jeremiah, "If you can find but one person who deals honestly and seeks the truth, I will forgive this city...They have lied about the Lord; they said, 'He will do nothing! No harm will come to us, we will never see sword or famine" (Jeremiah 5:1, 12). How wrong they were.

One time when Jeremiah was warning people with God's words in the temple itself, the chief priest had Jeremiah beaten and put in stocks at one of the gates leading into the temple. Did he decide to stop preaching and stay out of trouble? Just the opposite! He said, "But if I say, 'I will not mention him [God] or speak any more in his name, his word is in my heart like a fire, a fire shut up in my bones. I am weary of holding it in; indeed, I cannot!" (Jeremiah 20:9).

When they finally let him out of the stocks, the chief priest ordered him to tell the king all was well. But Jeremiah was true to God and declared that the priests and the king were evil. What courage! There were many false prophets trying to keep the king happy, and Jeremiah accused them of lying. "They speak visions from their own minds, not from the mouth of the

Lord. They keep saying to those who despise me, 'The Lord says you will have peace....no harm will come to you" (Jeremiah 23:16-17).

Death Threats

Then Jeremiah made a remarkable prophecy, something that only God knew, for only God knows the future. God told Jeremiah to tell the people that they would go into exile in Babylon (today's Iraq) for 70 years. The false prophets denied they would ever go into exile, but it happened just as prophesied. (See Jeremiah, 25th chapter.)

Things continued to get worse in the country, and Jeremiah kept prophesying, speaking the Word of the Lord. Once again, he was in the temple courtyard, and once again predicting terrible things were about to happen because the people refused to repent of their immoral lives and worship of imaginary gods. God warned Jeremiah, "Tell them everything I command you; do not omit a word." Jeremiah obeyed.

Immediately the priests who were supposed to be following God but were not, and the false prophets rushed at Jeremiah and seized him declaring, "You must die!" Immediately word was sent to the palace, and government officials assembled a quick court hearing. Some of the elders of the people stepped forward and said they should not be executing someone who is just speaking for the Lord God. The officials agreed and Jeremiah was set free.

Prophecies Of Hope

Did this close call, this brush with death stop him from ever preaching again? It did not! But his preaching was not always negative. A little at a time top officials and members of the royal family, then lesser officials were exiled to Babylon. Jeremiah wrote them a letter telling them that they were going to be there seventy years, and they should settle down, marry, have families, and seek peace where they were. Some day they would return to Jerusalem and rebuild it. Then he said something that we today take courage from:

" 'For I know the plans I have for you,' declares the Lord, 'plans to prosper you and not to harm you, plans to give you hope and a future' " (Jeremiah 29:11).

Among other words of comfort, Jeremiah made another remarkable prophecy about an eternal king ~ Jesus Christ. " 'In those days and at that time I will make a righteous Branch sprout from [King] David's line; he will do what is just and right in the land....This is the name by which it will be called: The Lord Our Righteousness' " (Jeremiah 33:15-16).

Ears That Would Not Hear

Later Jeremiah wrote a letter of warning to the most recent king. It was read by Jeremiah's assistant, Baruch. The king did not like what was in it. Baruch would read some of it, the king would cut that part off the scroll and throw it in the fire. Baruch would read some more, the king would cut that part off and throw it in the fire. Eventually, he had Jeremiah's entire letter burned up. Did this stop Jeremiah? No! He wrote another one just like it.

But the chief priest and his family was even madder. The high priest's grandson had Jeremiah thrown into a cistern. They lowered him by ropes down to the bottom, and Jeremiah sank down into the mud and was left there to starve to death. The priests who were supposed to be the kindest people of the land were the meanest people of the land. Even the king felt sorry for Jeremiah, and had him secretly taken out of the cistern, but still held under guard in protective custody. (See Jeremiah 38 and 39).

Finally, after Jeremiah had warned the people for twenty years, the king of Babylon came, took captive the remaining people and burned the city so no one could live there any longer. Wild animals took over the rubble. Why? Because people were living immoral lives and were worshiping all kinds of imaginary gods instead of the one God in heaven. Jeremiah had tried. He had done all he could.

Doom And Rebirth

Then he wrote Lamentations, the saddest book in the entire Bible.

"My eyes fail from weeping. I am in torment within, my heart is poured out on the ground because my people are destroyed...I became the laughingstock of all my people; they mock me in song all day long....My eyes will flow unceasingly; without relief, until the Lord looks down from heaven and sees....Those who were my enemies without cause hunted me like a bird. They tried to end my life in a pit and threw stones at me; the waters closed over my heard and I thought I was about to be cut off....With their own hands compassionate women have cooked their own children, who became their food when my people were destroyed....The Lord has given full vent to his wrath; he has poured out his fierce anger, He kindled a fire in Zion that consumed her foundations....Woe to us, for we have sinned".

Today, we read the life of Jeremiah and all he endured. If we did not have the rest of the Bible written after Jeremiah's time, we would not know that all God predicted through Jeremiah came true.

Seventy years after going into exile in Babylon,

the Jews were allowed to return to Jerusalem and rebuild the temple, and then the walls, and then the city itself. We can read about it in the writings of Ezra and Nehemiah, prophets who led the people back to their beloved Jerusalem. Though despised by the priests, most of the rulers and many of the people, today we recognize the courage Jeremiah held on to for over twenty years to declare the Word of God to people who did not want to hear it. To us today, Jeremiah was anything but a failure. He became our example of courage, and our hero.

15

YOU CAN BE A HERO ALONE
LIKE DANIEL & THREE FRIENDS

*I have been very zealous for the Lord God Almighty
....have rejected your covenant, broken down your altars,
and put your prophets to death with the sword.
I am the* **ONLY ONE** *left, and now they are trying to kill
me too.
(I Kings 19:10)*

It seemed that Daniel and his three friends were failures. By human standards they were. But by God's standards they were heroes.

Resentment Over Food

It started right away. They were among the young noblemen brought to Babylon (today's Iraq) by the king to be trained in Babylonian ways and serve in the palace. These Jewish young men were offered tables of food that would be the envy of any commoner. But the food included that which was forbidden by the Jews to eat. Because they could not always tell which animal which portions of meat came from, they asked to eat just vegetables. The king himself had selected the food, and the butler was afraid he would be executed for defying the king.

Daniel and his friends suggested they have a test: If, after ten days, they were weaker than the other young men, they'd consent to the king's diet. But, if they were stronger, all the others at the table of the young Jewish noblemen had to eat vegetables. At the end of the ten days, Daniel and his friends were stronger. This, of course, made everyone else at the table angry. How dare these four make things bad for everyone else?

This was the beginning of their unpopularity, even among their fellow Jews. Did Daniel and his friends decide they made a mistake because now they didn't have any friends? They could have. There was always time to change their minds.

Because Daniel was able to interpret a complicated dream of the king, and because he and his three friends were ten times wiser than the king's other advisers, Daniel was put in charge of the entire province of Babylon, and his three friends made administrators. (See Daniel 3.)

Resentment Over A Statue

Later the king made a huge statue 90 feet (30 meters) high made of gold. The leaders of the entire kingdom ~ 120 provinces ~ were ordered to come to a special ceremony and bow down to it. But Daniel's three friends refused. They were threatened and told they'd be thrown into a furnace if they worship the statue. They still refused. All they had to do was bow down this one time. That's all it took. They could have prayed to Jehovah God when they did it and say they were really bowing down to Jehovah. But they couldn't do this. They had to be examples to others of standing up for what they believed, standing up for the one true God.

They were thrown in the furnace that was so hot, the guards throwing them in were burned to death. Suddenly, the king leaped to his feet because he saw four men, all walking around in the fire unharmed, the fourth looking like the son of a god. He ordered the men to come out and the original three did. He looked them over and saw that nothing ~ not even their clothes or hair ~ was even singed. In fact, they didn't even smell like fire. Then the king ordered that no one in his entire kingdom would be allowed to say anything against the God of Daniel's three friends ~ Jehovah.

Many people were jealous of these four Jews ~ Daniel and his three friends. They had high positions in the kingdom and were Jews, not Babylonians. Further, they refused to worship the gods of the Babylonians. (See Daniel 3.)

Resentment Over A Prayer

Several years later, they got another chance to try to destroy them. This time they picked on Daniel. The governors of each of the 120 provinces had to report to Daniel, and they resented it. So they laid a trap for Daniel. They went to the new king and suggested an irrevocable edict requiring that no one would be allowed to pray to any god or man except the king. He was flattered and signed the irrevocable decree, even though it was punishable by being thrown into a den of hungry lions.

What most of them knew, but apparently the king did not know, is that Daniel prayed to Jehovah three times a day at his window facing west where Jerusalem was. Of course, all they had to do is watch Daniel's window, and eventually they saw him come to it and pray. Daniel knew they would be watching for him. But he prayed facing Jerusalem three times a day anyway, at the risk of his life. He could have decided to face Jerusalem when he prayed three times a day like usual, but just not go to his window to do it. After all, if he died, he could not stand up for Jehovah God any more. But he didn't. He refused to stop doing what he had always done.

Immediately the witnesses to Daniel praying in his window reported him to the new king. It was only then that he realized he had been trapped into condemning one of his closest advisors and friends. The edict could not be revoked.

So the king ordered Daniel before him. Daniel still had a chance. He could say he forgot. He could say it wasn't him the witnesses saw. He could say he changed his mind and decided never to pray to Jehovah God again. But he didn't do any of those things. He stayed true to God, even though he knew it meant his death.

So the king pronounced the death sentence on Daniel. He walked with him to the lion's den, telling him how much he had always valued his advice and friendship. They walked slowly. But eventually they arrived at the place of execution. He embraced Daniel, kissed him on each cheek, and sorrowfully, but hopefully said, "May your God, whom you have always served, rescue you." Then, as the king watched, a stone was rolled across the entrance until he could see Daniel no more, and the king walked sorrowfully away.

The king went back to his palace, but refused any food or any entertainment. He went to his bedroom and walked the floor with worry all night. In the morning at dawn, he was back at the den. Hoping against hope, he cried out, "Daniel! Servant of the living God! Has your God, whom you have always served, been able to rescue you from the lions?"

Then he heard it ~ Daniel's voice. "Oh king! Live forever! My God sent his angel, and he shut the mouths of the lions! They have not hurt me because I am innocent in his sight! Further, I have never done anything wrong before you, Oh, my king!"

The king was overjoyed and ordered that Daniel be brought out of the den. There was not a single scratch found on him because he had trusted in his God. (See Daniel 6.)

Daniel and his three friends were taken to Babylon and Jerusalem was burned. They could never return. They could have resented their captors. Instead, they became as helpful as they could. They turned their enemies into their friends. But, at the same time, they knew they would always have enemies among those who wanted their own religion, the religion of their family and friends. They did not want to change religions. Regardless, this did not change the loyalty of Daniel and his three friends to Jehovah God. When faced with death, they stood up for God anyway. They were heroes.

Multiple Choice Questions:

16

YOU CAN BE A HERO ALONE
LIKE ESTHER

*And who knows but that you [**ALONE**]
have come...for such a time as this?*
(Esther 4:14b)

It seemed that Esther was a failure. By human standards she was. But by God's standards she was a hero.

The first we hear of young Esther is that she was an orphan and had been adopted by an older cousin as his own daughter. Her cousin worked at the palace and would come home and tell Esther about all the goings on. She often wondered what it would be like to actually walk through the palace, or even just stand in one of the grand rooms.

Beauty Queen

One day her cousin came home with disturbing news: The queen had been exiled. But now, what to do for a new queen? Such intrigue. Eventually, there was beauty contest for a replacement. Esther was pretty to look upon, so she was taken to the palace for the beauty contest.

Her cousin knew about the politics around the palace and gave her good advice. He told her to take the advice of the eunuch in charge of the royal harem because he was a good man. He also advised Esther not to tell anyone that she was a Jew because Jews were very unpopular, especially those who had been brought as slaves from Palestine as their mutual great grandfather had been.

Esther was not only pretty to look upon, but she was delightful to talk to and just be around. She must have smiled a lot and made other people feel good about themselves. She must have been gentle, and perhaps even just a little bit shy. The Bible says she pleased the eunuch in charge of the harem, so he provided her with special beauty treatments and special food. He also gave seven maids to her, and assigned the best apartments in the harem to Esther.

Before Esther and all the other young ladies who had won the first part of the beauty contest were presented to the king, they had to undergo six months of treatments with oil of myrrh, and six months of learning how to use cosmetics and the best perfume for each young lady.

All this sounds wonderful. However, as each young lady completed her year of beauty regimen, she would be taken to the king to spend the night with him. The next morning, she would be taken to the harem of the concubines, never allowed to leave, and basically a prisoner the rest of her life, unless the king requested to see her again.

In the mean time, every day, her cousin (adoptive father) walked back and forth near the gate of the harem just to get snatches of information from maids

and servants going in and out. Then it came her
turn. The young ladies were allowed to take anything
with them to the king's palace that she wanted. Esther
asked the advice of the eunuch in charge of the harem,
and only took with her what he suggested she take.

Immediately the king fell in love with Esther. So
he selected her above all the other young ladies and
crowned Esther the new queen of King Xerxes of Persia!
(See Esther 2.)

Fearful Queen

But, as already seen, a person can rise very high
in the palace or be reduced to nothing by exile or
execution. After a few years, a plot was put together by
a government official to kill all Jews. He convinced the
king that the Jews were so different and difficult that
they refused to obey the king's laws. He told the king it
would be better in protecting his throne that all Jews be
exterminated. This official paid the king a huge bribe
because he hated the Jews so much. So, the king
accepted the bribe and made it a law that on a certain
day, all Jews were to be killed in every city and every
province of his kingdom.

Esther had not given her nationality. She had
always been a secret Jew. She secretly remembered the
Sabbath Day to keep it holy. She secretly prayed
toward Jerusalem three times a day as did Daniel, who
died about the time she became queen. She secretly
kept all of the Law of Moses that her cousin had taught
her growing up. She was contented to leave things quiet
and not stir up any trouble by revealing her true
identity. (See Esther 3.)

Her cousin sent a message to Esther explaining
the new law, and sent a copy of the law stating all Jews
were to be exterminated. She was shocked. Her cousin

sent word to her, begging her to go to the king and plead for mercy for her people.

Now she was both shocked and confused. She sent word back to her cousin that she could not just go to the king just because she happened to want to. For her to go to him without him requesting her could mean her death. Only if he held out his golden scepter to her could she escape death. She just couldn't take chances like that.

Her cousin sent this message back to her: *"Do not think that because you are in the king's house you alone of all the Jews will escape. For if you remain silent at this time, relief and deliverance for the Jews will arise from another place, but you and your father's family will perish"* (Esther 4:8).

Then he added one last but dynamic challenge to Esther: *"And who knows but that you have been brought to the kingdom for such a time as this?"* (Esther 4:9, KJV).

Is this why God changed so many things around in the palace? Just so Esther could be queen for the purpose of saving the Jews some day? Was this the whole purpose of her becoming queen?

But it meant revealing who and what she was? She would lose everything if she did. Even if she did save all the other Jews from being killed, she'd probably end up being exiled herself ~ or worse. She felt so alone. No one in the whole palace ever dreamed she was a Jew. She had managed to keep it a secret all her life. She couldn't tell it now. She just couldn't!

But she had been raised by a righteous man. Her adoptive-father knew when to tell everything that needed to be told, and now was the time for Esther to admit she was a Jew.

So finally she sent a message back to her cousin. "Gather all the Jews together in this city and fast for me for three days. My maids and I will fast too. Then, at the end of the three days, I will; go to the king.

"I will go to the king, even though it is against the law. And if I perish, I perish" (Esther 4:16).

Triumphant Queen

On the third day, Esther put on her royal robes and stood in the courtyard near the door leading into the throne room. The king was on his throne and happened to see her standing in the courtyard near the door. He raised his golden scepter to her, so she approached and touched the tip of the scepter according to law. (See Esther 4-5.)

She arranged to see him on two other occasions in private. Then, on another day, she went to the throne room again, fell at his feet and wept, begging him to put an end to the evil plan to kill all Jews. Perplexed, he held out his golden scepter to her. *"How can I bear to see disaster fall on my people? How can I bear to see the destruction of my family?"* (Esther 8:6) she begged.

"You a Jew?" the king must have responded. Esther continued to weep. Had she just declared her own death sentence? Would she be immediately sent to the dungeon and executed, even before the legal day to kill all Jews? What would happen to her now? She felt so alone, and silently begged God to give her strength.

But the king would not lose another wife. He loved Esther. So, even though he could not revoke his order to kill all Jews, he sent out a decree that the Jews could defend themselves. They did and lived. Esther, saved her nation with her courage. She was a hero alone.

17

YOU CAN BE A HERO ALONE
LIKE MORDECAI

A person should not compare himself with other people.
Each person should judge his own actions.
*Then he can be proud for what he [**ALONE**] has done.*
(Galatians 6:4)

It seemed that Mordecai was a failure. By human standards he was. But by God's standards he was a hero.

The Slave Who Pulled Himself Up

Mordecai's great grandfather, Kish, was a slave. He had been taken in chains from Palestine to Babylon by the Babylonian king (Esther 2:5-6). So, his great grandfather was born in slavery. Perhaps Mordecai's grandfather bought himself out of slavery and was a freedman. Each generation must have done a little to raise himself up in society.

The first we hear of Mordecai is that he was sitting at the king's gate (Esther 2:21). That was a position of importance. Anyone sitting at a city gate was among the elders who heard disputes and pretty much served as judges. (See Proverbs 31:23; Ruth 4:11a.)

One day, Mordecai learned of a plot against the king's life. He told the Queen who told the king. The king's life was saved and had ordered that it be written in his daily chronicles.

Mordecai was one step above sitting at the gate of a city. He was at the king's gate. Only royal officials were allowed to sit at the king's gate (Esther 3:2).

He Stood Alone for what was Right

This story took place soon after Daniel had died, the Daniel who had been the second highest nobleman of the land next to the king. (See Daniel 2:48; 5:29; 6:3). So, there had been Jews holding positions of importance in the court of the king. But they were always resented just because they were Jews (Daniel 3:12).

The king decided to make Haman highest in the kingdom, second only to the king, just as a previous king had made Daniel highest in the kingdom before him. Mordecai let it be known that he was a Jew. Perhaps Haman had already shown his disdain for Jews, for when Haman came through the king's gate, all the king's royal officials bowed down to him except Mordecai.

How impossible it is to hide when you're the only one standing. But that is what Mordecai did. He did not respect Haman and refused to bow down to him. He literally stood alone. He represented the thoughts of many people, but he was the only one with courage to act on his beliefs.

When His Life was Threatened, He Stood Alone

Day after day when Haman went back and forth to and from the palace, everyone bowed down to him but Mordecai. He stubbornly remained standing. The only man standing. The king had commanded that everyone bow before Haman, but day after day he refused. Alone he refused.

Of course, Haman was enraged and decided to execute Mordecai. But when he learned Mordecai was a Jew, it fed his other hatred, his hatred of all Jews. Haman bribed the king to send out an edict that, on a certain day, all Jews were to be executed throughout the kingdom. (See Esther 3.) Even then, with the death sentence hanging over all his people, Mordecai refused to bow down to Haman as he went in and out of the king's gate. He was the only one standing. He didn't even show fear in his presence. It completely enraged Haman, but he kept his peace because he knew Mordecai would be executed soon enough.

Still, it wasn't enough. He wanted a special punishment for Mordecai. He wanted to humiliate Mordecai, just as Mordecai had humiliated him. So he had a gallows built, seventy-five feet high, about as high as a seven-story building. All that was left to do was get the king's permission to hang Mordecai on it. It was late night, but he was so adamant about it, he couldn't wait until morning to get the king's permission to hang Mordecai. He went immediately to the palace.

The same night Haman began having the gallows built, and while on his way to the palace, the king couldn't sleep. So he ordered the book of his chronicles, the record book of his reign, be brought and read to him. He had completely forgotten that some time earlier Mordecai had reported an assassination plot against the king. Mordecai had overheard some officials plotting it at the king's gate. As a result of Mordecai's warning, the king's life was saved. (See Esther 2:21-23.) But, it troubled the king that he had never rewarded Mordecai for his loyalty.

The king needed some advice, so asked if anyone was in the royal court. Haman had just arrived, ready to ask permission to hang Mordecai on the gallows. The king sent for him and Haman was flattered that he did not have to wait until morning. The king asked what he should do to give special honor to someone. Egotistical Haman thought the king was talking about him. He said such an honored man should be given a royal robe that the king had worn, and be able to ride the king's horse with the royal crest on it, then be led through the streets with praises being proclaimed on the man.

The king liked the idea, and put Haman in charge of honoring Mordecai, not executing him. Haman was mortified. He went home that night enraged. The next morning he was given the royal robe and horse, and with Mordecai thus dressed and mounted, led him through the streets declaring the king's pleasure on Mordecai. Afterwards, he went home and told his wife and family that Mordecai was going to lead his downfall. (See Esther 6.)

Respect Stood Where Hatred Failed

But before he could plan a new plot to get rid of his mortal enemy, Mordecai, Haman was summoned back to the palace. There the king accused him to trying to molest his wife, Esther. So he had Haman hung on the same gallows he had built for Mordecai. (See Esther 7.)

Mordecai, the man who had dared to stand alone for what he believed to be right and proper was awarded the king's appreciation and trust. The king gave Mordecai his signet ring so he could save the Jews from the plot of Haman by declaring that they defend themselves. The king had Mordecai adorned in royal garments of blue and white, a purple robe, and a large crown of gold. (See Esther 8.)

Then he made "Mordecai the Jew" as he was always referred to, second in command in the kingdom. Why? It all started when Mordecai got the courage to stand alone literally, to refuse to bow down to an unprincipled man high in the government. He knew he could be executed for it, but he did it anyway, despite being descendant of a slave. He literally stood on his principles. At the time, all the officials and everyone else thought he was a loser and would never survive. But he did survive through the province of God, and today we consider him a hero.

18

YOU CAN BE A HERO ALONE
LIKE ANNA

*And then was a widow [**ALONE**] until she was eighty-
four.*
*She never left the temple, but worshiped night and day,
fasting and praying [**ALONE**].*
(Luke 2:37)

It seemed that Anna was a failure. By human
standards she was. But by God's standards she was a
hero.

Age 23, Widowed And Moved To The Temple

She was born around 90 BC and married around
74 BC. Seven years later, her husband died and she
was left a young widow. That was 67 BC. How lonely
she was. She was from the tribe of Asher, and her tribe
lived far away, northwest of Jerusalem on the shores of
the Mediterranean Sea. She was in Jerusalem. She
apparently never had any children. So there she was in
Jerusalem with no one; at least, no one of her family.
Her parents came to see her. She was only about 23
years old at the time. They probably urged her to move
back with them. But all her memories of her husband

were there in Jerusalem. (See Luke 2:36.)

So she stayed in her marriage home, surrounded by comforting things ~ furniture her husband had built for her, his clothes still hanging on hooks where he left them that last day. She saw him in the things and smelled him in his clothes. And so, though she was very lonely, she was comforted.

But one day, all that was destroyed. The great Pompeii brought battering rams and battered the temple and city gates. He also had machines that hurled great stones over the walls. She heard stories of the priests who kept offering their daily sacrifices, despite the dangers of being hit by one of the great stones hurled at the temple. How dedicated they were. Anna hoped she would have that kind of courage if such a time ever came for her. Little did she know....

Some time later, having broken through the gates and walls of the temple, Pompeii's soldiers cut the throats of everyone who had rushed to the temple for safety. But, even as the soldiers drew closer and closer to the great altar where the priests served, they refused to stop offering their sacrifices until they, too, were cut down. Then the slaughter extended to the rest of the city. A total of 12,000 inhabitants of Jerusalem were killed, and their houses were burned.

Now poor Anna had no where to go. Her house had been destroyed with all the others. So she did what everyone else did who wanted to stay in Jerusalem ~ moved to the temple grounds. The men helped rebuild the walls while the women nursed the survivors, cooked for the workers and did other things to help. There were apartments in the walls of the temple and Anna was able to secure one to share with some other women. Little did she know she would spend the rest of her life ~ 61 more years ~ there at the temple.

Age 52 And Still At The Temple

She wasn't so alone now. Anna was with other believers. Among their beliefs was that a Savior would come to free them of foreign powers, and even free them of their sins. How her people longed for that day to come. It had been predicted since the time of Adam and Eve. The promise was repeated during the time of Abraham, Isaac, and Jacob, then during the time of King David, and finally during the time of the many prophets who preached up until about 500 years earlier. The prophets were now silent about the promised Savior, but the earlier prophecies lived on. Oh, how Anna longed for their Savior. She felt the time was close. Everyone did.

But time passed. Anna was now 52 years old. Things had long ago gone back to some kind of normal. Then Caesar made Herod ~ later known as Herod the Great ~ King of Palestine. He was only half Jew and had been raised in Rome with Caesar's family, and the Jews resented him. So Jerusalem closed and locked its gates when he tried to come and take his place at the royal palace.

It was like Pompeii's raid all over again. Herod battered down the gate and his soldiers entered the city, swords waving. They killed so many that Herod had to get them to stop lest he "become king of a desert." Herod was the cruelest king they had had in centuries. Oh, how Anna longed for the Savior prophesied over the past 2000 years. Everyone did.

Just two years after taking control of Palestine, Herod did his wife a favor, and made her 17-year-old brother high priest. But he got to be too popular, so Herod had him killed and a few years later, had his wife killed because he thought she was trying to poison him.

Four years after that, he fell in love with another woman, but she was a commoner. So Herod made her father high priest so his intended bride would be of a higher class. The enemy had even infiltrated their religion. Oh, how Anna prayed for their Savior. Everyone did.

When Anna was around 68 years old, Mary was born. No one knew it yet, but Mary would some day be the mother of the longed-for Savior who Anna had been praying for for so long. By this time, Anna had become a prophetess herself. She, as did all other prophetesses, did not write anything, and did not prophesy in great sermons, but did prophesy in private to anyone who would listen to her.

As old age advanced, Anna got so she never left the temple. Instead, she worshipped, prayed and fasted night and day. (See Luke 2:37.) Please, Lord God Jehovah in heaven, send our Savior. We need him so much. How she longed for her Savior. Everyone did.

Age 84, And Finally The Savior Comes

Now Anna was 84 years old. As usual, she was praying. Sometimes she prayed sitting, sometimes kneeling, sometimes walking slowly around the temple grounds. Then she looked up and saw him: Her Savior. He was still a baby, but she knew. She was, after all, a prophetess and knew such things. She looked into her Savior's eyes and listened as the baby was blessed.

Mary and Joseph left with their baby, the Savior of the Jews, the Savior of the World. How excited Anna was! She couldn't wait to tell everyone. But apparently, no one believed her. "But he was finally born! I saw him!" There was no rush after them from others at the temple. There was no rush to the barn where baby Jesus had been born. No rush to celebrate.

Anna now, once again, felt very alone. She had tried to convince the other Jews who came her way that their Savior had finally been born, but no one was impressed. After all, Anna was an old woman now. She probably had just imagined it out of wishful thinking. "Please, listen to me" Anna must have begged. "He has been born! Our Hope, our Savior has been born!"

Things just went on as they had before, despite all of Anna's efforts. "All these years, these decades we at the temple and everywhere in our country have been praying for our Savior! Our prayers have been answered!" Where were all the believers? All those Anna had prayed with through all those years. Where were they now? Anna felt so alone.

There had been other signs he had been born. Shepherds spread the word. There was a strange star beaming down very close to Jerusalem in nearby Bethlehem. Everyone knew the Savior was supposed to be born in Bethlehem (Matthew 2:3-6). Despite Anna explaining that the Savior indeed was born in nearby Bethlehem, no one seemed to believe her. Anna stood by what she had said, for she was a prophetess. But no one believed her. She prophesied alone. No one paid any attention to her. But today, we look back and see that she was an unheralded hero.

19

YOU CAN BE A HERO ALONE
LIKE JOHN THE BAPTIST

*I am not **ALONE**.*
The Father who sent me is with me.
(John 8:16)

It seemed that John the Baptist was a failure. By human standards he was. But by God's standards he was a hero....

In Prison For His Beliefs

Here he was. Put in prison because of his beliefs (Mark 6:17). He had tried to spread the word about his beliefs and, at first, seemed to be succeeding. But now it was all over. He could no longer tell anyone. Now he sat in the dank, dark cell all alone except for the rats and a few other prisoners who no longer looked or felt very human.

Here he was. Put in prison where there were no crowds, no decision makers, no people to challenge his beliefs so he could explain them. Was it worth it? Would he have been better off not explaining so much at a time, so people would get used to him a little at a time? Could he have done anything different?

Maybe he should have just kept his mouth shut. Maybe he should have just kept his faith to himself. Maybe he shouldn't have thought he could make a difference in the world. Maybe....

Always Different

He'd been born into a family of religious leaders. His father was well respected in the religious community. His father was a priest, though in some parts of the world he probably would have been called an imam, a rabbi, a prophet, a monk. (Luke 1:5-10).

John had always known God wanted him for a special purpose. He had been miraculously born when his parents ~ like Abraham and Sarah ~ were too old to have children. His father had told this to him many times as he grew up. (Read about this in Luke 1:11-17.)

John was in line to be a priest himself. But he wanted to prepare people for a better religion ~ for Jesus, the Christ who would bring certain salvation and the Kingdom of Heaven to people.

So, instead of dressing like normal priests dressed, John did just the opposite. In fact, didn't dress like normal people either (Matthew 3:1-4). When he began preaching, he did not preach in a building. He preached next to a river so he could immerse people who repented of their sins. Baptism was a ritual cleansing. Soon he became known as John the Baptizer, or John the Baptist.

He kept telling people to get ready to become members of the new Kingdom of Heaven. This was another way of saying they should get ready for the beginning of the church, the Kingdom of Heaven on earth.

Outspoken Challenger

John was not always polite. He saw that he needed to shock people into seeing themselves the way God saw them. Many people decided to be baptized, but weren't sincere. They just wanted to look religious, even when they weren't. He called such people broods of snakes in Luke 3:7-8 ~

People came to be baptized by John. John said to them, "You are like poisonous snakes! Who warned you to run away from God's anger that is coming? You must do the things that will show that you have really changed your hearts and lives.

All kinds of people asked him what they should do to change their lives. Read about it in Luke 3:10-14 ~

The people asked John, "What should we do?"
John answered, "If you have two shirts, share with the person that does not have one. If you have food, share that too."
Even the tax collectors came to John. They wanted to be baptized. They said to John, "Teacher, what should we do?"
John said to them, "Don't take more taxes from people than you have been ordered to take."
The soldiers asked John, "What about us? What should we do?" John said to them, "Don't use force or lies to make people give you money. Be happy with the pay you get."

John even publicly declared the country's leaders were being immoral. Even Prince Herod, son of the former King Herod the Great, was not left out of John's warnings. Read about it in Mark 6:18-19 ~

Herodias was the wife of Philip, Herod's brother. But

then Herod married Herodias. John told Herod that it was not right for him to be married to his brother's wife.

This made Prince Herod so angry, he had John the Baptist imprisoned.

Reassurance

We do not know how long John remained in prison. We do know that John's followers did go see him there. They probably took food to him, possibly a warmer cloak to wear, and of course the latest news. They told him that Jesus was beginning to preach and baptize.

John was very glad. But he needed reassuring that he had not been imprisoned in vain. So he sent word to Jesus, "Are you the one I was telling everyone about?"

Jesus sent word back that he was healing people and spreading the good news of salvation. He added that John would be blessed if he did not falter in his beliefs. (See Matthew 11:1-6)

Waiting And Praying

So now, here was John in prison. Most of the time he thought about what he had told people. He wondered if it had been enough. Would his being in prison for his beliefs make his message stronger?

He leaned on his faith during those dark hours when one could hardly tell whether it was night or day outside. He recalled scriptures he had read through the years and repeated them over and over. Scriptures are God's Words; John needed to be reminded of what God had to say to him.

He also prayed. How could he think of so many things to say to God? His prayers were not memorized prayers. They were thoughts from his heart. He prayed for his countrymen, he prayed for people he had baptized and people who were enemies of God, he prayed for his family, he prayed for people throughout the world to be saved.

The scriptures were God talking to him. His prayers were him talking to God. In this way they had a kind of two-way conversation.

He did not know his immediate future. But he knew his distant future: He knew some day he would be able to join his Lord in heaven. He knew some day he would live forever in heaven. Oh, how he longed to be with God, the God of love.

Dying For His Beliefs

One evening he heard clanging of the outer gate into the prison. Then he heard the clanging of the door into his cell. Without a word, two soldiers led him out of his cell and deeper into the dungeon complex. John knew. He knew he was about to be executed and die. (Read about it in Mark 6:19-28.)

But it wasn't death that he saw in his mind. Death was just the door into heaven. How he welcomed the moment! He was ready. He had no doubts that he would close his eyes on earth and open them in heaven. Of course they would be spiritual eyes he would open, but it was all very real to him.

He had done what he could to spread the news of Jesus coming to save the world, and that people should repent of their sins and be baptized to get ready for the Kingdom of God. He had done the best he could. He had no regrets. And so, John the Baptizer was beheaded on earth and welcomed into heaven.

To most people, John had done everything wrong. He could have kept his mouth shut and not warned anyone. He could have gotten married and had a family and lived to a good old age. After all, with such a long life, he could have taught more people. He had exercised bad judgment, and he paid for it with his life. But to God, things were just the opposite. John had stood up for goodness and God, and had been willing to pay whatever price necessary to spread the word. The price he paid had drawn more attention to his message than a thousand sermons would have. John the Baptist was a hero.

20

YOU CAN BE A HERO ALONE
LIKE EPANET

*I am **LONE**ly like an owl living in the desert....*
*I am like **A LONE**ly bird on a roof.*
My enemies always insult me.
They make fun of me and curse me.
In the future, those people will praise the Lord.
Psalm 102:6-8, 18b

It seemed that Epanet was a failure. By human standards he was. But by God's standards he was a hero....

The First And Only Christian

Epanet lived in western Turkey in an area known in his time as Asia Minor. He was the only Christian in all of western Turkey. No one liked someone who went against the religion he had been born into. It wasn't done.

Here he was the only one who believed Jesus really was the Son of God. He'd often prayed for people to be more open to Jesus Christ, and for help to come.

He'd prayed this month after month, year after year.

How did it all come about?

Epanet had apparently traveled to Jerusalem for a Jewish holy day called Penetecost. While there, he heard a speech proving Jesus ~ who had been executed there a few weeks earlier ~ really was the Son of God and had come back to life.

Jesus' apostle Peter, told everyone *"Change your hearts and lives and be baptized, each one of you, in the name of Jesus Christ. Then God will forgive your sins, and you will receive the gift of the Holy Spirit."* There were 3000 people baptized that day. It seems Epanet was one of them. (Read all about it in Acts of the Apostles, chapter 2.) Then he went back home to western Turkey. This took place around 30 AD.

Some time later, the Apostle Paul wrote this: *"Say hello to my dear friend Epanetus. He was the first person to follow Christ in Asia [Minor]"* (Romans 16:5).

God's Assignment: Wait

Even though Epanet wanted to share the good news of Jesus with people where he lived, he soon found it was dangerous. His friends and family got angry because he had left the religion he was raised in. Many people even wanted to put him in prison or kill him. So finally he quit trying to tell people openly about his belief in Jesus.

At first he worshiped alone. But he never quit trying to convince his friends and family in secret. Eventually he was able to convert a hand full of believers. Acts of the Apostles 19:1 says later there were a few believers in western Turkey. This was

Epanet's tiny congregation. Jesus had promised his followers worldwide, *"For where two or three are gathered together in my name, there am I in the midst of them"* (Matthew 18:20). .

Epanet and the others must have often prayed for people around them to be more open to Jesus, and for help to come. He must have struggled to hold the little congregation together. But he was determined to hold fast, stand firm and do the right thing. He must have valued such scriptures as this: *"Wait for the Lord's help! Be strong and brave, and wait for the Lord's help!"* (Psalm 27:14).

Year after year Epanet prayed for help. Year after year it did not come. Another scripture he must have read often was this: *"Do what the Lord says and wait for his help. The Lord will make you the winner"* (Psalm 37:34).

The job given to him by God was to remain faithful alone year after year and keep the church alive. Remember, it only takes one person to be the church wherever they may live. And so he patiently waited and waited.

Finally help did come.   It came some 20 years later.

On Wings As An Eagle

Now it was around 50 AD. A very strong Christian who knew the Bible very well went to a major city in western Turkey called Ephesus. Acts of the Apostles 19:1 says that, when the Apostle Paul arrived at Ephesus, he found a few followers of the Lord Jesus Christ. Then Paul set up a religious school and taught everyone in western Turkey who wanted to learn about Jesus for two years.

How happy Epanet must have been! Maybe he told his Christian friends, "Didn't I tell you help would come some day?". Perhaps another favorite scripture of his was this:

But they that wait upon the Lord shall renew their strength;
they shall mount up with wings as eagles.
(Isaiah 40:31a KJV)

But after two years, there was a riot. The church had actually become so strong, the leaders of the religion most people previously believed declared, *"Paul has influenced and changed many people! He has done this in Ephesus and all over the country of Asia [Minor] !"* So unbelievers in Ephesus grabbed some of the Christians, forced them into their stadium, and threatened them. Thousands of the unbelievers shouted for two hours how great their old religion was. [See Acts 19-20]

Later Paul explained, *"Brothers and sisters, we want you to know about the trouble we suffered in the country of Asia [Minor]. We had great burdens there. The burdens were greater than our own strength. We even gave up hope for life. Truly in our own hearts we believed that we would die. But this happened so that we would not trust in ourselves."* (2nd Corinthians 1:8-9).

Paul left western Turkey, but the church had been built up at last; Epanet's dream of having many other souls saved and Christians to worship with had finally come true. It would be strong enough to stand even in the face of persecution.

The Dream At Last Fulfilled

Epanet had been the lone Christian in western

Turkey around 30 AD. Some sixty-five years later ~ when Epanet was very old or had died by then ~ there were seven congregations of the church in western Turkey. In fact, Jesus from heaven wrote through the Apostle John to these seven congregations. It is the very last book of the Bible ~ Revelation.

"This is the revelation of Jesus Christ....Christ sent his angel to show these things to his servant John.... From John, to the seven churches in the province of Asia [Minor]" (Revelation 1:1,4a).

Jesus then sent special messages to each of the seven congregations that existed in western Turkey, due in part to the refusal of Epanet to ever give up.

To the congregation in Ephesus, Jesus said, *"You continue to try without quitting. You endured {troubles} for my name. And you have not become tired of doing this."* (Revelation 2:3).

To the congregation in Smyrna, Jesus said, *"I know your troubles, and I know that you are poor. But really you are rich! I know the bad things that some people say {about you}"* (Revelation 2:9a).

To the congregation in Pergamum, Jesus said, *"You did not refuse to tell about your faith in me even during the time...my faithful witness was killed in your city"* (Revelation 2:13).

To the congregation in Thyatira, Jesus said, *"I know about your love, your faith, your service, and your patience"* (Revelation 2:19).

To the congregation in Sardis, Jesus said, *"You have a few people there in Sardis who have kept themselves clean. Those people will walk with me. They will wear white clothes, because they are worthy"*

(Revelation 3:4).

To the congregation in Philadelphia, Jesus said, *"I know that you are weak. But you have followed my teaching. You were not afraid to speak my name"* (Revelation 3:8b).

To the congregation in Laodicea, Jesus said, *"Here I am! I stand at the door and knock. If a person hears my voice and opens the door, I will come in."* (Revelation 3:20).

Not Weary In Well Doing

Epanet never gave up. Some of the people in larger congregations in Jerusalem, Rome and other places perhaps thought through all those early years, "If Epanet would just have more faith and work harder, his congregation would grow". How unfair for anyone to think this.

Surely Epanet knew what God had said through the prophet, "Who has despised the day of small things?" (Zechariah 4:10 KJV). Epanet did not grow bitter. He had faith that, if he just held it together long enough, his congregation would grow and thrive. Eventually, it did.

The unbelievers around Epanet must have considered him a fool to keep believing when no one else did. He didn't have to worship alone; he could return to their religion if he wanted to. But no one could get through to Epanet.

He stubbornly and faithfully held on to his belief in Jesus as the Son of God month after month, year after year. He was a spiritual giant of faith. We today take courage from his courage. To all who ever struggled alone and to God, Epanet was a hero.

21

YOU CAN BE A HERO ALONE
LIKE PAUL - I

*So [he] left and went into the hills **ALONE**.*
(John 6:15)

It seemed that Paul was a failure. By human standards he was. But by God's standards he was a hero....

House Arrest

It isn't easy being a Christian alone. But there he was arrested in Jerusalem and under house arrest, chained to a guard in Rome. People could come see him if they liked; he just couldn't go see them. (Read about it in Acts 28:16 and 30.)

How he longed to get out and tell people about the love of Jesus. It was burning in his heart. But it was illegal for him to go out of his "prison" and tell the wonderful story.

So there he was, limited by who he could talk to about Jesus and his love for their eternal souls. His soul cried out in frustration. He had to talk to these people. But how? It was impossible.

What is that in your hand?

Centuries earlier, God told Moses to lead the multitude of Israelites out of their slavery in Egypt. Moses objected with every argument he could think of. They had been enslaved for generations by one of the most powerful nations in the world. He wasn't a good speaker. No one would believe him. He might be arrested when he arrived. It was just impossible.

But God replied, "What is that in your hand?" (Exodus 4:2). In Moses' case, he had a simple shepherd's staff in his hand. God showed him how to perform miracles with his staff. Perhaps Paul thought about this. Perhaps Paul thought about all the things he could hold in his hand that might help him get the Good News out.

Then the answer came: In Paul's hand was a pen and parchment. Paul could write. And so he did.

Letter To Friends In Turkey

He wrote his Christian friends in Ephesus and called himself a prisoner of Christ Jesus (Ephesians 3:1).

He recalled with them how they were converted to Christianity in Ephesians 1:13-16 ~

You heard the true teaching—the Good News about your salvation. When you heard that Good News, you believed in Christ. And in Christ, God put his special mark on you by giving you the Holy Spirit that he promised. That Holy

Spirit is the guarantee that we will get the things God promised for his people.
This will bring full freedom to those people who belong to God. The goal of all this is to bring praise to God's glory.

He told them how to behave within their families at home in Ephesians 6:1,4 ~

Children, obey your parents the way the Lord wants. That is the right thing to do. Fathers, don't make your children angry. But raise your children with the training and teaching of the Lord.

He reassured them of how much God loved them and could accomplish through them in Ephesians 3:17-21 ~

I pray that Christ will live in your hearts because of your faith. I pray that your life will be strong in love and be built on love. And I pray that you and all God's holy people will have the power to understand the greatness of Christ's love. I pray that you can understand how wide and how long and how high and how deep that love is….With God's power working in us, God can do much, much more than anything we can ask or think of. To him be glory in the church and in Christ Jesus for all time, forever and ever. Amen.

Letter To Friends In Greece

He wrote his Christian friends in Philippi and explained how he was getting along in Philippians 1:12-14 ~

It is clear why I am in prison. I am in prison because I am a believer in Christ. All the Roman guards know this, and so do all the other people. I am still in prison, but most of the believers feel better about it now. And so they are much braver about telling people the message {about Christ}.

Do you see where he took advantage of the situation and began teaching his guards? They had no choice but to listen to him; they were chained to him!

But he must have gone through periods of discouragement. Maybe there was talk of executing him because of his faith, for he spoke, then, of his death in Philippians 1:20-21 ~

I hope that I will have the courage now, like always, to show the greatness of Christ in my life here on earth. I want to do that if I die or if I live. I mean that to me the only important thing about living is Christ. And even death would be profit for me.

Next, he tried to give them courage in case any of them were arrested. See Philippians 1:28-30 ~

And you will not be afraid of those people who are against you. All of these things are proof from God that you are being saved and that your enemies will be lost. God gave you the honor of believing in Christ. But that is not all. God also gave you the honor of suffering for Christ. Both these things bring glory to Christ. When I was with you, you saw the struggles I had {with people who were against our work}. And now you hear about the struggles I am having. You yourselves are having the same kind of struggles.

He ended his letter to them with something very amazing in Philippians 4:11-13 ~

I have learned to be satisfied with the things I have and with everything that happens. I know how to live when I am poor. And I know how to live when I have plenty. I have learned the secret of being happy at any time in everything that happens. I have learned to be happy when I have enough to eat and when I don't have enough to eat. I have learned to be happy when I have all the things I need and when I don't have the things I need. I can do all things through Christ, because he gives me strength.

Letter To More Friends In Turkey

He also wrote friends at Colossae, a city on a major trade route between seaports and the Euphrates River in the Middle East. He asked them in Colossians 4:3 ~

Also pray for us. Pray that God will give us an opportunity to tell people his message. I am in prison for doing this. But pray that we can continue to tell people the secret truth that God has made known about Christ.

He reminded them of Jesus giving them spiritual freedom by making it possible for them to go to heaven in Colossians 1:13 & 14 ~

God made us free from the power of darkness (evil). And he brought us into the kingdom of his dear Son (Jesus). The Son paid the price to make us free. In him we have forgiveness of our sins.

He warned them to stay away from human philosophies that lead them from Christ in Colossians 2:8-10 ~

Be sure that no person leads you away with false ideas and words that mean nothing. Those ideas come from people, not Christ. Those ideas are the worthless ideas of people in the world. All of God lives in Christ fully (even in Christ's life on earth). And in Christ you are full. You need nothing else. Christ is ruler over all rulers and powers.

He closed his letter with a final request in Colossians 4:18 ~ *Remember me in prison.*

Good Out Of Bad

Paul was in a very bad situation. He had been arrested and imprisoned several different places. In Jerusalem he had been accused by Jews and taken prisoner by the Romans (Acts 21:30-37). Next, he was transferred to a prison in Caesarea in today's Lebanon (Acts 23:23-24). He stayed in prison for two years there (Acts 24:27). Finally, he was sent to Rome for trial (Acts 25:9-12).

Nothing was turning out right for Paul. He had so much Good News to share about Jesus Christ. Why had God allowed this bad situation to get out of hand and get even worse?

To people of the world, Paul's situation could not possibly be worse than it was. But he turned a bad situation into something wonderful for us today. If he had not been imprisoned, perhaps we would not have had the encouraging words he wrote during this bad time. Paul became a hero!

22

YOU CAN BE A HERO ALONE
LIKE LYDIA

I was sad and lonely.
I was defeated and away from my people.
So who gave me these children?
*Look, I was left **ALONE**.*
Where did all these children come from?
(Isaiah 30:17)

It seemed that Lydia was a failure. By human standards he was. But by God's standards she was a hero.

Oh, Lydia was rich and all that. She was the envy of a lot of people. But it was only a private envy. She had a big house, a real show place, because she was an exporter of purple cloth, a rarity at the time. Actually, people resented Lydia for having all that wealth because she was in the wrong religion. How could the gods have blessed her when she worships the who claims he is the only God in existence?

Hated For Being A Jew

Thus far, Lydia had lived her life as a Jewess. People hated the. Regardless, everyone in her household was a loyal Jew. Some she had converted herself, and some had been raised in that religion as she had been.

She knew her house was being watched. Lydia was not one to confront people. She just wanted to be left alone to worship God in the way her conscience dictated, along with the directives of the Law of Moses. She didn't want to insult people who didn't believe like she did, although she did pray for them to be enlightened.

So, when the seventh day of the week came along. Lydia always took her household outside the city away from peering eyes, and worshipped by a river. Their worship consisted of prayers, reading the law and the prophets, and singing the psalms. They liked to sing, but needed privacy to do it. The river front outside of the city gave them that privacy.

Clandestine Worship

This Saturday was not any different from any other. Knowing the house may be watched, first two servants left with water jugs as though going to the town well for water. But once at the well, they kept walking through the city gate and eventually to the river bank. A butler in the household left through the front gate and began walking in the wrong direction, circled around, and eventually ended up going out the city gate to the river bank. Later, Lydia herself left with two of her maids. They walked through the market a few minutes, went around to another residential neighborhood, then eventually to the city gate where they left and went to the river bank. There were already several in the household there, but not everyone had arrived yet. Normally it took two hours for everyone in her household to arrive so they could worship together. They were patient with each other. It was always worth it.

Now, all assembled, Lydia's steward led the group in opening prayer. Then they began to sing. In the middle of their second psalm, a small group of strangers approached them. Had they been discovered? Would they be turned in to the authorities?

A man named Paul seemed to be their leader and spokesman. There seemed to be a few wives in the group, but all hung back while Paul introduced himself and his friends. He said he couldn't help but overhear their songs, actually psalms of David whom they all love. Yes, Paul was a fellow Jew, although he had moved on to greater things. What greater things could there be than the one true God, Maker of heaven and earth?

Then A Hated Christian

Lydia invited Paul and his group to sit with them, and they and her household sang familiar psalms of David together. After a little while, Lydia asked if anyone of their guests would like to say something, They did. Paul recalled with them all the prophecies of a Savior, a divine King who would save everyone from Satan's punishment for our sins. They were all familiar with the prophecies because they had been made in the Jewish scriptures for thousands of years.

Then he told them the prophecies had all come true in Jesus, the Christ. One by one he went through Jesus' life and showed how all the prophecies had been fulfilled by him. He ended by explaining that Jesus had died in their place for their sins, then came back to life, thus overcoming death for everyone.

"This is fascinating! This is wonderful!" Lydia and the others told each other. She was the first to speak up to Paul and his friends. "What shall we do? How can we become Christians too?" Paul explained they could be baptized right there in the river if they wanted to. They wanted to! And so they did. Right then and there, they were all baptized.

Afterwards, Lydia invited them to her home. "Come! There is so much more we want to know! Share our first days as Christians with us!" So Paul and his companions and their wives accepted her invitation. Of course it took them all nearly three hours to gradually go one or two or three at a time to her house in such a way that people watching her house didn't get suspicious. (See Acts 16:13-15.)

FEAR FOR THEIR LIVES

Not long after, when Paul and one of his friends were on their way to the river for prayer and scripture reading, they were seized and dragged to the market place because of a miracle Paul had performed. "These men are Jews and are throwing our city into an uproar by advocating Jewish customs that are illegal for Romans!" Paul and his friend were stripped and beaten severely, then thrown into prison.

Word of what happened spread across the city like wildfire. It wasn't long before someone in Lydia's household heard what happened and rushed back to tell Lydia. No one else had left to go to the place of prayer yet over by the river. She gathered her household around as well as Paul's friends who had stayed at her house. "We shall pray for them." And they did. All night they prayed.

About mid-morning the next day there was a knock on Lydia's gate. It was Paul and his friend! But a soldier was with them. Had they tortured Paul to get him to tell that Lydia was a worshipper of the one God and not the local gods of the city? Had Paul turned them in to the authorities in order to escape further punishment? Lydia stared alternately at Paul and the soldier. Chills went down her spine. She waited for the chains to be pulled out.

Grinning and knowing what Lydia must be thinking Paul hurriedly explained the jailer had become her brother in Christ during the night.. The jailer asked if his family could join Lydia's household at their place of prayer by the river when they worshipped from now on. (See Acts 16:16-40.)

True Amidst Persecution

The next day, Paul and his friends left. Lydia continued to carry on. The two households got to know each other and of course worshipped together ~ A Jewish household and a Gentile household.

Eventually, they were discovered because it was getting so difficult to hide their growing group who prayed by the river. In fact, there got to be so many of them, Paul wrote them a letter some years later, beginning with, "To all the saints in Christ Jesus at Philippi, together with the overseers and deacons....You stand firm in one spirit, contending as one man for the faith of the gospel without being frightened in any way by those who oppose you....It has been granted to you on behalf of Christ, not only to believe on him, but also to suffer for him, since you are going through the same struggle you saw I had" (Philippians 1:2, 28-30).

Having been discovered meeting by the river, they began changing their meeting place. Sometimes they met in a warehouse, sometimes in a member's home, sometimes outside of town in a cave. Always moving around to avoid detection. Not always successful, sometimes losing business as Lydia did, sometimes losing jobs, sometimes being imprisoned on trumped-up charges, but never forsaking Jesus Christ, their Savior.

23

YOU CAN BE A HERO ALONE
LIKE AQUILA AND PRISCILLA

We couldn't come to you,
but it was very hard to wait any longer.
*So we decided to stay ____ **ALONE**.*
(I Thessalonians 3:1)

It seemed that Aquila and Priscilla were failures. By human standards they were. But by God's standards they were heroes....

We do not know when or where they became Christians. We do know they had first been Jews. So perhaps they were converted to Christianity and belief that Jesus really was the Son of God on a trip to Jerusalem. The first day of the church's existence was the Day of Pentecost in Jerusalem and 3000 people were baptized that day.   Many were from Pontus in today's Turkey where Aquila had been born, and many were from Rome where they lived at the beginning of our story (Acts of the Apostles 2:9-10).

The Turmoil Begins In Italy

Aquila and his wife Priscilla lived at Rome at least for awhile as Christians. Did they think about how wonderful their lives would be from then on with their new belief in Jesus and hope of heaven? Maybe their lives were wonderful at first.

But eventually Claudius Caesar ordered all Jews to leave Rome (Acts 18:1-3a). Claudius had made proselytizing by any religion illegal. Christians often tried to convert Jews.

So Aquila and Priscilla left. Were they allowed time to sell their home, or did they have to just desert it? Were they allowed time to sell their other possessions so they would have funds to travel with and settle down somewhere else? Where would they go? What would they do?

They Move To Greece

Aquila and Priscilla decided to settle in the seaport city of Corinth in southern Greece. They were tent makers by trade. They hoped the many sailors would want small tents to take with them as shelter whenever they sailed to another country for trade or war. They hoped the herdsmen who lived up in the hills would want tents. They hoped travelers to and from the Middle East and Far East would want tents. Bravely, they set up their business and probably lived in the back of their shop.

One day they had a visitor. His name was Paul. He was a tentmaker too and wondered if he could go in with them as a partner. They were excited about this because Paul was also a Christian like them. Further, Paul was a teacher of Christianity. (See Acts 18:3b.)

Their new friend, Paul, brought turmoil back into

their lives. He taught the Jews every Saturday at their local synagogue. But the Jewish leaders didn't like him taking over their followers, so became very abusive toward him. Of course, whatever happened to Paul also happened to some extent to Aquila and Priscilla. All this reminded them of the problems the Jews and Christians had trying to proselytize each other before being kicked out of Rome.

The Jews gave Paul many problems, trying to ruin his reputation and probably trying to get people to not buy any of the tents he made or that Aquila and Priscilla made. They even hauled Paul to court for proselytizing. Probably Aquila and Priscilla went to court to be with their friend, partner, and Christian brother.

Finally Paul gave up on the Jews and his heart ached. But he didn't give up on everyone; he spent the next year and a half teaching the Greeks about Jesus. Certainly Aquila and Priscilla did what they could to encourage this man of God, even though their occupation may have suffered as a result. (You can read all about this in Acts of the Apostles 18:4-17.)

But maybe they lived amid too much turmoil. Perhaps life would be easier for them if they moved somewhere else.

They Move To Turkey

This time, they moved to another seaport city in today's Turkey, the city of Ephesus. Their faith and understanding of Jesus, the Son of God, continued to grow. One day a Jew from Alexandria, Egypt, came to Ephesus and began teaching about Jesus, but did not realize baptism was for forgiveness of sins. Aquila and Priscilla went to hear him speak. Let's read about what happened in Acts of the Apostles 18:24-26 ~

24A Jew named Apollos came to Ephesus. Apollos was born in the city of Alexandria, Egypt. He was an educated man. He knew very much about the Scriptures. 25Apollos had been taught about the Lord (Jesus). Apollos was always very excited when he talked to people about Jesus. The things Apollos taught about Jesus were right. But the only baptism that
Apollos knew about was the baptism that John taught [only for repentance, not forgiveness].
26Apollos began to speak very boldly in the synagogue. Priscilla and Aquila heard him speak. They took him to their home and helped him understand the way of God better.

Later Paul rejoined Aquila and Priscilla in Ephesus, probably staying and working with them as he had before. He stayed two years. During that time, Paul wrote two letters to the church they had left behind in Corinth. Both letters, inspired by God, became part of the New Testament. In I Corinthians 16:19, Aquila and Priscilla sent their greetings back to their Christian friends in Corinth.

Paul continued to teach about Jesus, no doubt with the continued encouragement of Aquila and Priscilla. He not only upset the Jews, but this time, he also upset the worshipers of a popular goddess.

Suddenly there was a riot! People from all over the city rushed at two of Paul's traveling companions and brought them into the arena so they could condemn them to die. They shouted for over two hours. Paul wanted to go into the arena and defend them. But his other friends, including Aquila and Priscilla, wouldn't let him go to the arena. Instead, they hid him for awhile. Finally they convinced him to leave Ephesus.

Just how dangerous had it become for Christians

in Ephesus? When Paul wrote the church in
Corinth, he said he had nearly fought wild beasts in
Ephesus (I Corinthians 15:32). The people there had
apparently threatened to throw him to the lions to be
torn apart.

Aquila and Priscilla left Ephesus too. We know
this because, when Paul wrote the church in Ephesus,
he made no mention of greeting Aquila and Priscilla,
even though they had become close friends by then.
Where to next?

They Move Back To Italy

Home. They apparently wanted to go back home
to Rome, back to their family roots. Claudius Caesar
did not rule very long. Perhaps they moved back when
he died. Perhaps they thought it would be safer then.
When they got back, they got busy teaching people
about Jesus Christ. One by one people decided to
become Christians. They started with just the two of
them. But, by the time their friend, Paul, wrote to the
church in Rome, he said the church met in their home.
This is what he said in Romans 16:3-5 ~

*3Say hello to Priscilla and Aquila. They work together
with me in Christ Jesus.*
*4They risked their own lives to save my life. I am
thankful to them, and all the non-Jewish churches are
thankful to them.*
5Also, say hello to the church that meets at their house.

But the next Roman emperor after Claudius was
much more cruel. He was Nero Caesar. Under Nero,
persecution of Christians grew worse and worse. A book
entitled *Foxe's Book of Martyrs* tells in chapter two some
of what Nero did to the Christians:

Nero even refined upon cruelty, and contrived all manner

of punishments for the Christians that the most [evil] imagination could design. In particular, he had some sewed up in skins of wild beasts and then worried by dogs until they expired. Others he dressed in shirts made stiff with wax, fixed to axletrees, and set [them] on fire in his gardens in order to illuminate them.

There is a possibility, since the church met in the home of Aquila and Priscilla, that they were among those Nero tortured to death for being Christian. We never heard of them again after their move back to Rome.

Peace Amid Turmoil

Their life as Christians meant a life of moving, encouraging and escaping, moving, encouraging and escaping. To their old friends back in Rome, Aquila and Priscilla had never been as successful as they might have been. They could have played it safe and never become Christians. Instead, they chose a religion no one liked.

Never could they call any place home for long after they became Christians. Never could they have a peaceful life after they became Christians. Always their life was in turmoil, at least on the outside. But that was the viewpoint of people who did not have the hope of heaven as did Christians. To other Christians who knew Aquila and Priscilla, and to us today, they were heroes.

24

YOU CAN BE A HERO ALONE
LIKE PAUL - II

*The first time I defended myself, no person helped me.
Every person left me [**ALONE**].
I pray that God will forgive them. But the Lord stayed
with me.
The Lord wanted all the non-Jews to hear that Good
News. So I was saved from the lion's mouth.
The Lord will save me when any person tries to hurt me.
The Lord will bring me safely to his heavenly kingdom.
(2nd Timothy 4:16-18)*

It seemed that Paul was a failure. By human standards he was. But by God's standards he was a hero....

Released From Prison

Paul was released from imprisonment in Rome after the events in our previous lesson, and saved from lions. But the close call he experienced in nearly being executed did not stop him once he was freed.

There never seemed to be a time when Paul was not spreading the Good News of Jesus' death to pay the penalty for our sins and resurrection for our liberty from death. Paul was like Jesus who " came to **find** lost people and save them." (Luke 19:10).

Goes Back To His Old Ways

This way of life had begun years earlier, soon after his conversion to Christianity. Paul had been an anti-Christian terrorist. He had gone from city to city to find Christians and haul them to prison to be sentenced to death. But in Damascus, Syria, he had been convinced that Jesus really was the Son of God. Everyone was astonished ~ both the Christians who had expected to be arrested by him, and the Jews who had expected to help him find Christians to arrest.

But Saul [Paul] became more and more powerful. He proved that Jesus is the Christ [Messiah Savior].   His proofs were so strong that the Jews who lived in Damascus could not argue with him. After many days, some Jews made plans to kill Saul [Paul] ...But Saul [Paul] learned about their plan. One night some followers that Saul had taught helped him leave the city (Acts 9:22-25).

Later, Paul went to a city called Antioch in today's Turkey. He preached there and several Jews became Christians. But the rest of the Jews, especially their leaders, became jealous and had him expelled from the entire region (Acts 13:49-52).

So Paul went to another city called Iconium and taught that Jesus was the Son of God. Many Jews and non-Jews (Gentiles) believed and became Christians. Once again, the Jewish leaders became angry and tried to get enough people stirred up to stone Paul to death. He heard about it and left town before they could. (Read about it in Acts of the Apostles 14:1-6.)

The angry Jews from Antioch and Iconium just followed him to the next city, Lystra. After teaching and converting many, the angry Jews stirred up a crowd who finally stoned him and dragged him outside of the city, leaving him for dead. But the new Christians went to him and helped him. Then Paul did an amazing thing: He got up and went back into the city! (Read Acts 14:19-20)

At another time, Paul went to a city named Philippi in Greece. Several people there became Christians. What happened next? People who did not like Christians hauled him before a Gentile court and lied about him. *The men brought Paul and Silas to the leaders and said, "These men are Jews. They are making trouble in our city" …. Then the leaders tore the clothes of Paul and Silas and told some men to beat Paul and Silas with rods. The men beat Paul and Silas many times. Then the leaders put Paul and Silas in jail.* (Acts 16:20-23). You will never guess what Paul and his Christian friend did while in stocks in prison: They prayed and sang hymns (Acts 16:25)!

Eventually they were released. Did they go into hiding? No, Paul and his Christian friend just went on down the road to the next city, and another after that, and another after that. Trouble followed him where ever he went. People marched, falsely accused, rioted, and did everything they could think of to stop Paul from telling people the Good News that Jesus was the Son of God. But Paul was stubborn and refused to stop.

When He Was Weak, He Was Strong

Just how much persecution did Paul go through? In his letter to the Corinthians about half way through his ministry, he said, *I have been in prison more often. I have been hurt more in beatings. I have been near death many times.* Next, he listed what he had been through so far:

Five [5] times the Jews have given me their punishment of 39 hits with a whip.
Three [3] different times I was beaten with rods.
One [1] time I was almost killed with rocks.
Three [3] times I was in ships that were wrecked, and
One [1] of those times I spent the night and the next day in the sea.

He concluded, *I have been in danger from rivers, from thieves, from my own people (the Jews), and from people who are not Jews. I have been in danger in cities, in places where no people live, and on the sea.... I have done hard and tiring work, and many times I did not sleep. I have been hungry and thirsty. Many times I have been without food. I have been cold and without clothes.* (Read all about it in II Corinthians 11:23-27.)

Was Paul complaining or bragging? Neither one. He explained, *So I am happy when I have weaknesses. I am happy when people say bad things to me. I am happy when I have hard times. I am happy when people treat me badly. And I am happy when I have problems. All these things are for Christ. And I am happy with these things, because when I am weak, then I am truly strong* (II Corinthians 12:10).

Loyal To The Death

Finally, Paul knew his enemies were about to succeed in executing him for his faith. His attitude toward his death is an example for Christians worldwide and in all ages (II Timothy 9:6-8):

My life is being given as an offering for God.
The time has come for me to leave this life here.
I have fought the good fight.

I have finished the race.
I have kept the faith.
Now, a crown (reward) is waiting for me....

PAUL'S ADVICE FOR US TODAY

Jesus had taught that, if someone hits us on one cheek, we are to turn the other cheek so they can hit it too. Further, he said we are to pray for people who persecute us and actually love them! (Read all about this in Matthew 5:10, 39, 44-45). It is amazing the number of persecutors who have been convinced of the love of Jesus Christ by "turning the other cheek" and decided to become Christians too.

Paul wrote this to one congregation that had been going through a lot of persecution (Philippians 1:28-29):

And you will not be afraid of those people who are against you. All of these things are proof from God that .... God gave you the honor of believing in Christ. But that is not all. **God also gave you the honor of suffering for Christ.** *Both these things bring glory to Christ.*

He went on to say toward the end of his encouraging letter, (Philippians 3:20):

But our homeland is in heaven. We are waiting for our Savior to come from heaven. Our Savior is the Lord Jesus Christ. He will change our humble bodies and make them like his own glorious body.

Troublemaker And Hero

Often Paul went through persecutions alone. Did he not have friends to protect him? He had plenty of friends. But he was always going to strange new places where he did not know anyone at all, and therefore, had no protection.

He said in Romans 15:20, *I always want to tell the Good News in places where people have never heard of Christ.*

The faith of this one man who so many people hated, this one man who people had tried for years to shut up is still being talked about centuries later all over the world. It seemed to people of the world that Paul was nothing but a troublemaker. How dare he challenge them to question their life-long beliefs! But in the eyes of God and of people who believed him and became free in Christ, he was a hero.

25

YOU CAN BE A HERO ALONE
LIKE LUKE

For…has deserted me…has gone…has gone….
ONLY *Luke is with me.*
(2nd Timothy 4:10-11)

It seemed that Luke was a failure. By human standards he was. But by God's standards he was a hero.

Here he was. Getting up every day, fixing a small meal for two, and taking it over to the prison. His old friend Paul was there. Everyone else was gone. No one else was left to help old Paul in his dying weeks and days. Things had not always been that way.

Slave & Physician

Who was Luke anyway? His full name was Lucanus. It was a name usually found with slaves. Because he had a slavish name, he may have been born of slave parents, and raised a slave. Or he was captured in war and given a slave's name.

Lucanus ~ Luke ~ was a physician (Colossians

4:14). In Bible times, physicians were always slaves and they always served just one rich family.   In Bible times, slaves were sometimes educated and elevated, wearing good clothes, living in good homes, and having great responsibilities. He must have been the personal physician of someone important enough that he was able to pay for Luke's education.

Freedman

By the time Luke met Paul, he may have been a freedman. This is what often happened to the more advanced and intelligent slaves. Usually, they were freed because of their loyalty and doing something special, more often than not saving the life of their master or a loved one of their master. It is easy to believe that Luke was freed because he did indeed save someone's life. It is also easy to believe Luke was a freedman because he was free to travel with Paul so many places over a period of years.

We do not know exactly when he was converted, but he joined Paul on a missionary journey when he was near the northwest coast of today's Turkey in Troas, more anciently called Troy. All through the book of the Acts of the Apostles, reference is made to Peter, Paul, Barnabas, and many others as "they". But in Acts 16:9 and 10, it says of Paul and his traveling companions, that they went to Troas. Paul saw a vision of a man across the Aegean Sea in Macedonia, Greece, begging him to come to Macedonia to help them. "After Paul had seen the vision, WE got ready at once to leave for Macedonia."

Personal Physician of Paul

Luke remained with Paul and his companions from northern to southern Greece, then over to today's western Turkey in Ephesus, then back to Greece, then back to Troas (Troy) (See Acts 16-21, and finally across the Mediterranean Sea to Palestine and Jerusalem. Luke stayed nearby when Paul was imprisoned in Jerusalem and Caesarea. And when he finally appealed to go to Rome as a Roman citizen and his case be heard by Caesar himself, Luke was there with him.

Luke was with Paul "when it was decided that we would sail for Italy", when their ship wrecked and they almost drowned, when they wintered, stranded, in Malta, and when they finally arrived in Rome. Luke was there through it all. It was two years before Caesar finally heard Paul's case, and Luke was there (Acts 22-28).

Historian

Educated Luke was not idle, just standing by and watching things during this time. Luke wrote one of the biographies of Jesus, the Gospel of Luke. His is the only biography written by a non-eye witness. His was written based on the evidence. He was not only not an eye witness, but he was not a Jew (Colossians 4:11, 14). The Gospel of Luke was written in chronological order giving the names of Roman rulers at the time, as all good historians did, and sent it to a friend, perhaps in order to convert him to Christianity.

Many have undertaken to draw up an account of the things that have been fulfilled among us, just as they were handed down to us by those who from the first were eyewitnesses and servants of the word. Therefore, since I myself have carefully investigated everything from the beginning, it seemed good also to me to write an orderly account for you, most excellent Theophilus, so that you may know the certainty of the things you have been taught (Acts 1:1-4).

Apparently some time after the apostle Paul's trial before Caesar (refer to Acts 28:30), Luke decided to follow up with an account of the apostles' activities to get the church started. So, he wrote Acts of the Apostles which begins thusly:

In my former book, Theophilus, I wrote about all that Jesus began to do and to teach until the day he was taken up to heaven after giving instructions through the Holy Spirit to the apostles he had chosen (Acts 1:1-2).

At the time of Paul's first imprisonment in Rome, he wrote several letters to congregations he had established. When he wrote the congregation in Colossae and a brother there, Philemon, he said,

Prepare a guest room for me, because I hope to be restored to you in answer to your prayers. Epaphras, my fellow prisoner in Christ Jesus, sends you greetings. And so do Mark, Aristarchus, Demas and Luke, my fellow workers.

Later Paul wrote that no one supported him at his first defense. Everyone deserted him. But he was delivered. (2nd Timothy 4:16-17). Now Paul was imprisoned again and it looked like he would not be released this time.

I am already being poured out like a drink offering, and the time has come for my departure. I have fought the good fight. I have finished the race. I have kept the faith. Now there is in store for me the crown of righteousness which the Lord, the righteous Judge, will award to me on that day (2nd "Timothy 4:6-8).

Loyal to the End

Apparently Luke felt guilty for deserting Paul at his first defense. He was determined to never let old

Paul go through it again alone, even if it mean his own imprisonment. And so, here he was preparing decent food every day to take to Paul, maybe some soap and water to clean himself, and perhaps ointment for the insect and rat bites he may have been suffering since he said he was "suffering, even to the point of being chained like a criminal" (2nd Timothy 2:9). Daily, he probably also brought him a clean tunic and robe to wear and took the filthy ones home with him to lovingly wash the vermin out of and hang in the sun to dry and sterilize.

Everyone else was gone. Timothy seemed to still be in Ephesus on the west coast of today's Turkey (1st Timothy 1:3). Demas, who had been with him when he first went to Rome had deserted him because he loved the world too much. Crescans went to Galatia, a large section of today's Turkey. Titus went to today's Yugoslavia. "Only Luke is with me" (2nd Timothy 4:9-10).

All the excitement gone. All the crowds. All the friends and enemies. All the sunshine and clean water and air. Everyone gone. Now only Luke was there with the old soldier of the Lord. And so he continued on, day after day, getting up, gathering food and supplies, going over to the smelly, filthy prison, being frisked for weapons, being humiliated by crude guards, and sitting quietly with old Paul. Being Paul's last friend.

They talked of days gone by. Sometimes Paul dictated a letter which Luke was able to write out for him. Often they prayed together for the congregations Paul and established and which Luke was there to help with. Often Luke must have interrupted Paul's prayers to pray for Paul. Sometimes they may have sang their old hymns together. Perhaps softly lest Paul be beaten, or loudly to make sure all the other prisoners could hear and perhaps believe on this strange Lord Jesus Christ they were just now learning about.

Luke knew he was taking chances associating with Paul. What if they just kept him? Paul was closely guarded and chained. It would be easy enough to not unlock the outer gates for him. But Luke stayed true because everyone needs a friend at the end. Luke was determined to be that friend, no matter what the cost. His friends thought he was taking too many risks and may end up being executed along with Paul as his accomplice.   But to us today, we see that he was being a hero.

26

YOU CAN BE A HERO ALONE
LIKE JOHN

I...your brother and companion in the suffering and kingdom
and patient endurance that are ours in Jesus,
*was on the island [**ALONE**]*
because of the word of God and the testimony of Jesus.
(Revelation 1:9)

It seemed that John was a failure. By human standards he was. But by God's standards he was a hero.

Alone

Life wasn't fair. John was an apostle of Jesus. He could perform miracles. He could remember everything Jesus had ever said ~ another miracle. (See Matthew 10:1-4, 19.) Not only that, but he was the last of the twelve apostles still living. Seekers everywhere wanted to hear what he had to say. But now, it was not to be. Now he was being punished for spreading the Christian religion, something that was illegal nearly every place he went. Now John was in exile on an island near Turkey ~ the Isle Patmos ~ and all alone.

         You Can Be A Hero Alone
(Read about this in Revelation 1:9-10).

How did he spend his time? Much of it was spent "in the Spirit." The New Testament says in several places that being "in the Spirit" refers to the good Christian life (Luke 10:21, Romans 14:17-18, II Corinthians 6:6, Ephesians 2:21-22). What else does it mean?

Prayer

Luke 10:21 says Jesus rejoiced in the Spirit and thanked God for good that had come. John must have walked along the beaches of that island trying to think of things to thank God for. Certainly, he had much to complain about. But, being "in the Spirit", he tried to think of the good.

Of course, he thanked God for the shelter where he laid his head at night and where he got in out of the rain and cold wind. It may have just been a shack provided for him; after all, he was on the island as punishment. But shelter was shelter, whether made of gold or clay. He also had clothes to wear. They may have been rags, but at least they were clothes. He also had food to eat. It may not have been very much, and it may have had no taste or tasted bad, but at least it was food.

He prayed for people. Who was on John's prayer list? He certainly prayed for all the Christians he knew, and even Christians he didn't know ~ in his home town, in his nation, in other parts of the world. He didn't know all their names, but God did.

John also prayed for non-Christians. He knew that God loves sinners (I John 4:10, 19) and Christians are to pray in the Spirit for the lost (Jude 1:20-23). He probably also prayed for the non-believing families of believers, for former neighbors, for government authorities who had punished him.

What posture did John take when he prayed? People in his society often prayed with their heads bowed down to the ground. But, since Christians are to be constantly in prayer, he probably also prayed standing up, sitting down, even walking around. The posture did not matter so much, as long as he prayed.

Song

What else did John do while "in the Spirit"? Colossians 1:8 says a person is "in the Spirit" when he tells about the love of God.   Elsewhere in that same writing, it says Christians are to sing with gratitude in their hearts (Colossians 3:16).

Here he was in exile and probably not living in very much comfort. But John still had much to be thankful for. After all, like every other human, he was a sinner (Romans 3:23). Now he was saved. Saved from what? Saved from an eternity in hell: Hell, the home of Satan; hell, the place where there is no light, no love, no smiles (Matthew 25:30, 46). He had been saved from ultimate bad so he could enter ultimate good in heaven: Heaven, the home of God; heaven, the place where there is light, love, singing (Revelation 22:3-5).

Where did the songs come from? He apparently sang some of David's psalms found in the Bible. Where did the hymns and spiritual songs come from mentioned in Colossians 3:16? Maybe he created his own. Maybe there were popular folk tunes that he liked, so he expressed his gratitude for salvation, for Jesus, for heaven in some of those folk tunes. Maybe he just chanted by putting some of Jesus' words to those simple tunes. Maybe he changed the type of songs he sang through the day.

Words Of God

One writer of the New Testament said that a person is "in the Spirit" by sharing the Truth with love (II Corinthians 6:6-7). Another writer said a person is "in the Spirit" by sharing the Word of God (Hebrews 6:4-5).

How many hours must he have walked along the beach recalling Jesus' words, repeating them over and over in his mind. They had been words of wisdom, encouragement, warning, enlightenment, love. He could never tire of recalling those words of Jesus. But how could he share them?

John also wrote parts of the Word of God. He had not only been provided shelter, clothes and food on the island, but also pen and parchment. John apparently wrote many letters. Perhaps a guard would deliver one now and then.

There are five letters that he wrote that still exist. One was the life of Jesus Christ with an emphasis on Jesus being the Word of God (John 1:1-4,14).   Another letter also centered around the fact that Jesus was the Son/Word of God, and carried warnings to anyone who did not believe this, calling such a person an "anti-Christ" (I John 4:2-3). A third and fourth letter were sent to friends and are short.

John's final inspired letter that still exists is called Revelation. It tells of a vision he had while on the Isle of Patmos. Here he was alone, but "in the Spirit" remembering all Jesus' words and activities. Suddenly his old friend, his Lord appeared and greeted him. It wasn't an ordinary greeting, for Jesus now was shining like the sun and his voice was like a trumpet. John fell at Jesus' feet trembling. (Read about it in Revelation

1:9-17.)

But then Jesus did something special. He touched John. Together again. John was now probably over 90 years old. He had probably been around age 30 when he was with Jesus on earth. For sixty long years John had told others about Jesus. For sixty long years he suffered for telling people Jesus really was the Son of God (Revelation 1:9.) For sixty very long years, John had remained faithful.

Now, at last, they were together again. Jesus told John "Write" (Revelation 1:19). What John wrote at this time became the last book of the Bible ~ Revelation. It tied together things of the past and the future ~ prophecy and fulfillment.   It described heaven.

Lord's Supper

What else does it mean to be "in the Spirit"? When John saw Jesus again, he did so on the "Lord's Day". This phrase is not used elsewhere in the Bible. But we can easily figure it out. Jesus came back to life and overcame death on Sunday, the first day of the week. (Read about it in John chapter 20.)

The Kingdom of Heaven, the Church, began on Sunday. (NOTE: Jesus was crucified the day before Passover [John 19:14, 31, 42 ~ a "special Sabbath"], and the church began on the day of Pentecost [Acts 2:1] which was 50 days after the day of Passover.)

What special thing did Christians do on the first day of the week? Acts of the Apostles 20:7 says they met on the first day of the week to break bread. In the original language of the New Testament, it says they met every first day of the week to break bread in a religious sense. Just what did they do? The night before Jesus' crucifixion, he gave his apostles bread and told them to eat a bite of it in remembrance of his body sacrificed for sinners on the cross. Then he gave them some red wine (grape juice) to take a drink of in remembrance of his blood shed for sinners on the cross. He told them to do this until he returned at the end of the world. (Read about it in I Corinthians 11:23-26.)

Alone But Not Alone

So here was John walking around alone in exile on this island. For the most part he didn't have anyone to talk to except the guards. He had so much he could be doing and telling, but it was no longer possible. The government had made sure of that. But we today view what John accomplished, even while alone, and to us he is a hero.

QUICK SURVEYOF BIBLE FOR MEDITATION

Being the only Christian in your area, or being par of a very small group of Christians is hard. It is almost impossible to remain a loyal Christian all alone. But it can be done. To help you I your struggle, here are 52 easy weekly Bible studies and worship guides it is an easy survey of the entire New Testament of the Bible.

OPTION 1 is the Bible Class for families and friends who wish to study and worship together in a home or smaller congregations with few leaders or someone who cannot find any other Christians to study the Bible and worship with

If you are in a country where it is illegal for you to meet for Christian worship, but know other Christians who want to study and worship together in secret, you might want to consider meeting in a different home each week. Even then, people who attend should arrive at different times in order to not arouse suspicion of neighbors. Or you could go out of town and meet in a cave or other natural shelter hidden from people.

OPTION 2 is a conclusion of worship for group meetings. But, it is ALSO FOR those living in a home where the others are violently against Christianity and will do bad things to you if they knew you had become a Christian.

Therefore, you have to hide behind a locked doo to worship. So, skip down and do only option 2 which is the most important part of Sunday worship. (We can sing, pray, read scripture any day of the week. But Sunday is set aside for the Lord's Supper, as shown by the Apostle Paul in Acs 20:6ff.)

You should be able to complete the short Bible reading about Jesus' crucifixion, whisper two scripture hymns, and partake of the two emblems – unleavened bread and red grape juice – of the Lord's Supper in about 15 minutes. Perhaps you can hide on the roof or in the bathroom or basement.

DOWNLOAD the BIBLE into your native language onto a flash drive. If you are living in a country where it is illegal for you to own a Bible, hide your flash drive in a jar and bury it in your yard in case your home is ever searched

MEMORIZE verses from the Bible. It may be the only Bible you have some day.

FOR SONGS: Sing in your native language a Bible verse, with each phrase being a different musical note. (Perhaps sing a phrase and let your family repeat it. Then sing the next phrase and let your family repeat it. Etc.) Or you could sing the Bible verse to a familiar tune your family knows. Or sing a few lines of a poem about Jesus someone in your family wrote.

Of course, if you are fearful of being discovered, whisper your songs, or sing them in your mind.

FOR THE LORD'S SUPPER: If you don't have grape
juice available, soak raisins (dried grapes) in water to
plump them and get the juice from it. For the bread, it
needs to be unleavened. Some crackers, pita bread, any
kind of flat bread are possible sources. Otherwise,
make your own with flour and water, baked in an oven
or lightly fried.

NO COPYRIGHT: This material does not have a
copyright. Therefore, feel free to send copies to smaller
congregations with few leaders or home congregations.

A NOTE TO MISSIONARIES AND ENCOURAGERS: Feel
free to scan and send each Sunday's easy Bible study
and worship guide over the internet. But be CAREFUL.
In your subject line, do not use words such as Bible,
Jesus, Christian, Church, Baptism, etc.

It is suggested that you attach this as a document and
be password protected with a word known only to the
sender and receiver. The recipient should delete your
message from both their email and computer history.

Sunday 1

Birth & Adult Baptism of Jesus (Matthew 1-4)

Option 1 – Worship in a Group

READ ALOUD MATTHEW 1:18-25

1:18 - What was Jesus' mother's name?

1:18 - Mary was not married to Joseph yet. She became pregnant by the power of who?

1:20-21 - Who named Jesus? What does his name mean?

READ ALOUD MATTHEW 2:1-23

2:1 - What town was Jesus born in?

2:2 - The wise men from the east were from around Iraq, Iran, and India. They came because they saw a special _________ in the sky in the direction of Israel.

2:7-8 - What evil king of the Jews told the wise men the exact city the baby king was born in?

2:11 - What gifts did the wise men bring to the baby king (who was really going to be a king of people's souls, but they didn't know that yet)?

2:14 - Both the wise men and Joseph were warned in a dream to flee because the evil king was sending soldiers to kill all babies. What country did Joseph take his wife and her baby to?

2:23 - Years later after the evil king died, Joseph moved his family back to Israel. What town did they move to?

READ ALOUD MATTHEW 3:13-17

3:13 - What was the name of the river Jesus was baptized in?

3:15 - Jesus told John he wanted to be baptized to fulfill all what?

3:16 - When Jesus was baptized, he went down into and came up out of the what?

3:16 - God's Spirit descended on Jesus in the form of a what?

3:17 - A voice out of heaven declared, "This is My ______________ in whom I am well pleased."

READ ALOUD MATTHEW 4:1-11

4:2 - How long did Jesus go without food in the wilderness?

4:3 & 11 - The tempter came to him. Who was the tempter?

4:3 - While Jesus was hungry, the devil tempted him to turn stones into what?

4:6 -   Next the devil took him to the roof top of the temple and tempted him to throw himself down so the __________ could save him.

4:8 - Third, the devil tempted him to worship him so he could control all the __________ of the world.

4:4 & 7 & 10 - Each time Jesus refused to obey the devil by telling him what was ______ in the scriptures.

4:11 - Finally, the devil left Jesus alone, and he was helped by who?

Option 2 – Alone Among Enemies or Continue Worship in a Group

LORD'S SUPPER:

 You Can Be A Hero Alone
Sing or whisper HEBREWS 12:14

Read MATTHEW 26:26-30, about Jesus and the very first "Lord's Supper"

Take a bite of unleavened bread, representing Jesus body tortured on the cross for us.

Pray silently about Jesus' sacrifice, dying in your place for your sins.

Take a sip of grape juice, representing Jesus' blood that dripped away on the cross for you,

Pray silently about your own sins and desire to live more as God wants you to.

Sing or whisper 1st PETER 3:18a

COLLECTION:

Prayer: Thank God for your blessings.

Set aside a little money to be used to buy a flash drive to put Bible study material on it, or help someone in need that you know.

CLOSING PRAYER

GOD BLESS AND KEEP YOU SAFE UNTIL NEXT SUNDAY

Sunday 2

Famous Sermon On the Mountain (Matthew 5-7)

Option 1 – Worship in a Group

READ ALOUD MATTHEW 5:1-47

5:7 - What did Jesus say the reward will be to merciful people?

5:8 - What did Jesus say the reward will be people who are pure in heart?

5:12 - Good people are often insulted, lied about, and persecuted on earth. Jesus said we should rejoice because our reward is where?

5:16 - Jesus said being a light means showing your __________ works.

5:21-22 - Jesus said that we are guilty of what if we call someone bad names?

5:38-39 - Most people say you should take revenge. If someone knocks your tooth out, you should knock their tooth out. But Jesus said we should __________ our enemies.

READ ALOUD MATTHEW 6:1-4

6:1 - Jesus said people who do good works to show off get

their reward from _____, but not from God.

6:3 - When we give to the poor, we are not to let our ____ hand know what our ____ hand is doing. What do you think that means?

READ ALOUD MATTHEW 7:1-6

7:2 - We should be careful how we judge other people because they will do what?

7:3 - People who accuse someone else of having some tiny bad thing in their life, often have a __________ bad thing in their own life.

7:5 - Is it easy to see ourselves as others do?

7:6 - Jesus said we are not to waste our time giving something holy to what kind of people?

READ ALOUD MATTHEW 7:7-14

7:7 - If we are seeking holiness in our life, we have to do what?

7:9 - Good fathers do not give their children __________ when they ask for bread.

7:10 - God is a perfect heavenly ___________ and will do more for us than our own loving fathers.

7:12 - This verse is called the "Golden Rule". We are to treat others how?

7:14 - Jesus said the gate to heaven is ________ and hard to go through, while the gate to hell is ________ and easy to go through.

READ ALOUD MATTHEW 7:15-23

7:15 - Jesus warned that false prophets will look like spiritual ________, but are really spiritual ___________.

7:17 - If a prophet demands people die for him, he is not acting like Jesus who did what for us?

7:21 - Just because a religious leader prays a lot to the Lord, does that alone save him?

7:22 - Just because someone performed miracles in the name of the Lord, does that prove he's saved?

7:23 - What will Jesus say to these false prophets on the Day of Judgment?

READ ALOUD MATTHEWE 7:24-28

7:24 - What kind of person is able to put his soul on a spiritual foundation of rock?
7:26 - What kind of person puts his soul on a spiritual foundation of sand?

Option 2 –Alone Among Enemies or Continue Worship in a Group

LORD'S SUPPER

Sing or whisper ACTS 2:24

Read MATTHEW 27:27-37 about soldiers beating Jesus, mocking him, then nailing him to a cross.

Take a bite of unleavened bread, representing Jesus body tortured on the cross for us.

Pray silently about Jesus' sacrifice, dying in your place for your sins.

Take a sip of grape juice, representing Jesus' blood that dripped away on the cross for you,

Pray silently about your own sins and desire to live more as God wants you to.

Sing or whisper ACTS 2:38

COLLECTION

Prayer: Thank God for your blessings.

Set the money aside to be used to buy a flash drive to put Bible study material on it, or help someone in need that you know.

CLOSING PRAYER

GOD BLESS AND KEEP YOU SAFE UNTIL NEXT SUNDAY

Sunday 3

Selects 12 Apostles, Then Warns Them (Matthew 10)

Option 1 – Worship in a Group

READ ALOUD MATTHEW 10:1-4

10:1 - What two kinds of miracles did Jesus give his 12 apostles power to do?

10:2 - Who was Simon Peter's brother? Who was James' brother?

READ ALOUD MATTHEW 10:5-15

10:5-6 - At that time there were Gentiles (non-Jews), Samaritans (half-Jews), and Jews (Israelites). Jesus told his 12 apostles to go to the cities of who?

10:7 - They were to tell everyone in every city that what was going to arrive very soon?

10:8 - To convince people their words were true, they were to heal the _______, raise the _______ and cash out ___________.

10:9-10 - They were not to take along extra _______, _________ or _______.

10:14 - Were they to curse anyone who refused to believe them?

READ ALOUD MATTHEW 10:16-23

10:16 - Jesus was sending them to teach people who wanted to tear them apart like __________.

10:16 - So, they were to be as mild as _______, but clever as __________, and harmless as __________.

10:17 - He warned that they would be treated how?

10:18 - When they were put on trial, instead of defending themselves, they were to ____________ about the kingdom of God.

10:21 - He predicted that family members would do what to each other?

10:22 - He said they would be ____________ by everyone.

10:23 - When things got to bad, they were to go to

____________________________.

READ ALOUD MATTHEW 10:24-42

10:27 - Jesus taught them in private, but they were to spread his teachings when?

10:28 - Who were the only ones they were to fear? (Memorize this verse.)

10:32 - Jesus promised that everyone who confessed him before people, Jesus would confess them before who? (Memorize this verse.)

10:34-36 - Jesus told them that spreading Christianity would even make their __________ their enemies.

10:38 - Jesus said anyone who does not take up his own ____________ as Jesus was going to do was not worthy of him.

10:42 - Anyone who gives a cup of water to you shall not lose his __________.

Option 2 – Alone Among Enemies or Continue Worship in a Group

LORD'S SUPPER:

Sing or whisper 1ST CORINTHIANS 11:24

Read MATTHEW 26:36-46 about Jesus' agony in a garden the night before he was crucified.

> Take a bite of unleavened bread, representing Jesus body tortured on the cross for us.

> Pray silently about Jesus' sacrifice, dying in your place for your sins.

> Take a sip of grape juice, representing Jesus' blood that dripped away on the cross for you,

> Pray silently about your own sins and desire to live more as God wants you to.

Sing or whisper 1ST CORINTHIANS 11:25

COLLECTION

Prayer: Thank God for your blessings.

Set the money aside to be used to buy a flash drive to put Bible study material on it, or help someone in need that you know.

CLOSING PRAYER

GOD BLESS AND KEEP YOU SAFE UNTIL NEXT SUNDAY

Sunday 4

Farmers & a Judge (Matthew 13)

Option 1 – Worship in a Group

READ ALOUD MATTHEW 13:1-17

13:13 - Jesus said he told earthly stories to teach spiritual things. Some people do not understand them because they don't have spiritual ____________ to want to see spiritual things and spiritual ____________ to want to hear spiritual things.

13:15 - Some people have hearts that are

____

13:17 - Those people don't want God to ____________ them because they don't want to admit that they sin.

READ ALOUD MATTHEW 13:18-23

13:18-19 - In this story, Jesus called the seed planted the ________ of God, also called the __________ of the Kingdom of God.

13:19 - Seed that falls by the side of a road to stick to the bottom of people's shoes and and taken onto the ____________ to be trampled.

13:19 - Who do you think the evil one is who takes the Word out of people's heart?

13:20-21 - People who quickly accept God's Word, then lose

interest are like _________ hearts.

      13:21 - What causes such people to fall away from God?

      13:22 - What do the weeds represent chokes the word of God out of people's hearts?

      13:23 - What does a person do whose heart is good soil for the Word of God?

READ ALOUD MATTHEW 13:24-30

      13:25 - Our enemies can ruin good seed we've planted just by planting what afterward?

      13:31-32 - The Word of God can be planted small, but grow into what? (Some people wear a mustard seed as a necklace to remind them of this.)

      13:33 - The Word of God in one heart can reproduce the Word in what way?

      13:37 - Jesus sometimes called himself the Son of God and the Son of Man. How could he be both?

      13:38 - The field Jesus sows the Word of God in is what?

      13:38 - Since the good seeds in this story are the children of God, people who are bad seeds are the children of who?

      13:39 - At the end of the world, who will bring in the crop of all human souls?

      13:40 - What will God do to people who are not his children?

      13:41 - There will be some people in the Kingdom of God who are false children because they cause God's true children to

_______.

      13:43 - But the true righteous children of God will
_____________ as the sun.

READ ALOUD MATTHEW 13:44-52

      13:44 - We should treat he kingdom of heaven like a
_____________ that may be hidden.

      13:44 - If we realize how valuable the kingdom is, we will do what to have it?

      13:44 - The kingdom of heaven is also like fine what?

      13:47-48 - How is the kingdom of heaven like a __________ in the sea?

      13:49-50 - At the end of the world, the angels will take the bad fish out and throw them into a __________.

Option 2 –Alone Among Enemies or Continue Worship in a Group

LORD'S SUPPER:

Sing or whisper ECCLESIASTES 7:20

Read MATTHEW 26:36-46 about Jesus' agony in a garden the night before he was crucified.

Take a bite of unleavened bread, representing Jesus body tortured on the cross for us.

Pray silently about Jesus' sacrifice, dying in your place for your sins.

Take a sip of grape juice, representing Jesus' blood that dripped away on the cross for you,

Pray silently about your own sins and desire to live more as God wants you to.

Sing or whisper ROMANS 3:23

COLLECTION

Prayer: Thank God for your blessings.

Set the money aside to be used to buy a flash drive to put Bible study material on it, or help someone in need that you know.

CLOSING PRAYER

GOD BLESS AND KEEP YOU SAFE UNTIL NEXT SUNDAY

Sunday 5

John is Beheaded & a Storm is Stopped (Matthew 14)

Option 1 – Worship in a Group

READ ALOUD MATTHEW 14:1-12

14:1-2 - Herod, a governor and son of King Herod, heard Jesus was performing miracles, he thought Jesus was who risen from the dead?

14:3-4 - The previous year, John the Baptist had been preaching against Herod for marrying his brother's who?

14:5 - Governor Herod wanted to kill John the Baptist, but was afraid because people believed John was a what?

14:6 - Governor Herod had a birthday party and his new wife's daughter ___________ in front of him.

14:7-12 - He told the girl he would give her whatever she wanted as a reward. What did she ask for?

READ ALOUD MATTHEW 14:13-21

14:13 - Jesus was so sad when he heard that John the Baptist had been killed in prison, he did what to be alone?

14:14 - But when he got there, a large crowd was waiting for him, wanting him to do what for them?

14:15 - That night, Jesus' apostles wanted to send the crowds away to buy what for themselves?

14:16-18 - But Jesus told his apostles to feed them, even though all they had was what?

14:19-21 - Jesus fed how many men with that little bit of food?   Adding a wife and two children for each man, about how many people total did Jesus feed by miracle?

READ ALOUD MATTHEW 14:22-33

14:22-23 - Jesus sent the crowds away and sent his twelve apostles away so he could do what alone?

14:24 - But his apostles were on the boat about 6 kilometers out in the Lake of Galilee where what was happening?

14:25 - Jesus knew what was going on, so miraculously did what to get to them in their boat?

14:26 - His apostles saw Jesus and thought he was a what?

14:27 - What did Jesus say to get them to quit being afraid of him?

14:28-29 - The apostle Peter was so excited he did what?

14:30 - But when Peter quit looking at Jesus and started looking at the stormy wind and waves, he began to what?

14:31 - Jesus held out his hand and helped Peter. Even though Peter had more faith than any of the other apostles, Jesus told him he had what?

14:32 - Once Jesus and Peter got into the boat, what happened to the stormy wind?

14:33 - Realizing Jesus could actually control nature, they bowed down to him in the boat and said he was who?

READ ALOUD MATTHEW 14:34-36

14:34-35 - When they landed on the other side of the lake and were recognized, what did people do?

14:36 - All they had to do to be healed was to touch what?

Option 2 – Alone Among Enemies or Continue Worship in a Group

LORD'S SUPPER

Sing or whisper 1ST JOHN 4:9

Read MATTHEW 27:45-54 about the darkness in the middle of the day when Jesus was crucifixion what happened when he died, and what the Roman captain said about Jesus after seeing it all.

Give a bite of unleavened bread to everyone in your family who has been baptized into Jesus

Everyone pray silently about Jesus' sacrifice, dying in their place for their sins.

Pass out a sip of grape juice to everyone who has been baptized into Jesus.

Everyone pray silently about their own sins and desire to live more as God wants us to.

Sing or whisper 1ST JOHN 4:10

COLLECTION

Prayer: Thank God for your blessings.

Set the money aside to be used to buy a flash drive to put Bible study material on it, or help someone in need that you know.

CLOSING PRAYER

GOD BLESS AND KEEP YOU SAFE UNTIL NEXT SUNDAY

Sunday 6

Children, Backsliders, Forgiveness (Matthew 18)

Option 1 – Worship in a Group

READ ALOUD MATTHEW 18:1-6

     18:1 - Jesus' disciples asked him who should be considered greatest in what?

     18:2 - He replied that the greatest is like a what?

     18:3 - In what way can adults be like children?

     18:5 - He also warns people who are mean to children, saying it would be better that they ________ than face him on the Day of Judgment.

READ ALOUD MATTHEW 18:7-14

     18:7 - What did Jesus call people who make us fall away from our faith?

     18:8-9 - Although he may not have meant it literally, what did he say we should do to a part of our body if it causes us to fall from our faith?

     18:10 - What special being in heaven watches out for little children?

     18:11 - Jesus called himself the Son of Mankind because he was God in a human body for awhile. Why did he come to earth?

18:12-13 - A good shepherd does what special thing if one of his sheep falls away from the flock?

18:14 - Jesus is like our shepherd. God the father does not want any of us, his sheep, to ______.

READ ALOUD MATTHEW 18:15-20

18:15 - If a brother or sister in Christ is committing sins that are noticed by others, what should we do?

18:16 - If s/he does not listen and change, what should we do?

18:17 - If s/he still doesn't listen, everyone in the ___________ should be told, and that person shunned so they will miss your love and fellowship and return.

18:20 - Memorize this: "Where 2 or 3 are gathered together in My name, I am there in their midst."

READ ALOUD MATTHEW 18:21-35

18:21 - Peter asked Jesus if a Christian sins against us, how many times we should forgive him. Peter suggested how many times should be enough?

18:22 - Jesus said no. He said we should forgive the same sin by the same person how many times?

18:23-24 - Jesus told a story of a slave who owed millions of pieces of money to his master, but the slave what?

18:25-26 - His master demanded he sell his wife and children into slavery so he could repay the debt, but the man owing the money did what?

18:27 - So his master felt sorry for him, erased the debt, telling him he didn't owe him anything, because he F___________ the debtor.

18:28-30 - But this same slave went to someone who owed him a little bit of money and did what to him?

18:31-34 - When the master of the first slave heard about it, he handed his slave over to be tortured until he could do what?

18:35 - This was a parable to explain that our heavenly Father will hand us over to be tortured in hell if we do not do what?

Option 2 –Alone Among Enemies or

Continue Worship in a Group

LORD'S SUPPER

Sing or whisper HEBREWS 9:26

READ MATTHEW 28:1-7, 11-15 about Jesus coming back to life, appearing to the 5 women who had supported him in his travels (including his mother) and how the High Priest bribed the guards to say his body was stolen while they were sleeping.

Take a bite of unleavened bread, representing Jesus body tortured on the cross for us.

Pray silently about Jesus' sacrifice, dying in your place for your sins.

Take a sip of grape juice, representing Jesus' blood that dripped away on the cross for you,

Pray silently about your own sins and desire to live more as God wants you to.

Sing or whisper REVELATION 7:14

COLLECTION

Prayer: Thank God for your blessings.

Set the money aside to be used to buy a flash drive to put Bible study material on it, or help someone in need that you know.

CLOSING PRAYER

GOD BLESS AND KEEP YOU SAFE UNTIL NEXT SUNDAY

Sunday 7

How to Treat Your Family
(Matthew 19)

Option 1 – Worship in a Group

READ ALOUD MATTHEW 19:1-12

19:3 - Some people asked Jesus if it was okay to _________ for any reason they want to.

19:6 - Since God said husband and wife are to be one, they are no longer ______.

19:6 - "What _________ has joined together, let _____ ______________ separate."

19:8 - Moses had allowed divorce only because their __________ were __________.

19:9 - Jesus said that the only reason a person can divorce is if their spouse committed __________________.

19:9 - If a person divorces for the wrong reason, then remarries, that person is still married in the eyes of God and is ______________________________ with the illegal spouse.

19:12 - Some have decided never to marry for several reasons. The best reason to not marry does this so s/he can spend more time helping in the kingdom of __________________.

READ ALOUD MATTHEW 19:13-15

19:13 - Some parents brought their little children to Jesus so he could _______ for them.

19:14a - His apostles thought Jesus was too important and told the parents not to do this. Jesus said "____________

_____________ _____________."

19:14b - Why? Because children are automatically in the ___________ of _____________.

READ ALOUD MATTHEW 19:16-26

19:16 - A young man came to Jesus and asked what?

19:17 - Jesus told him to do what?

19:18-19 - Jesus listed all of Moses' Ten Commandments relating to the treatment of other people.

19:20 - The young man said he obeyed all those commandments. But he felt he was still what?

19:21 - Jesus saw the emptiness in his heart, so told him to do what?

19:22 - The young man left very sad because he was very _____________ and couldn't give up his possessions to be saved in eternity.

19:23 - Jesus warned people that it is hard for who to enter the kingdom of heaven?

19:24 - It is so hard, that a camel can walk through _________________ easier.

25-26 - When his followers said that made it impossible for a rich man to go to heaven, Jesus replied that with __________ all things are __________________.

READ ALOUD MATTHEW 19:27-30

19:27 - Jesus' apostle Peter said he had left how much to follow Jesus?

19:29a - List the things Jesus said Christians have to sometimes leave in order to be Christians.

19:29b - But, if they do, they will receive how much more of those same things and people in the kingdom of heaven?

____

19:29b - In what way can the church be a substitute for these things?

Option 2 –Alone Among Enemies or Continue Worship in a Group

LORD'S SUPPER

Sing or whisper HEBREWS 4:15

Read MARK 14:12-21 where Jesus predicts his betrayal

Take a bite of unleavened bread, representing Jesus body tortured on the cross for us.

Pray silently about Jesus' sacrifice, dying in your place for your sins.

Take a sip of grape juice, representing Jesus' blood that dripped away on the cross for you,

Pray silently about your own sins and desire to live more as God wants you to.

Sing or whisper HEBREWS 7:25

COLLECTION

Prayer: Thank God for your blessings.

Set the money aside to be used to buy a flash drive to put Bible study material on it, or help someone in need that you know.

CLOSING PRAYER

GOD BLESS AND KEEP YOU SAFE UNTIL NEXT SUNDAY

Sunday 8
Enemies Try to Trap Jesus
(Matthew 22)

Option 1 – Worship in a Group

READ ALOUD MATTHEW 22:1-14

22:1 - What is an earthly story with as heavenly meaning?

22:2 - Inviting people into the kingdom of God is like a king inviting people to his son's what?

22:3 - But those who were invited to come did what?

22:4-5 - Twice the king sent servants out to beg the invited guests to come. What did they do instead?

22:6 - What else did the invited guests do to the servants with the message?

22:7-8 - The king killed all those who killed his servants, saying they were not _______ to come to the wedding feast.

22:9-10 - So he invited many strangers where?

22:11-12 - The king provided festive wedding clothes to the guests, but one did not change what?

22:13 - The guest who came but refused to change was cast into outer darkness. What do you think this outer darkness represented?

22:14 - God calls everyone to enter his kingdom, but very few come, so very few are what?

READ ALOUD MATTHEW 22:15-22

22:15-16 - The Pharisees, a Jewish sect, hated Jesus, so decided to trap him. The bait they set was to flatter him and tell him what?

22:17 - They asked him if it was lawful to pay what to the hated foreign occupation government, the Romans?

22:18 - Jesus called him what?

22:19-21 - Jesus told them to give coins made by Caesar to who?

READ ALOUD MATTHEW 22:23-33

22:23 - The Sadducees were another Jewish sect and they believed what?

22:24-25 - According to Jewish law then, if a man died with no children, his _______ was supposed to impregnate the widow and name them after the deceased husband.

22:26-28 - The Sadducees tried to trap Jesus by asking him, "If the widow is married to seven brothers and never has a child, who will she be _______________ to in heaven?"

22:29-30 - Jesus replied that in heaven people will be like the ________ and not _________

22:31-32 - Jesus proved there was life after death by saying God IS the God of who? Were they still alive 1500 years after they lived on earth?

READ ALOUD MATTHEW 22:36-46

22:36-38 - Jesus said the greatest commandment was what?

22:39-40 - Jesus said the second greatest commandment was what?

22:42 - Christ means Messiah, the eternal king who was to take the punishment of people's sins from them. Jesus is often called Jesus Christ. Whose human descendant did they say the Christ was?

22:43-44 - Jesus said David called his "son" (his descendant) Lord, meaning God.

22:45 - David called Christ God because this descendant was also the Son of God.

Option 2 – Alone Among Enemies or Continue Worship in a Group

LORD'S SUPPER

Sing or whisper ISAIAH 53:5a

Read MARK 14:22-31 where Jesus shows how to keep the "Lord's Supper"

Take a bite of unleavened bread, representing Jesus body tortured on the cross for us.

Pray silently about Jesus' sacrifice, dying in your place for your sins.

Take a sip of grape juice, representing Jesus' blood that dripped away on the cross for you,

Pray silently about your own sins and desire to live more as God wants you to.

Sing or whisper ISAIAH 53:7

COLLECTION

Prayer: Thank God for your blessings.

Set the money aside to be used to buy a flash drive to put Bible study material on it, or help someone in need that you know.

CLOSING PRAYER

GOD BLESS AND KEEP YOU SAFE UNTIL NEXT SUNDAY

Sunday 9

A Wedding, a Rich Man & a Judge (Matthew 25)

Option 1 – Worship in a Group

READ ALOUD MATTHEW 25:1-12

25:1 - In Jesus' time, the groom and friends paraded through the street to the bride's house, and her maids met them near her house. In Jesus story, how many bride's maids went to meet the groom?

25:2-4 - How many took extra oil for their lamps?

25:5-6 - The maids fell asleep waiting, and the groom's parade didn't come into sight until when?

25:7-9 - By then the maids' lamps had gone out. What did the unprepared maids want the prepared maids to do? Why didn't they?

25:10 - While the foolish maids were trying to buy more oil at the midnight oil when all the shops were closed, the groom came and what did the wedding party do then?

25:11-12 - Jesus said this is like when he will come to call the church to him (he often called the church his bride) to take everyone to heaven. What will happen to people who are unprepared?

READ ALOUD MATTHEW 25:14-33

25:14 - The rich man who went on a journey and left his slaves in charge are like what person who was about to be crucified and go on a journey to heaven?

25:15-18 - What did the three slaves do with the talents given them to take care of his estate while he was gone?

25:19-23 - When the master returned, what did he tell the two who had doubled the talents he'd given them?

25:24-25 - Rather than think of his master as good, the one who received just one talent claimed his master was what?

25:26-28 - The master was angry because the slave with one talent did what with it?

25:29-30 - Although we are children of God, in a way we are like slaves because we are expected to do good works and teach others. What will happen to us if we do not?

READ ALOUD MATTHEW 25:31-46

25:31 - When Jesus returns, who is he going to have with him?

25:32-33 - Is Jesus going to set up another kingdom on earth when he comes, or is he going to immediately declare it is the Day of Judgment? Where will he sit?

25:34-38 - Jesus will reward people who did what to him?

25:39-40 - In what way do we do these things to Jesus?

25:41 - Those who do not will be sent to the eternal fire which will also have who in it?

25:42-46 - Summarize what Jesus said.

Option 2 – Alone Among Enemies or Continue Worship in a Group

LORD'S SUPPER

Sing or whisper 1ST CORINTHIANS 6:11b

READ MARK 14:32-50 about Jesus begging his Father at the last minute to not make his death necessary, and his arrest.

Take a bite of unleavened bread, representing Jesus body tortured on the cross for us.

Pray silently about Jesus' sacrifice, dying in your place for your sins.

Take a sip of grape juice, representing Jesus' blood that dripped away on the cross for you,

Pray silently about your own sins and desire to live more as God wants you to.

Sing or whisper ISAIAH 1:18

COLLECTION

Prayer: Thank God for your blessings.

Set the money aside to be used to buy a flash drive to put Bible study material on it, or help someone in need that you know.

CLOSING PRAYER

GOD BLESS AND KEEP YOU SAFE UNTIL NEXT SUNDAY

Sunday 10

John Baptist & Miracles (Mark 1)

Option 1 – Worship in a Group

READ ALOUD MARK 1:1-8

1:1-3 - This is a prophecy made 700 years earlier of John the Baptist. What prophet did God make this prophecy through?

1:5 - A person cannot receive forgiveness of their sins until they do what two things? (Hint: One is an attitude; one is an action.)

1:6 - John the Baptist lived like a hermit in the wilderness. He dressed just like a prophet hundreds of years earlier named Elijah. How did John dress, and what did he eat?

1:7 - But John did not take glory for himself. He said he was preparing people for the appearance of one so wonderful, he was not worthy to do what?

1:8 - Christians are baptized with water, but, after Jesus died and came back to life, he made it possible for Christians to receive what at their baptism?

READ ALOUD MARK 1:9-13

1:9-10 - John baptized in the Jordan River. Did he sprinkle water on people and call it baptism? What did he do to baptize them?

1:10 - When Jesus was baptized, what appeared in the form of a dove and rested on him?

1:11 - Then a voice from heaven announced that Jesus was who?

1:13 - Jesus was _________ by _________ for how long after his baptism?

1:13 - Sometimes after our own baptism, Satan tempts us. Why do you think he does that?

1:13 - Jesus did not eat during this time. After resisting Satan, who came to help him?

READ ALOUD MARK 1:14-21

1:14-15 - Did Jesus say the kingdom of God was going to begin thousands of years after he died and returned to heaven? When did he said it would begin?

1:16-18 - When he called Simon and Andrew to be his apostles, he said they would no longer be ______________, but would become ______________ of men.

1:19-20 - Who else did Jesus call to be his apostles at this time?

READ ALOUD MARK 1:21-28

1:21-24 - While Jesus was preaching, a demon shouted through someone in the audience saying Jesus was who? If demons believe and are still lost because they did not follow Jesus' rules, is it possible for people to believe but still be lost?

1:25-25 - Jesus did not ask the demon to come out of the man. He didn't do a lot of ceremonies to get the demon to come out of the man. Jesus simply said 7 words. What were they?

READ ALOUD MARK 1:29-34

1:31 - What immediately left Peter's mother-in-law? Was it gradual?

1:34 - That evening, everyone in the _______ came to him and he did what?

READ ALOUD MARK 1:35-45

1:35-37 - The next morning before daylight, what did Jesus do?

1:38 - Jesus told his apostles he wanted to go to other _______________ to do what?

1:39 - Did Jesus ever perform a miracle without preaching? ______ Why do you think that was?

1:41-42 - Did Jesus only heal people whose symptoms were on the inside? How long did it take for a person to be healed? (This is a test for true healings.)

1:43-48 - So many thousands came to see Jesus, he could no longer teach where? Where did he go to receive people?

Option 2 – Alone Among Enemies or Continue Worship in a Group

LORD'S SUPPER

Sing or whisper ISAIAH 9:2

Read MARK 14:53-65 about Jesus' illegal trial in the middle of the night.

Take a bite of unleavened bread, representing Jesus body tortured on the cross for us.

Pray silently about Jesus' sacrifice, dying in your place for your sins.

Take a sip of grape juice, representing Jesus' blood that dripped away on the cross for you,

Pray silently about your own sins and desire to live more as God wants you to.

Sing or whisper ISAIAH 9:6

COLLECTION

Prayer: Thank God for your blessings.

Set the money aside to be used to buy a flash drive to put Bible study material on it, or help someone in need that you know.

CLOSING PRAYER

GOD BLESS AND KEEP YOU SAFE UNTIL NEXT SUNDAY

Sunday 11

Terrorists, Demons, Farmers & Lights (Mark 3-4)

Option 1 – Worship in a Group

READ ALOUD MARK 3:13-19

3:14-15 - Jesus selected twelve men to preach and what else? [NOTE: The only time we know of demon possession was during the lifetime of Jesus and his apostles. It never occurred over the 4000 years before him, or the 2000 years since.]

3:17 - Which two were brothers and who Jesus nicknamed "Sons of Thunder."

3:18 - During Jesus' lifetime, religious terrorists were called religious zealots (had a lot of zeal). Do you think it would ever be possible today to convert a terrorist like Jesus did? Why?

3:19 - A hypocrite is someone who pretends to be good when he is really bad. Should we refuse to be a Christian because we heard of one who was a hypocrite? Even who had a hypocrite among his closest friends?

READ ALOUD MARK 3:20-34

3:22 - Some religious leaders couldn't deny Jesus cast out demons, so they told him he cast them by because he was the _____________ of demons.

3:23 - Jesus asked them, "How can __________ cast out himself?"

3:28 - Jesus said that all sins can be forgiven but blaspheming who? John 14:14 & 17 calls the Holy Spirit the Word of God. So, if we despise the Bible that tells us how to be saved, is it possible for a person who ask forgiveness for despising the Bible?

4:31-34 - Jesus was teaching in a house so crowded that, when Jesus' mother and brothers came to see him, they had to send word to him that they were there. Who did Jesus say were his mother and brothers?

4:35 - Who did Jesus say were his brothers and sisters? Are you obeying God? If so, who is your "big brother"?

READ ALOUD MARK 4:1-9

4:1 - Sometimes so many people crowded around Jesus, wanting to hear his words of wisdom, if he was by a lake, he taught from a what?

4:2 - A parable is a heavenly story with an __________ meaning.

4:4 - A farmer spread seed, but some fell near a road and who ate it?

4:5-6 - Some seed fell on rocky ground, sprouted quickly, but it didn't have any ______, so was scorched by the __________.

4:7 - Some seed fell among ________ that chocked it out.

4:8 - Still other seed was planted in good soil and yielded ___, ___. and even ____ times more than the seed that had been planted.

READ ALOUD MARK 4:10-20

4:14 - Jesus said the seed is a symbol of the __________ of God.

4:15 - The birds that takes away the seed are a symbol of who?

4:16-17 - Seed that blooms quickly because it has no root is like people who accept the Word of God with __________ at first, then fall away when they experience what?

4:18-19 - The thorns are symbols of what things that choke out the Word of God from someone's life?

4:20 - The Seeds in the good soil are like good hearts of people who hear, believe, and then follow up by making more

______________.

READ ALOUD MARK 4:21-25

4:21 - Common sense says we don't light a ______ and then hide it under a ______.

4:22 - Our light cannot be ____________. When we do good, who will see it?

4:24-25 - If God measures out many talents to someone who uses those talents to spread the Kingdom, even _____________ talents will be given to him.

Option 2 – Alone Among Enemies or Continue Worship in a Group

LORD'S SUPPER

Sing or whisper ISAIAH 25:8

Read MARK 15:1-15 where Governor Pilate talked with Jesus, then tried to set him free.

Take a bite of unleavened bread, representing Jesus body tortured on the cross for us.

Pray silently about Jesus' sacrifice, dying in your place for your sins.

Take a sip of grape juice, representing Jesus' blood that dripped away on the cross for you,

Pray silently about your own sins and desire to live more as God wants you to.

Sing or whisper ISAIAH 5:8

COLLECTION

Prayer: Thank God for your blessings.

Set the money aside to be used to buy a flash drive to put Bible study material on it, or help someone in need that you know.

CLOSING PRAYER

GOD BLESS AND KEEP YOU SAFE UNTIL NEXT SUNDAY

Sunday 12

A Woman, a Little Girl & Rejection (Mark 5-6)

Option 1 – Worship in a Group

READ ALOUD MARK 5:21-43

5:22 - A synagogue is like a Jewish church building. ______ was an elder for the synagogue where Jesus was visiting.

5:23 - He begged Jesus to help his __________ who was about to ______.

5:25 - On Jesus' way, a woman saw him who had been bleeding for ______ years.

5:26 - She had spent all her money on _______ who couldn't help her.

5:24 & 28 - She couldn't get close to Jesus, so reached out and touched his ______.

5:29 - What happened to her immediately?

5:30 - Did Jesus know what happened?

5:34 - So Jesus looked for her and she came forward. Jesus explained that what had healed her?

5:35 - But, because of the few minutes delay, what happened to the little 12-year-old girl?

5:36 - Did Jesus tell the father to just give up?

5:38 - By the time they arrived at the father's house, the house was full of people doing what?

5:39 - But Jesus told them the girl hadn't really died, but was really what?

5:40 - What did all the people in the house do?

5:41 - Jesus took the girl's parents and Peter, James, and John and went to her bedside. There he talked to the dead girl and said what?

5:42 - So what did the dead girl do?

5:43 - Jesus was not a show-off and bragger. What did he tell the people at the house to tell other people?

READ ALOUD MARK 6:1-6

6:1 - Then Jesus went back to his what?

6:2 - At his local synagogue, he preached and performed a few miracles. What did his neighbors say about it?

6:3 - What was Jesus' occupation?

6:3 - His mother was Mary. What were the names of his four brothers?

6:3 - What other family members lived in the town?

6:4 - They got jealous of Jesus, and Jesus said a prophet gets honored everywhere except where?

6:5-6 - Because of their unbelief, he only did a few what?

READ ALOUD MARK 6:7-13

6:7 - Jesus gave his 12 apostles power over what?

6:7 - Then he sent them out without him to ___________ in pairs.

6:8-9 - He told them not to take what with them?

6:10 - This was to be a test to make them find believers to

_____________.

6:11 - If there were no believers in a town, they were supposed to do what?

6:12 - The apostles preached that people should do what?

6:13 - What kinds of miracles did they perform?

Option 2 – Alone Among Enemies or Continue Worship in a Group

LORD'S SUPPER

Sing or whisper ISAIAH 50:6

Read MARK 15:16-26 about Jesus' treatment between being sentenced to death and being nailed to his cross.

Take a bite of unleavened bread, representing Jesus body tortured on the cross for us.

Pray silently about Jesus' sacrifice, dying in your place for your sins.

Take a sip of grape juice, representing Jesus' blood that dripped away on the cross for you,

Pray silently about your own sins and desire to live more as God wants you to.

Sing or whisper ISAIAH 43:1

COLLECTION

Prayer: Thank God for your blessings.

Pass around a basket or cup, allowing even little children a chance to give a few coins too.

Set the money aside to be used to buy a flash drive to put Bible study material on it, or help someone in need that you know.

CLOSING PRAYER

GOD BLESS AND KEEP YOU SAFE UNTIL NEXT SUNDAY

Sunday 13

Legalists, Deafness, Demons
(Mark 7)

Option 1 – Worship in a Group

READ ALOUD MARK 7:1-37

7:1 - Scribes were people who copied important documents and scripture before the time of mechanical print. So they knew the law as much as lawyers did.

7:2 - The Scribes were following Jesus around trying to catch him doing something against the law. they caught him doing what with what?

7:3 - Was hand washing before meals in the scriptures or creed of elders?

7:4 - What other creeds of the elders did they keep?

7:5-6a - When the Scribes and Pharisees criticized Jesus for eating without washing his hands, he called them what name?

7:6b - Hypocrites honor God with their _______, but not with their _______.

7:7a - Hypocrites worship god in what?

7:7b - Hypocrites teach people to obey the creeds of _______.

7:8 - By keeping their creeds and traditions, they neglected what?

READ ALOUD MARK 7:9-23

7:10 - The Law of Moses said anyone who did not honor their parents was to be punished how?

7:11 - But the Scribes claimed that whatever they might have spent on elderly parents is really whose money?

7:12 - By saying it is God's money, they claim they can't spend the money to help their __________.

7:13 - Therefore, they break God's law of Moses in order to keep the elder's creeds and __________.

7:15 - Jesus said what is on the ______ of our body makes him unclean.

7:18 - Also, whatever does into a person's ______ does not make him unclean, but what goes into a person's __________ does.

7:21 - What are four things that come out of a person's heart that are bad?

7:22 - What are eight more deeds that come out of a person's heart that are bad?

READ ALOUD MARK 7:24-30

7:24-25 - Jesus went to Tyre, which today is in Lebanon, to hide from Jewish religious leaders wanting to kill him, but what happened anyway?

7:26 - The country was Phoenicia, but controlled by Syria. She was not a Jew, but kept asking Jesus to do what?

7:27 - Jesus called the Jews the children. Jews considered non-Jews what to be like what?

7:28 - She was willing to take what?

7:29 - So, just the crumbs of Jesus' healing ability did what for her daughter?

READ ALOUD MARK 7:31-37

7:31 - Decapolis was a province with ten big cities in it on the east of the Sea of Galilee in Palestine.

7:32 - Some people brought Jesus a man who couldn't __________ or __________.

7:33- 35 - Jesus touched his ears and tongue, and then what happened?

7:36 - Jesus told them not to ______ because he was trying to hide from the Jewish religious leaders who wanted to kill him.

Option 2 – Alone Among Enemies or Continue Worship in a Group

LORD'S SUPPER

Sing or whisper 1ST KINGS 8:46

READ MARK 15:27-39 giving details of Jesus' crucifixion and how he was treated even on the cross

Take a bite of unleavened bread, representing Jesus body tortured on the cross for us.

Pray silently about Jesus' sacrifice, dying in your place for your sins.

Take a sip of grape juice, representing Jesus' blood that dripped away on the cross for you,

Pray silently about your own sins and desire to live more as God wants you to.

Sing or whisper LEVITICUS 17:11

COLLECTION

Prayer: Thank God for your blessings.

Set the money aside to be used to buy a flash drive to put Bible study material on it, or help someone in need that you know.

CLOSING PRAYER

GOD BLESS AND KEEP YOU SAFE UNTIL NEXT SUNDAY

Sunday 14

Feeds 5000, Heals Blind, Escapes Death (Mark 8)

Option 1 – Worship in a Group

READ ALOUD MARK 8:1-9

8:1-2 - Thousands of people followed Jesus so they could hear him preach for how many days with nothing to eat? Do you think you would want to do that?

8:3 - Jesus was afraid if he sent them home now, they would do what on their way?

8:4 - What kind of place had Jesus been preaching?

8:5 - Among Jesus and his twelve apostles, they had how many loaves of bread left?

8:6, 8 - Jesus broke them up, blessed them, and put them in baskets for his apostles to do what?

8:7 - They also found a few what, which Jesus blessed and were passed around among the people?

8:9 - How many people did Jesus feed with the few loaves and fishes?

READ ALOUD MARK 8:10-21

8:10-11a - Then Jesus and his apostles entered their boat and went to another district where who came to argue with him?

8:11b - Although Jesus had just given a great sign he was the Son of God, the Pharisees pretended he didn't, and demanded a different what?

8:15 - Jesus called the Pharisees and Prince Herod (son of Herod the Great) leaven, and told his apostles to beware of them. What do you think he meant?

8:18 - Jesus said sometimes people have eyes that do not see and ears that do not hear? What do you think he meant by that?

8:19 - He reminded them of a miracle he performed just a few days earlier where he fed how many people? How much food was left over?

8:20 - He reminded them of the miracle he had just performed that day where he fed how many people? How much food was left over?

8:21 - Jesus had power to heal people, but he also had power to make what grow without being in the ground? Do you think these two miracles were signs of who Jesus was?

READ ALOUD MARK 8:22-30

8:22 - In what town on the Sea of Galilee did a blind man come to Jesus asking him to touch him?

8:23 - Did Jesus heal him there in the town, or take him away from people to do it in private?

8:26 - After healing him, Jesus told him to go home and not return where?

NOTE: It was getting more dangerous for Jesus; Herod and the Pharisees were trying to arrest and kill him. So, he didn't stay in towns very long.

8:27a - Jesus escaped to another province with a city and suburbs named after Caesar and Governor Philip. What was the name of the city?

8:27b-28 - His apostles told him some people thought he was what two prophets?

8:29 - Peter said he was who?   (The word "Christ" means "Messiah" means anointed one, or crowned one.)

8:30 - Jesus told them to do what about their knowledge of who he was? With people trying to kill him, why do you think he said this?

READ ALOUD MARK 8:31-38

8:31a - If you think of man as opposed to God, would Mary, Jesus, mother, be considered "man"? So, even though Jesus was the Son of God, his father, he was the son of who as his mother?

8:31b - Jesus predicted that soon he would be condemned to die by who?

8:31c - But what would he do after he was killed?

8:32 - Saddened and shocked, Peter took Jesus aside and tried to get him to change his mind about what?

8:33 - Jesus told Peter he was speaking for who? What would have happened if Jesus had not taken our punishment for our sins?

8:34 - Memorize what Jesus said in this verse. What can be your cross?

8:35 - In what way will we save our life if we lose our life?

8:36-37 - When we're putting money first in our life, we are doing what to our soul?

8:38a - If we are shamed of Jesus now, what will Jesus do?

8:38b - Jesus will return to take us to heaven with who else?

Option 2 –Alone Among Enemies or Continue Worship in a Group

LORD'S SUPPER

Sing or whisper JOHN 1:29

READ MARK 15:40-16:8 - About Jesus burial, then Jesus coming back to life on Sunday morning, then angels appearing to Jesus' mother Mary, Jesus aunt Salome, and 3 other women who had supported him in his travels.

Take a bite of unleavened bread, representing Jesus body tortured on the cross for us.

Pray silently about Jesus' sacrifice, dying in your place for your sins.

Take a sip of grape juice, representing Jesus' blood that dripped away on the cross for you,

Pray silently about your own sins and desire to live more as God wants you to.

Sing or whisper JOHN 3:16

COLLECTION

Prayer: Thank God for your blessings.

Set the money aside to be used to buy a flash drive to put Bible study material on it, or help someone in need that you know.

CLOSING PRAYER

GOD BLESS AND KEEP YOU SAFE UNTIL NEXT SUNDAY

Sunday 15

Glowing, Voice from Heaven, Epileptic, (Mark 9)

Option 1 – Worship in a Group

READ ALOUD MARK 9:1-13

9:1 - If the kingdom of God was to appear during the apostle's lifetime, what does this say about people who claim the kingdom of God will appear when Jesus returns?

9:2-3 - On a mountain with Jesus' closest friends, Jesus' form changed and looked like what?

9:4 - What two men who had died centuries earlier appeared to talk to Jesus? Which one introduced the great Law the Jews always kept? Which one introduced the age of prophets?

9:6 - How did Peter, James and John react when they saw him?

9:7 - God spoke out of heaven and said what?

9:8 - When Moses (representing the Old Law), and Elijah (representing the old prophets) disappeared, this meant that from now on, we are to live by what who said?

9:9-10 - When Jesus said he was going to die and come back to life, did they think he would literally, or symbolically?

9:12-13 - As they grasped how Jesus was the Son of God, they said a second Elijah was supposed to come first, but Jesus said he had. He was someone who was killed by Herod for introducing Jesus as the great King of the Jews. Do you remember from earlier lessons who that was?

READ ALOUD MARK 9:14-29

9:17-18, 20-22 - What kind of disease do you think the evil spirit put into the boy? (NOTE: There were no demons in people after the time of the apostles. Jesus has control over all of them now.)

9:23-24 - One of the most-remembered scriptures in the Bible is what the boy's father begged for Jesus to do for him. What did the boy's father cry out? How can you apply that to your life?

9:25-27 - Then what did Jesus do?

9:28-29 - Jesus' apostles admitted they could not do what? Jesus rebuked them and told them they had forgotten to do what?

READ ALOUD MARK 9:30-37

9:31 - Once again Jesus warned his apostles he was going to do what?

9:32 - Why do you think they didn't understand what he had just told them plainly?

9:33-34 - His own apostles still thought the Kingdom of God was going to be established in Jerusalem and be an earthly kingdom. So they argued about what?

9:35 - Memorize Jesus' answer.

9:36-37 - Some people claim children need to be baptized. But Jesus said we must be like a child to be received by who?

READ ALOUD MARK 9:38-50

9:38 - Do you remember when Jesus sent 72 people out to preach for him, and gave them power to perform miracles? When his 12 apostles saw that, they thought what?

9:40 - Memorize what Jesus said in this verse.

9:41 - Even if we do what in Jesus name, we will be rewarded?

9:42 - If someone causes a child to disbelieve, will he please God?

9:43-48 - If your hand, foot or eye causes you to stumble, it is better to do what than to keep it and enter hell?

9:50 - Salt is used as a preservative so meat doesn't spoil. What can be our salt to preserve our soul so it does not spoil?

Option 2 – Alone Among Enemies or Continue Worship in a Group

LORD'S SUPPER

Sing or whisper JOHN 10:11

READ MARK 16:9-20 where Jesus came back to life, appeared to Mary Magdalene, two followers walking to Emmaus, and returned to heaven in the presence of his 11 remaining apostles.

Take a bite of unleavened bread, representing Jesus body tortured on the cross for us.

Pray silently about Jesus' sacrifice, dying in your place for your sins.

Take a sip of grape juice, representing Jesus' blood that dripped away on the cross for you,

Pray silently about your own sins and desire to live more as God wants you to.

Sing or whisper HEBREWS 13:20

COLLECTION

Prayer: Thank God for your blessings.

Set the money aside to be used to buy a flash drive to put Bible study material on it, or help someone in need that you know.

CLOSING PRAYER

GOD BLESS AND KEEP YOU SAFE UNTIL NEXT SUNDAY

GOD BLESS AND KEEP YOU SAFE UNTIL NEXT SUNDAY

Sunday 16

Miracle Baby John the Baptist
(Luke 1)

Option 1 – Worship in a Group

READ ALOUD LUKE 1:1-4

1:1-2 - Luke was an educated man (physician) who wrote the life of Christ based on what who told him?

1:3-4 - Luke decided to __________ everything carefully so he could discover the write down the exact __________ of what he had been told.

READ ALOUD LUKE 1:5-25

1:5 - The priest, Zacharias, served during the time of what king?

1:5 - His wife's name was __________ and she descended from __________, the very first high priest of the Jews centuries earlier.

1:7 - They had never had any __________ and they were __________ in years.

1:9-10 - Zacharias was chosen to burn __________ in the __________, while a multitude of people stood outside doing what?

1:11 - Who did he suddenly see?

1:12 - How did Zacharias react to him?

1:13 - What did he announce to the priest?

1:15 - He was predicted to be great in the sight of _____, will never drink _______, and will be filled with the _____ __________ even before birth.

1:17 - He was to be a prophet like the great __________.

1:18 - Zacharias did not believe right away because he was

_______.   1:20 - So the angel said he would be _______________ until his birth.

1:24 - When he returned home, his wife Elizabeth became pregnant, and stayed ______ for _________ months.

READ ALOUD LUKE 1:26-38

1:26 - Six months later, the same __________, Gabriel, went to a city named ________.   1:27 - He appeared to a virgin named ________, a descendant of ________ and Abraham.

1:31 - He told her she was going to bear a _______ and name him

_____________.

1:32 - The child will be the Son of __________.

1:33 - The child will some day become a king, and his kingdom will last ___________.

1:35 - Some Muslims claim the Holy Spirit was Gabriel. Did Gabriel say he was going to be the father of the child?

1:37 - Once again, Gabriel said the child will be the Son of

__________.

READ ALOUD LUKE 1:39-45; 56-66

1:39-40 - Immediately, Mary rush to the home of who_______? Both were pregnant with miracle babies!

1:43 - Elizabeth called Mary the __________ of the Lord.

1:56 - Mary stayed with Elizabeth for how long?

1:57-59 - Elizabeth's relatives said her baby should be named after his father.

1:60-61 - Elizabeth said he would instead be named __________.

1:62-63 - So the relatives and neighbors made signed to Zacharias as to what the child should be named, and Zacharias wrote his name on what?

1:64 - As soon as he wrote the name, Zacharias was able to do what?

1:66 - The relatives and neighbors were so amazed, they asked each other what?

Option 2 – Alone Among Enemies or Continue Worship in a Group

LORD'S SUPPER

Sing or whisper JOHN 18:12

READ LUKE 22:14-20 where Jesus showed us how to keep the Lord's Supper.

Take a bite of unleavened bread, representing Jesus body tortured on the cross for us.

Pray silently about Jesus' sacrifice, dying in your place for your sins.

Take a sip of grape juice, representing Jesus' blood that dripped away on the cross for you,

Pray silently about your own sins and desire to live more as God wants you to.

Sing or whisper JOHN 13:3

COLLECTION

Prayer: Thank God for your blessings.

Set the money aside to be used to buy a flash drive to put Bible study material on it, or help someone in need that you know.

CLOSING PRAYER

GOD BLESS AND KEEP YOU SAFE UNTIL NEXT SUNDAY

Sunday 17

Angels, Shepherds, & Miracle Baby Jesus (Luke 2)

Option 1 – Worship in a Group

READ ALOUD LUKE 2:1-7

2:1 - Who decreed that a census be taken of the entire Roman world?

2:3 - Everyone was to go to his own home town to do what?

2:4 - Joseph lived in _________ in the northern province of Galilee, and registered in _________ in the southern province of Judea.

2:5-7 - Jesus was born there and laid in an animal's feed _________ in a barn because there was no room for them in the _____________.

READ ALOUD LUKE 2:8-20

2:8-10 - An _________ appeared to _________ and announced good news of great joy for all people.

2:11 - That day in the city of _________, the Savior of the world was born, Christ the _________.

2:13-14 - Suddenly there were many _________ praising God

and declaring _______ on earth.

2:15-16 - So the shepherds went to ______ Jesus.

2:17-18 - Then the shepherds _______ everyone about it, but no one else tried to go see the miracle baby.

READ ALOUD LUKE 2:26-38

2:21 - On the ______ day after his birth, the baby was _________ and given the name _________.

2:25-26 - There was a man named __________ in Jerusalem who had the Holy ________ in him who revealed he would not ___________ before he saw the ____________.

2:27-28 - Simeon went to the temple where he took Jesus in his _________.

2:30 - He prayed that his eyes had seen God's _________.

2:31-32 - The baby was to be a light, not only to Jews (Israelites), but also to ___________ (non-Jews).

2:34 - Simeon predicted that when this baby is grown many will _______ spiritual because of him, and many will ______ spiritually because of him.

2:35 - Events in the child's adult life will _________ Mary's heart.

2:36a - A prophetess was in the temple too named __________.

2:37b - She was _______ years old, and never left the temple but prayed and fasted _______ and ________.

2:38 - She told everyone that the Savior had been born, but what did they do? [Nothing.]

READ ALOUD LUKE 2:39-52

2:39-40 - Jesus grew up in what town?

2:41-42 - Every year Jesus' parents went to the Feast of Passover, but they didn't let Jesus go until he was how old?

2:43-45 - After the Feast, his parents headed back to Nazareth, but who stayed behind?

2:46a - They looked for Jesus for _______ days.

2:46b - Mary and Joseph found him in the ___________ courts listening to and asking questions of the religious _______________.

2:47-49 - When they finally found Jesus, he said, "Why were you _________ for me? Didn't you know I would be

___________________ my heavenly Father?" So, even at this young age, Jesus knew who he was.

2:50-52 - Then they returned to _____________ where Jesus grew in stature and ________ and favor with men and ________.

Option 2 – Alone Among Enemies or Continue Worship in a Group

LORD'S SUPPER

Sing or whisper JOHN 19:2

READ LUKE 22:39-53 - Jesus prays in an olive grove not to be crucified, and then is arrested.

Take a bite of unleavened bread, representing Jesus body tortured on the cross for us.

Pray silently about Jesus' sacrifice, dying in your place for your sins.

Take a sip of grape juice, representing Jesus' blood that dripped away on the cross for you,

Pray silently about your own sins and desire to live more as God wants you to.

Sing or whisper JOHN 19:6

COLLECTION

Prayer: Thank God for your blessings.

Set the money aside to be used to buy a flash drive to put Bible study material on it, or help someone in need that you know.

CLOSING PRAYER

GOD BLESS AND KEEP YOU SAFE UNTIL NEXT SUNDAY

Sunday 18

Farming, Lamps, a Woman & a Dead Girl (Luke 8)

Option 1 – Worship in a Group

READ ALOUD LUKE 8:1-15

8:2-3 - What three wealthy women traveled with Jesus' apostles and also supported them?

8:5 - What happened to the seed sown on a path?

8:6 - What happened to the seed sown among rocks?

8:7 - What happened to seed sown among thorns?

8:8a - What happened to seed sown in good soil?

8:8b-10 - What did Jesus mean when he said, "He who has ears to hear, let him hear"?

8:11 - In Jesus' parable, what did the seed represent?

8:12 - Seed sown on a path is snatched our of hearts like a bird by who?

8:13 - Seed sown in rocky hearts have to _______, so fail during times of ________.

8:14 - Seed sown in thorny hearts is choked out by what?

8:15 - Seed sown in good and noble hearts produces what?

READ ALOUD LUKE 8:16-21

8:16 - Where do people not put a lamp?

8:17 - What spiritual light do you think Jesus was really talking about?

8:18 - If we listen to Jesus' words, we will be given _______, but those who do not because of hard deaf ears will have Jesus' words taken where?

8:21 - Jesus had an earthly family where he grew up. But who did he say his mother and brothers are?

READ ALOUD LUKE 8:22-25

8:22-23a - Jesus fell _______ in the middle of a _______.
8:23b - What suddenly happened out there?
8:24a - What did Jesus' disciples yell at him?
8:24b - So Jesus just got up and told the storm to do what?
8:25b - His disciples became _________ because even the _________ obeyed him.

READ ALOUD LUKE 8:26-39

8:26-27 - On the other side of the lake, they met a man who had a _______ in his mind, and had not ____ clothes, and was living in a _______.

8:28 - When he saw Jesus, the ______ in his mind called Jesus who?

8:29a - What did Jesus command?

8:29b - The _____ in his mind that also possessed his boyd that became so strong he had been able to break ______.

8:30 - The demon was made up of many other demons, like drops of rain come together in a pail. What did he say his name was?

8:32-33 - Jesus let the demons go into what kind of animals?

8:37 - After that, the man's mind was calm and he did what with Jesus?

8:38-39 - The man wanted to stay with Jesus, but Jesus told him to go home and do what?

READ ALOUD LUKE 8:40-56

8:41 - A synagogue was a Jewish place of Bible study and worship. Who came to Jesus and begged him to go to his house?

8:42 - Why? How old was she?

8:43 - On his way to the house, a woman was in the crowd on the street who had been bleeding how long?

8:44 - What did the woman do that she was healed of her bleeding?

8:46 - Jesus knew a miracle had happened because he could feel what go from him?

8:48-49 - The woman's _______ healed her, but the dead girl was healed without having any _______.

8:52 - At the dead girl's house, Jesus told everyone to stop _______ because the girl was just _______.

8:53 - The mourners suddenly started _______ at Jesus.

8:54-56 - The girl's _____ returned to her when Jesus told her what?

Option 2 – Alone Among Enemies or Continue Worship in a Group

LORD'S SUPPER

Sing or whisper JOHN 19:30b

READ LUKE 22:54-65 - The apostle Peter denies knowing Jesus, guards mock Jesus.

> Take a bite of unleavened bread, representing Jesus body tortured on the cross for us.

> Pray silently about Jesus' sacrifice, dying in your place for your sins.

> Take a sip of grape juice, representing Jesus' blood that dripped away on the cross for you,

> Pray silently about your own sins and desire to live more as God wants you to.

You Can Be A Hero Alone

Sing or whisper JOHN 19:33

COLLECTION

Prayer: Thank God for your blessings.

Set the money aside to be used to buy a flash drive to put Bible study material on it, or help someone in need that you know.

CLOSING PRAYER

GOD BLESS AND KEEP YOU SAFE UNTIL NEXT SUNDAY

Sunday 19

Training His 12, & a Hated Foreigner
(Luke 10)

Option 1 – Worship in a Group

READ ALOUD LUKE 10:1-24

10:1 - Jesus selected 72 followers to preach ahead of him where? If each pair preached in one town, how many towns were they to preach in?

10:2 - "The harvest is _______, but the workers are ______." Jesus said we are to ask the Lord of the harvest what? Will you pray for that for your community?

10:3 - Jesus warned them that they were going to be like lambs among what?

10:4 - They were not to take time to spend ______ or talk to people ______________.

10:7 - They were to select a house to stay in and accept whatever _______ they gave them as payment for their work.

10:9a - Jesus gave them the power to do what?

10:9b, 11b - What does it mean that the kingdom of God is near?

10:10, 12 - Sodom was an Old Testament town that God burned down because of immorality. What did Jesus say about the town that turned against one of his preachers?

10:16 - He who listened to the preachers he sent out was really listening to who? He who rejected the preachers he sent out was really rejecting who?

10:17 - When the 72 returned, they said even _______ submitted when rebuked in Jesus' name. (NOTE: We have no indication in scriptures that demons possessed anyone before or after Jesus' time.)

10:18 - Jesus said he saw who fall from heaven?

10:19 - Jesus told the preachers that, instead of rejoicing over their miraculous powers, they should rejoice that their names were where?

10:21 - While everyone was so happy at what they had accomplished, even Jesus was full of what?

10:22 - The Son of God reveals who?

READ ALOUD LUKE 10:25-37

10:25 - An expert in the Law of Moses asked Jesus what he must do to have what?

10:27 - Jesus asked the expert what he thought it took. He expert said we should love _____ and our _______ as ourself.

10:28 - When the expert asked who his neighbor was, Jesus told a parable about a Samaritan ~ a half-breed neither Jews or Gentiles liked.

10:30 - A man was traveling between ______ and ______ when he was ____ and ____ by _______.

10:31 - A priest saw him laying on the road and did what?

10:32 - A Levite (assistant to priests) saw him laying on the road and did what?

10:33-34 - But a hated Samaritan saw him and did what?

10:35 - What did the hated Samaritan do the next day?

10:36-37 - Who was the true neighbor? The priest, the Levite, or the hated Samaritan?

READ ALOUD LUKE 10:38-42

10:38 - Who opened her home to Jesus and his disciples?

10:39 - Who was her sister, and what did the sister do?

10:40 - But Martha was busy in the kitchen doing what?

19:41 - Jesus comforted Martha and told her not to _____ about doing so many things for him.

19:42 - The thing Jesus wanted Martha to do the most was

to do what _______ was doing.

Option 2 –Alone Among Enemies or Continue Worship in a Group

LORD'S SUPPER

Sing or whisper JOHN 20:1

READ LUKE 22:66-71 - Jesus admits in the Jewish court that he is the Son of God.

Take a bite of unleavened bread, representing Jesus body tortured on the cross for us.

Pray silently about Jesus' sacrifice, dying in your place for your sins.

Take a sip of grape juice, representing Jesus' blood that dripped away on the cross for you,

Pray silently about your own sins and desire to live more as God wants you to.

Sing or whisper JOHN 20:18

COLLECTION

Prayer: Thank God for your blessings.

Set the money aside to be used to buy a flash drive to put Bible study material on it, or help someone in need that you know.

CLOSING PRAYER

GOD BLESS AND KEEP YOU SAFE UNTIL NEXT SUNDAY

Sunday 20

Fear, Wealth, Sudden End of World (Luke 12)

Option 1 – Worship in a Group

READ ALOUD LUKE 12:1-12

12:1b - How can hypocrisy be like leaven?

12:3 - Jesus warned that, whatever we say in the dark will be heard in the ______, and whatever we whisper in closets will be shouted on _______.

12:4 - Do not be afraid of people who can only kill the

_________.

12:5 - Instead, fear anyone who can cause you to die and go to ________.

12:7 - We are so valuable to God, he even numbers the very ______ on our ______.

12:8 - Jesus was the son of man in two ways: His other was a _ _ man, and he was a son of mankind through his mother.

12:8-9 - If we confess Jesus before _____ and the ______, Jesus will confess us before them

12:10 - John 14:17 calls the Holy Spirit the Sprit of _______, and John 17:17 says God's ________ is Truth. Therefore, if we blaspheme (deny) the Bible, it is impossible to ________ us because we don't think we've done anything wrong.

12:11 - Christians will sometimes be taken before religious leaders and government _________.

12:11-12 - Why are we not to worry what we will say in our defense at that time?

READ ALOUD LUKE 12:13-34

12:13-15 - We are to beware of ______ because our life does not consist of ________.

12:16-17 - A rich man had such a productive crop, he couldn't store it all. What could he have done instead of store his food?

12:18 - He decided to tear down his barns and build _________ _________.

12:19 - The rich fool told himself to ______, _______, and be ________ because he had so many possessions.

12:20 - But God knew that that very night he would _______ and leave behind his possessions to someone else.

12:21 - In what way could he have used his riches for God?

12:22-23 - We are not to worry about what we will ______ or _______, for life is more than _______ and _______.

12:24 - After all, God does not let even little _______ go hungry.

12:25-26 - Who can add a single ______ to his life? So why worry?

12:27 - Consider the _______ and how they _______. But the richest man in the world was never clothed like one of them.

12:28 - If Gods clothes the ______ in the field that lasts only a few weeks, how much more will he ________ us?

12:29 - So do not keep _________.

12:30 - After all, ______ knows you need them.

12:31 - Memorize this verse.

12:32 - God has already chosen to give us the _________.

12:33 - Store up ______ in ________ where thieves and moths cannot destroy them.

12:34 - Memorize this verse.

READ ALOUD LUKE 12:35-48

12:35-36 - Be good slaves so when your ________ returns, you will be able to _______ the door for him.

12:37-38 - The master himself will serve such good _________.

12:39-40 - Jesus will return to get us at the end of the world at an _______ we do not _______.

12:42-44 - When Jesus returns and finds us working hard, we will be put in charge of _______ his _________.

12:45-46 - The slave who treats other slaves bad will be surprised because Jesus will return at an _______ he does not expect.

12:47-48 - Some people believe these two verses indicate there will be levels of punishment in hell. What do you think?

READ ALOUD LUKE 12:49-59

12:49-53 - Jesus knew ahead of time that some believers within a _______ will believe in him and some will not.

12:54-55 - Jesus said we can tell before it _____ on the earth, and whether it will be a hot _______, but we pretend we do not know how to stop bad from happening.

12:57-59 - Jesus encouraged people going through a dispute to settle it before they get to _______ where their punishment will be worse.

Option 2 –Alone Among Enemies or Continue Worship in a Group

LORD'S SUPPER

Sing or whisper JOHN 20:19

READ LUKE 23:1-12 where former enemies became friends because they had the same problem,

> Take a bite of unleavened bread, representing Jesus body tortured on the cross for us.

> Pray silently about Jesus' sacrifice, dying in your place for your sins.

> Take a sip of grape juice, representing Jesus' blood

that dripped away on the cross for you,

Pray silently about your own sins and desire to live more as God wants you to.

Sing or whisper JOHN 20:20

COLLECTION

Prayer: Thank God for your blessings.

Set the money aside to be used to buy a flash drive to put Bible study material on it, or help someone in need that you know.

CLOSING PRAYER

GOD BLESS AND KEEP YOU SAFE UNTIL NEXT SUNDAY

Sunday 21

A Lost Sheep, Lost Coin, Lost Son (Luke 15)

Option 1 – Worship in a Group

READ ALOUD LUKE 15:1-10

15:1-2 - The self-righteous who bragged how good they were complained that Jesus ate with who? Are we likely to be able to save people we do not associate with?

15:3-4 - If a good shepherd has 100 sheep and loses one, what will he do?

15:5-6 - Afterwards, will he keep it a secret? What will he do?

15:7 - There is more joy in _______ over a sinner who repents than ______ self-righteous people who brag about how good they are.

15:8 - If a woman has ten _______ _________, and loses one, what will she do?

15:9 - After she founds what she lost, what will she do?

15:10 In heaven, there is joy in the presence of _______ over one _______ who repents.

READ ALOUD LUKE 15:11-32

15:11-12 - A did what with his two sons?

15:13 - Then the younger son went to a ___________ where he _________ his money doing bad things.

15:14-15 - Then a famine hit and he had to go to work doing what?

15:16 - He even wanted to eat what the ______ ate, but wasn't allowed to.

15:17 - Then he remembered home and how who had plenty to eat?

15:18 - He decided to return home and admit he had sinned against ________ and ________.

15:19 - He also decided he was not worthy to be called his father's ____, but was worthy only to be a _______ in the household.

15:20 - But his father was watching for him and _______ to meet him.

15:21-22 - After the son repented, his father ordered what to be done to his sinful son?

15:23 - Then he ordered a fattened calf to be sacrificed: True or False?

15:24a - To the father, his son had been _______, but had come back to _______.

15:24b - To the father, his son had been _______, but finally had been _________.

15:25-26 - When the older son came in from the field, he heard the sound of _______ and asked a ________ what was happening.

15:27-28 - How did the older son react when he learned what was happening?

15:29a - The older son went to their father and complained that he had always done what?

15:29b - But their father had never done what for the older son?

15:30 - What did he say the younger son had been doing while away from home?

15:31 - The father responded that how much belonged to the older son?

15:32 - Did the father think he had a choice whether to rejoice over his younger son? How do you think our heavenly Father reacts when a sinner comes back to him?

Option 2 – Alone Among Enemies or

Continue Worship in a Group

LORD'S SUPPER

Sing or whisper 1st PETER 1:19

READ LUKE 23:13-25 Jesus interrogated by Governor Pilate and Herod.

Take a bite of unleavened bread, representing Jesus body tortured on the cross for us.

Pray silently about Jesus' sacrifice, dying in your place for your sins.

Take a sip of grape juice, representing Jesus' blood that dripped away on the cross for you,

Pray silently about your own sins and desire to live more as God wants you to.

Sing or whisper 1st PETER 2:24

COLLECTION

Prayer: Thank God for your blessings.

Set the money aside to be used to buy a flash drive to put Bible study material on it, or help someone in need that you know.

CLOSING PRAYER

GOD BLESS AND KEEP YOU SAFE UNTIL NEXT SUNDAY

Sunday 22

A Dead Good Man & a Dead Bad Man (Luke 16)

Option 1 – Worship in a Group

READ ALOUD LUKE 16:1-31

16:1 - A rich man had a manager (steward) who was doing what with the rich man's possessions?

16:2 - So the rich man demanded his manager give an _______ of all his possessions.

16:3-4 - The manager knew he was going to be fired, so decided to make people so happy who owed his master money, they will do what for the manager?

16:5-7 - So the manager told the people who owed his master oil and wheat, they only had to pay back _________ of it.

16:9 - Just like the manager who helped others cheat his master made friends with the cheats, we should make friends with good people so that, when things go bad for us, other Christians will receive us into what?

16:10-11 - If a person is good with little things, he will be good with ________ things. If a person is not good with _______ things, he will not be good with ______ things.

16:12 - If you are not good with someone else's things, who will ______ something to own yourself?

16:13 - The two masters we cannot serve at the same time are what?

16:14-15a - God knows what?

16:15b - That which men love is ___________ to God.

16:16a - The Law of Moses and the prophets of the old testament were in effect until ________ the Baptist.

16:16b - Everyone was trying to force their way into the ___________ of God.

16:17 - It was easier for _________ and __________ to pass away than one letter of the Law of Moses to fail.

16:18 - But Jesus went above the Law of Moses and said people can't just divorce for any reason. If they do, then remarry, they commit what?

READ ALOUD LUKE 16:19-31

16:19 - A man was so rich, he lived like a king every _______.

16:20 - A poor man named Lazarus laid at his gate every day covered with ________.

16:21a - Lazarus longed to just eat what fell from the rich man's ________.

16:21b - The dogs did what to Lazarus?

16:22a - The poor man died and was carried away by who to be with Abraham?

16:22b - Did the same thing happen to the rich man when he died?

16:23 - In hades (hell), the rich man was in _________ and could see the good happening to poor Lazarus.

16:24 - The rich man begged Abraham to send Lazarus to do what?

16:25 - What did Abraham reply?

16:26 - Although some people teach you can go from hades to heaven, this verse teaches what?

16:27-28 - So, the rich man begged Abraham to send someone to warn his what?

16:29 - Abraham replied they've got the Bible (Law of _______ and ________), so have all the warning they need.

16:30 - The rich man replied that they would listen if someone talked to them who had done what?

16:31 - Who rose from the dead later on, and people even today will not listen to him?

Option 2 – Alone Among Enemies or Continue Worship in a Group

LORD'S SUPPER

Sing or whisper LUKE 22:19

READ LUKE 23:26-38 where Simon from Cyrene in Libya carried Jesus cross, then Jesus was crucified.

Take a bite of unleavened bread, representing Jesus body tortured on the cross for us.

Pray silently about Jesus' sacrifice, dying in your place for your sins.

Take a sip of grape juice, representing Jesus' blood that dripped away on the cross for you,

Pray silently about your own sins and desire to live more as God wants you to.

Sing or whisper LUKE 22:20

COLLECTION

Prayer: Thank God for your blessings.

Set the money aside to be used to buy a flash drive to put Bible study material on it, or help someone in need that you know.

CLOSING PRAYER

GOD BLESS AND KEEP YOU SAFE UNTIL NEXT SUNDAY

Sunday 23

Children, Bad Examples & End of World (Luke 17)

Option 1 – Worship in a Group

READ ALOUD LUKE 17:1-5

17:1 - Give an example of someone being a stumbling block for you to share the love of Jesus Christ with another person.

17:2 - Jesus sometimes calls us little ones. What would it be better to happen to someone who causes us to stumble than to face judgment?

17:3-4 - One stumbling block is someone who keeps sinning. Jesus says we must forgive a truly repentant person how much?

17:5 - A mustard seed is one of the smallest seeds. Give a spiritual example of what we can do in a spiritual sense if we have faith the size of a mustard seed.

READ ALOUD LUKE 17:7-10

17:7 - Even though we are children of God, we should consider ourselves slaves of God. Should we, as slaves, expect praise before God is praised?

17:8 - We must praise God before what?

17:9 - Should we expect God to thank us for everything we do for him?

17:10 - What should we think about before bragging how

much we've done for God?

READ ALOUD LUKE 17:11-21

17:11-12 - How many lepers went into a village to meet Jesus?

17:13-14a - When they asked Jesus to have mercy on them, Jesus told them to show themselves to health officers of Jesus' day. Who were the health officers?

17:14 - What happened on their way to the health officers? How much faith did they have to go there before being healed?

17:15-16 - How many healed lepers returned to Jesus glorifying God?

17:17-19 - The only one who returned was a hated half-breed called a what? Jesus called this person a what, in order to shame the other nine who were Jews?

17:20-21 - Is the kingdom of God a place? Who do you think is the head of the kingdom of God?

READ ALOUD LUKE 17:22-37

17:22-24 - Jesus said a day would come when people will seek the Son of Mankind (Jesus, son of the huMAN, Mary) everywhere. Are we to believe them?

17:25 - Jesus warned that he was going to suffer what?

17:26-27 - The Son of Man will return at the end of the world to take the saved back to heaven with him, when lost people are doing what?

17:28-29 - What rained down on Sodom during the days of Lot after they had been warned?

17:30-31, 34-36 - On that day two will be doing something together and one suddenly _________ to heaven.

17:33 - Give the spiritual meaning to losing one's life in order to save it.

Option 2 – Alone Among Enemies or

Continue Worship in a Group

LORD'S SUPPER

Sing or whisper LUKE 22:63

READ LUKE 23:39-49 - Criminals crucified with Jesus, darkness in the land three hours, a Roman centurion believes in Jesus.

Take a bite of unleavened bread, representing Jesus body tortured on the cross for us.

Pray silently about Jesus' sacrifice, dying in your place for your sins.

Take a sip of grape juice, representing Jesus' blood that dripped away on the cross for you,

Pray silently about your own sins and desire to live more as God wants you to.

Sing or whisper LUKE 22:64-65

COLLECTION

Prayer: Thank God for your blessings.

Set the money aside to be used to buy a flash drive to put Bible study material on it, or help someone in need that you know.

CLOSING PRAYER

GOD BLESS AND KEEP YOU SAFE UNTIL NEXT SUNDAY

Sunday 24

Self-righteous, Humble, & Blind
(Luke 18)

Option 1 – Worship in a Group

READ ALOUD LUKE 18:1-8

18:1-2 - Jesus told a parable about a certain _____ who did not respect God or man.

18:3 - A poor widow kept coming to him over and over again, asking for what?

18:4 - Finally, the judge agreed to help her, not because he cared what happened to her, but because of what?

18:6-7 - If the unrighteous judge did this, how will God respond to your cries?

18:8 - So, when Jesus comes to judge the world, will he find anyone left on earth with faith?

READ ALOUD LUKE 18:9-17

18:9 - Jesus told another parable to warn people who thought they were very, very _____, and viewed everyone else with what?

18:10-11 - Pharisees were people who would do anything to look righteous to other people, even to bragging how often they prayed and fasted. The Pharisee in Jesus' parable bragged he was not what?

18:12 - What did the Pharisee brag to God that he did for God?

18:13a - The hated tax collector was so humble, he didn't even lift up what?

18:13b - Instead, he begged God to do what? Can you memorize his six-word prayer?

18:14a - Who was just before God? The bragger or the humble one?

18:14b - Explain "He who elevates himself will be lowered; He who lowers himself will be elevated".

18:15 - When parents brought their _______ to Jesus, his twelve disciples got mad at them for bothering Jesus.

18:16a - Jesus told them to do what?

18:16b - The ___________ of ______ belongs to children. Do you think this proves that, when children die, they are automatically saved?

18:17 - Jesus said we had to have the faith and trust of a _______ in order to receive the kingdom of God.

READ ALOUD LUKE 18:18-34

18:18 - A ruler sincerely asked Jesus what to do in order to inherit what?

18:19 - Who is the only good one in the world?

18:20 - Jesus repeated five of Moses' Ten Commandments, indicating they are still in effect in the Christian era. What were they?

18:21 - What did the ruler brag about?

18:22 - Jesus told him to do something so he wouldn't be so proud. What was it?

18:23 - The ruler quit bragging because of what?

18:24-25 - Jesus said it was easier for a camel to go through what than a rich man to enter the kingdom of God?

18:26 - Since everyone has something they value, his hearers said what?

18:27 - Jesus said what about impossibilities?

18:28 - Then Peter said that he and the other disciples had done what?

18:29-30 - Perhaps they were discouraged for leaving everything for Jesus, because Jesus replied with what encouraging words?

18:31-33 - Then Jesus told them he was going to give up even more than his disciples, because he was going to go through what five terrible things?

18:34 - Why don't you think his twelve disciples understood what Jesus was telling them?

READ ALOUD LUKE 18:35-43

18:35 - What was the blind man beside the road doing?

18:36-37 - When he heard the noise of the crowd, he was told who was passing by?

18:38-39 - What did the blind man begin yelling over and over and over?

18:40-41 - What did the man tell Jesus he wanted?

18:42 - What allowed the man to be healed?

18:43 - Did the formerly blind man desert Jesus then?

Option 2 – Alone Among Enemies or Continue Worship in a Group

LORD'S SUPPER

Sing or whisper LUKE 23:18

READ LUKE 23:50 - 24:12 - Jesus is buried, then comes back to life.

Take a bite of unleavened bread, representing Jesus body tortured on the cross for us.

Pray silently about Jesus' sacrifice, dying in your place for your sins.

Take a sip of grape juice, representing Jesus' blood that dripped away on the cross for you,

Pray silently about your own sins and desire to live more as God wants you to.

Sing or whisper LUKE 23:23

COLLECTION

Prayer: Thank God for your blessings.

Set the money aside to be used to buy a flash drive to put Bible study material on it, or help someone in need that you know.

CLOSING PRAYER

GOD BLESS AND KEEP YOU SAFE UNTIL NEXT SUNDAY

Sunday 25

A Tax Collector, the King, & Cheaters
(Luke 19)

Option 1 – Worship in a Group

READ ALOUD LUKE 19:1-10

19:1-2 - In Jericho lived a very rich chief _______ __________ named Zaccheus (Zack-ee-us)

19:3 - When Jesus came to town, Zaccheus tried to see him, but couldn't. Why?

19:4 - So Zaccheaus ran ahead of the crowd following Jesus and climbed a ________ _________.

19:5 - Jesus was impressed that he was willing to humble himself just to see Jesus, so he told Zaccheus he was going to do what?

19:6-7 - The others in the crows complained because they called Zaccheus a ________.

19:8a - So Zaccheus stopped in front of the crowd and said he was going to do what with the poor?

19:8b - And if he had cheated anyone, how much was he going to give back to that person?

19:9a - Jesus said _______ had come to Zaccheus' household.

19:9b - After all, even this "sinner" no one liked was a descendant of what person that everyone respected?

19:10 - Jesus said he had come to earth to _______ and _______ the lost. How can you seek the lost around you who may want to hear the truth about Jesus?

READ ALOUD LUKE 19:11-27

19:11 - Everyone thought the kingdom was earthly and was going to appear where?

19:12 - Jesus told a parable about a nobleman who went to a _____ distant country to claim a new kingdom.

19:13 - Before he left, he gave _____ slaves how _____ pieces of money.

19:15 - When he returned, he demanded to know what the slaves had done with what?

19:16 - The first slave invested his piece of money and earned how much?

19:17 - So the nobleman said he did so well, he was going to let that slave rule over what in the new kingdom?

19:18 - The second slave invested his piece of money and earned how much?

19:19 - So the nobleman said he did so well, he was going to let that slave rule over what in the new kingdom?

19:20 - The third slave earned how much with his piece of money?

19:21 - The third slave had cruelly judged the nobleman, accusing him of what?

19:22 - So the nobleman said he was going to judge the resentful slave by his own what?

19:23 - If he wasn't going to invest the money, the slave should at least have done what?

19:24-25 - Then the nobleman ordered that the one piece of money he'd given the resentful slave be given to which other slave?

19:26 - Jesus said, whoever has earned a lot will be given a lot. Whoever has earned nothing will have what done to him? How can you apply the pieces of money to your life if you call them talents instead?

19:27 - Verse 14 says the other slaves didn't want the nobleman to rule over him. What did the nobleman do to his enemies? How can you apply this to the Day of Judgment?

READ ALOUD LUKE 19:28-44

19:28 - Then Jesus headed in the direction of what city?

19:29-31 - Jesus told two of his disciples to go ahead to a nearby village and get a what?

19:32-35 - What did the disciples put on it as a saddle for Jesus?

19:36 - As Jesus rode closer to Jerusalem, people began putting what on the road to be walked on?

19:37 - Then the whole crowd following Jesus began to do what?

19:38 - What did they call Jesus?

19:39-40 - Some of the self-righteous Pharisees told Jesus to get his followers to quit saying that. But Jesus said, if they didn't what would cry out?

19:41-42 - As he approached Jerusalem, he grew very sad and _____ because the people in the city did not understand _______.

19:43-44 - Jesus warned the people that some day their _____ will surround the city, then pull the city down to the _______.

READ ALOUD LUKE 19:45-48

19:45 - Once in Jerusalem, Jesus went to the temple and drove out who?

19:46 - He shouted at them that they had made the temple a what? Really, the temple was supposed to be a what?

19:47 - Even though he taught daily in the temple, the chief priests tried to do what to Jesus?

19:48 - But they couldn't because they couldn't find anything wrong Jesus said or did, and the people did what?

Option 2 –Alone Among Enemies or Continue Worship in a Group

LORD'S SUPPER

Sing or whisper LUKE 23:33

 You Can Be A Hero Alone

READ LUKE 24:13-35 - Jesus appears to two believers after his resurrection.

Take a bite of unleavened bread, representing Jesus body tortured on the cross for us.

Pray silently about Jesus' sacrifice, dying in your place for your sins.

Take a sip of grape juice, representing Jesus' blood that dripped away on the cross for you,

Pray silently about your own sins and desire to live more as God wants you to.

Sing or whisper LUKE 23:34

COLLECTION

Prayer: Thank God for your blessings.

CLOSING PRAYER

GOD BLESS AND KEEP YOU SAFE UNTIL NEXT SUNDAY

Sunday 26

Words Become Flesh & Blood, God Arrives (John 1)

Option 1 – Worship in a Group

READ ALOUD JOHN 1:1-5

1:1 - In the beginning of the world was __________ that was with God and was God. Are your words with you, and do your words reveal you?

1:2 - Was the Word called an it or he?

1:3 - Compare this verse with Genesis 1. Whenever God spoke that was Jesus before he became flesh?

1:4a - Whenever God spoke in Genesis something came into being, many of which were alive. Therefore, in God's Word is _____. Compare this with John 5:26 and John 11:25.

1:4b-5 - In what way is the world full of darkness? How is Jesus the Light of the world?

READ ALOUD JOHN 1:6-13

1:6 - Whose son was John? Look this up in Luke 1:21-24, 63.

1:7 - What did Jesus call himself in John 8:12?

1:8 - Sometimes people thought John was the Light of the

world. Sometimes he had to explain what to people?

1:9 - What and who does 2nd Corinthians 4:6 say the Light is?

1:10 - In what way was the world made through Jesus, the Word?

1:11 - If Jesus, the Word, made the world, he owns the world. So, who is this verse talking about?

1:12 - If we believe in Jesus, we become __________ of God by adoption.

1:13 - Does that mean God has a wife, or is it spiritual?

READ ALOUD JOHN 1:14-18

1:14a - What other time did God walk on earth? See Genesis 3:8.

1:14b - Even though believers in the Word (Jesus) get to be children of God by adoption, Jesus, the Word, was the only _______ Son of God, the only produced Son of God. Compare this also with Colossians 1:13.

1:15 - Compare this verse with 1st Timothy 3:16. God is called who in Titus 2:13.

1:16 - Compare this verse with Colossians 1:18-19 and Colossians 2:9.

1:17 - What did Jesus do to the Law of Moses when he died on the cross? See Colossians 3:14

1:18 - Compare this verse with Hebrews 1:1-8

READ ALOUD JOHN 1:19-28

1:19-20 - Christ means messiah. Messiah means anointed one. In Bible times, a person was anointed to be high priest or king. Jesus was both.

1:21-22 - The Jewish leaders wanted to know who John was. They asked if maybe he was the prophet _____ raised from the dead, but he said no.

1:23 - In days before paved highways, people went out and repaired their highways and make them straight for when a king came. Who was the king John was making the highway straight for?

1:24-27 - John said he was not worthy to do what to the One who was introducing to the world?

1:28 - John was baptizing in what river that still has that

name today?

READ ALOUD JOHN 1:29-34

      1:29 - When Jesus came to John, what did John call Jesus? Why?

      1:30 - Again, John said Jesus existed _______________.

      1:31-32 - To make sure John announced the right person, what did God send from heaven to descend on Jesus?

      1:33a - It represented the Holy ______ of God.

      1:33b - John said Jesus would be able to baptized in the

________________.

      1:34 - John testified that Jesus was who?

Option 2 – Alone Among Enemies or Continue Worship in a Group

LORD'S SUPPER

Sing or whisper LUKE 23:44

READ LUKE 24:36-53 - Jesus appeared alive to his apostles, then returned to heaven.

        Take a bite of unleavened bread, representing Jesus body tortured on the cross for us.

        Pray silently about Jesus' sacrifice, dying in your place for your sins.

        Take a sip of grape juice, representing Jesus' blood that dripped away on the cross for you,

        Pray silently about your own sins and desire to live more as God wants you to.

Sing or whisper LUKE 23:46

COLLECTION

Prayer: Thank God for your blessings.

Set the money aside to be used to buy a flash drive to put Bible study material on it, or help someone in need that you know.

CLOSING PRAYER

GOD BLESS AND KEEP YOU SAFE UNTIL NEXT SUNDAY

Sunday 27

Reborn in Water & Spirit, Lamb of God (John 3)

Option 1 – Worship in a Group

READ ALOUD JOHN 3:1-21

3:1a - The Pharisees were of a Jewish religious sect that led the Jews in Jesus' time. Who was one of the rulers?

3:1b - He was afraid of his fellow Pharisees, so this man went to see Jesus when?

3:2 - What signs do you think Jesus was performing to make people realize he was from God?

3:3 - This man was a ruler in the kingdom of the Jews, but Jesus said there was a better kingdom of God, but to be a citizens, one had to be what?

3:4 - Nicodemus did not realize yet that Jesus spoke of spiritual things in physical terms. So he asked Jesus how he could do what?

3:5 - Jesus explained that, to be born again, requires both ________ and the ________ of God. He was speaking of baptism.

3:6 - That which is born of the flesh is flesh. That which is born of the Spirit is ________.

3:7-8 - Can we see the wind? Can we hear it? Can we see what the wind does? How is the wind like the Spirit of God and being born again?

3:9-11 - Jesus said he had seen such rebirths? Who was baptizing at that time?

3:12 - If we are not baptized, we do not understand what happens to us after baptism. Compare this with Acts 2:38.

3:13 - Jesus said who had descended from heaven? In what way was his mother Mary a woMAN. Who was Jesus' Father?

3:14-15 - Read Numbers 21:6-9 to understand what pole Moses lifted up in order to save people from being killed. Jesus predicted he would be lifted up on a pole to give people eternal life. What do we call that pole Jesus died on?

3:16 - This is the most popular verse in the Bible among Christians. Memorize it.

3:17 - Jesus did not come into the world to condemn sinners, but to do what for sinners?

3:18 - In verse 13, Jesus called him the Son of Man. In this verse, he called himself the Son of _______.

3:19 - What happened in the darkness in the world?

3:20 - This verse explains why many people hate Christians. What is it?

3:21 - Who is drawn to the Light?

READ ALOUD JOHN 3:22-36

3:22-23a - Jesus and his twelve disciples went to preach near who else that was preaching?

3:23b - What was he doing there?

3:24 - Later on, John was arrested and then what happened to him?

3:25-26 - What was Jesus and his disciples doing at that same time?

3:27-28 - John had to keep telling people he was not the _________. Remember, that word means Messiah, and Messiah means anointed one.

3:29 - Who was the bridegroom John was referring to? See Ephesians 5:28-29.

3:30-31 - Jesus came from __________, but John came from the earth.

3:32-33 - What Jesus saw there he tells people about, but many people did not what?

3:34-35 - The Father in heaven gave all things to who while on earth?

3:36a - He who believes in the Son of God has what?

3:36b - Belief and obedience go together. If someone does not believe, he will not obey. If he does not obey, what will happen?

Option 2 – Alone Among Enemies or Continue Worship in a Group

LORD'S SUPPER

Sing or whisper LUKE 23:49

READ JOHN 13:1-20 - Jesus washes his disciples feet, then shows how to keep the Lord's Supper after he left the earth.

Take a bite of unleavened bread, representing Jesus body tortured on the cross for us.

Pray silently about Jesus' sacrifice, dying in your place for your sins.

Take a sip of grape juice, representing Jesus' blood that dripped away on the cross for you,

Pray silently about your own sins and desire to live more as God wants you to.

Sing or whisper LUKE 23:52-53

COLLECTION

Prayer: Thank God for your blessings.

Set the money aside to be used to buy a flash drive to put Bible study material on it, or help someone in need that you know.

CLOSING PRAYER

GOD BLESS AND KEEP YOU SAFE UNTIL NEXT SUNDAY

Sunday 28

Loved by Outcasts, Saves a Dying Boy (John 4)

Option 1 – Worship in a Small Group

READ ALOUD JOHN 4:1-26

4:1-4 - The province between the provinces of Judea in the south and Galilee in the north was called what?

4:5 - The city of Sychar was located near land that Jacob (Israel) gave to which son who had been prime minister of Egypt 1500 years earlier.

4:6a - A well outside of town was called __________'s well.

4:6b - Jesus was tired, so sat down by the well. If the Jewish first hour was 9 AM, what time was it when Jesus sat down by the well?

4:7 - Even though it was not polite for a man to talk to a woman in public, Jesus said what to the woman?

4:8 - Who was Jesus waiting for?

4:9 - Not only was the person a woman, but she was a Samaritan. What did Jews think of Samaritans?

4:10 - Jesus then explained to the woman that, if she understood who he was, she would ask him for what?

4:11-12 - The woman objected that Jesus did ot have anything to do what with water?

4:13-14a - Jesus replied that anyone drinking his water will never do what?

4:14b - Jesus further explained that his water will give what?

4:15 - Did the woman want Jesus' water?

4:16-18a - Jesus told her to go get her husband. When she said she did not have a husband at that time, Jesus replied that she had had _____ husbands.(probably widowed many times).

4:18b - Further, Jesus told her that the man she was living with at that time what not who?

4:19 - The woman realized Jesus was a __________.

4:20 - She wondered if he was a prophet from there in Samaria or from the temple in __________.

4:21 - Jesus said the day was coming when people wouldn't have to go to this mountain or to __________ to worship the Father in heaven.

4:22 - Salvation was from the Jews in the sense that the Jewish prophets prophesied a Jew would bring salvation to the world. What was Jesus' nationality?

4:23-24 - Then Jesus explained that the location of worship was not important, but true worshipers worshiped in _______ and in _______.

4:25 - This woman believed the Messiah would come some day. What else did she call the Messiah?

4:26 - What did Jesus reply?

READ ALOUD JOHN 4:27-45

4:27 - When Jesus' twelve disciples returned, they were surprised at what?

4:28-29 - Immediately the woman left, went into the city, and told everyone she thought she had actually met who?

4:30 - What did the men of the city do?

4:31-32 - Jesus used every opportunity to make a spiritual point from a physical event. He told his disciples he had what that they didn't know about?

4:33-34 - Jesus explained that his food was to do what?

4:35 - What time of year does it seem Jesus was in Samaria?

4:36-38 - If Jesus was the sower of the seed (Word), he considered what group the reapers?

4:39 - At first, the people of the city believed in Jesus because of whose testimony?

4:40 - So Jesus stayed there and taught for how long?

4:41-42 - Then many more believed because of what?

READ ALOUD JOHN 4:46-54

4:46a - In Cana, Jesus miraculously turned water into ______. In those days, it was not fermented like it is today after the invention of bottles.

4:46b - A royal official living in another city called Capernaum had a son who was ______.

4:47 - He official went to Jesus in Cana and begged him to do what?

4:48-49 - The official interrupted Jesus' preaching and begged Jesus to go to his son before his son ______.

4:50 - We have long-distance phone calls today. Jesus healed the boy who was in the town of ______, even though Jesus was still in the town of ______.

4:51-53 - The official's servants met him on his way home and said his son was healed exactly when?

4:54 - Turning water into wine was Jesus' first miracle. What was Jesus' second miracle?

Option 2 – Alone Among Enemies or Continue Worship in a Group

LORD'S SUPPER

Sing or whisper LUKE 24:2-3

READ JOHN 13:21-35 - Jesus predicts that he will be betrayed and killed.

Take a bite of unleavened bread, representing Jesus body tortured on the cross for us.

Pray silently about Jesus' sacrifice, dying in your place for your sins.

Take a sip of grape juice, representing Jesus' blood that dripped away on the cross for you,

Pray silently about your own sins and desire to live more as God wants you to.

Sing or whisper LUKE 24:5

COLLECTION

Prayer: Thank God for your blessings.

Set the money aside to be used to buy a flash drive to put Bible study material on it, or help someone in need that you know.

CLOSING PRAYER

GOD BLESS AND KEEP YOU SAFE UNTIL NEXT SUNDAY

Sunday 29

1 with God, 2 Resurrections, 4 Proofs (John 5)

Option 1 – Worship in a Group

READ ALOUD JOHN 5:18-24

5:18 - What two reasons were the Jewish leaders trying to kill Jesus?

5:19 - Adults have children who are just like them. God had who as a Son who was just like him?

5:20 - Since the one God has Mind, Word, and Spirit, in what sense does the Mind tell his Words what to say? Do the Words have to obey the Mind?

5:21 - God the Father (Mind) raises the dead, so God the Son (Word) can do what?

5:22 - A judge pronounces sentences with words. So, since Jesus was the Word, the Father has given him all what?

5:23 - Everyone who honors God the Father, automatically honors God the ___________.

5:24a - Anyone who believes the Word believes the originator of his words. Who is that?

5:24b - Jesus does not judge those who believe, because believers have already passed from ___________ to ___________.

READ ALOUD JOHN 5:25-39

5:25 - In what sense are we dead if we do not listen to Jesus, the Word?

5:26 - God is life. Satan is death. Since God the Father and God the Spirit are life, who else is life?

5:27 - In what sense was Jesus the Son of God but also the son of mankind?

5:28-29 - Some day Jesus will call everyone out of their tombs to be judged. Compared this with 1st Thessalonians 13:15-17.

5:30 - As God the Mind (Father) instructs his Words (Son), the Son does the will of who?

READ ALOUD JOHN 5:31-47

5:31-32 - One cannot testify about _______.

5:33 - One of Jesus' witnesses was _______ the Baptist.

5:34-35 - His witness was like a _______ burning to give _______ to people.

5:36 - An even greater witness was Jesus' miracles, which he called his _______.

5:37-38 - Another witness of Jesus' divinity was the Father who testified through his _______ which they heard spoken through _______.

5:39 - A final witness of Jesus' divinity was the __________ which prophesied about Jesus' birth, life, and death.

5:40 - But some who did not want to believe in Jesus refused to believe and have eternal _______.

5:41-42 - Even though Jesus did not need the love of men, many people did not have the love of _______ in them.

5:43 - Jesus did not come in his own name (the Word), but in the name of his _______.

5:44a - But men are more likely to believe someone who declares his own____.

5:44 - How many Gods did Jesus say there were?

5:45-47 - Jesus said they didn't believe in him because they didn't believe _______ who prophesied about him.

Option 2 –Alone Among Enemies or Continue Worship in a Group

LORD'S SUPPER

Sing or whisper LUKE 24:36

READ JOHN 18:1-11 - How Judas betrays Jesus

Take a bite of unleavened bread, representing Jesus body tortured on the cross for us.

Pray silently about Jesus' sacrifice, dying in your place for your sins.

Take a sip of grape juice, representing Jesus' blood that dripped away on the cross for you,

Pray silently about your own sins and desire to live more as God wants you to.

Sing or whisper LUKE 24:39

COLLECTION

Prayer: Thank God for your blessings.

Set the money aside to be used to buy a flash drive to put Bible study material on it, or help someone in need that you know.

CLOSING PRAYER

GOD BLESS AND KEEP YOU SAFE UNTIL NEXT SUNDAY

Sunday 30
Walks on Water, is Bread of Life

Option 1 – Worship in a Small Group

READ ALOUD JOHN 6:1-14

6:1-2 - When Jesus went to the other side of the Sea of _________, a large crowd followed him because they had seen the miracles hew had performed on who?

6:3 - Jesus and his disciples sat down where?

6:4 - The ___________ feast was nearby when the Jews ate unleavened bread and lamb as a sacred meal.

6:5 - When he saw the large crowd coming their way, He asked Philip what?

6:6 - Why did he ask Philip this?

6:7 - He said it would take more than how much money to buy enough ______ for the crowd to eat?

6:8 - Who was Peter's brother?

6:9 - This brother found a boy with how much food and brought him to Jesus?

6:10 - How many people were in the crowd?

6:11 - Jesus divided up the boy's lunch and divided it up, and the people were able to eat how much?

6:12-13 - How much did they have left over from the boy's lunch?

6:14 - The Old Testament scriptures had prophesied a divine Prophet, and the people decided who was that Prophet?

READ ALOUD JOHN 6:15-21

6:15a - The people decided right then and there to make Jesus be their what?

6:15b - Why do you think Jesus hid himself so they couldn't make him an earthly king?

6:16-17 - That night, his twelve disciples went down the mountain to the Sea of Galilee to cross back to the town of ______.

6:18 - On their way, a strong ______ did what?

6:19a - They rowed their boat out how far?

6:19b - Suddenly, they saw Jesus ______ on the water toward them.

6:20 - Jesus called to them over the wind, what?

6:21 - As soon as Jesus climbed into the boat in the middle of the Sea of Galilee, what happened?

READ ALOUD JOHN 6:22-40

6:22-25 - The people followed Jesus in their own boats to what town?

6:26 - Does it sound like the people just wanted another free meal?

6:27 - Jesus told them to not try so hard to get food that does what?

6:28-29 - When the people asked what the work of God was, he said it was to do what?

6:30 - After all he had done for them, they pretended he hadn't done anything for them and demanded he do what?

6:31 - Compare what they said with the description of manna in Exodus 16:4 in the Old Testament.

6:32 - Jesus said it wasn't really ______ who gave them the bread from heaven but God, the Father.

6:33 - But there is another bread that gives life to who?

6:34 - Did the crowd want that bread?

6:35 - Jesus said who was the bread of life and water of life?

6:36 - They'd heard and seen Jesus, but still they did ______ believe.

6:37-38 - In what sense does the Word (God the Son) have to obey the Mind (God the Father)?

6:39 - On the last day of the world, Jesdus is going to ______ up all believers.

6:40 - Who has eternal life?

READ ALOUD JOHN 6:41-58

6:41 - Who did Jesus say once again was the bread of life who has come down from heaven?

6:42 - Some objected because they knew his earthly father whose name was _______. (Some people claim his earthly father died when he was a child, but this proved he was still alive when Jesus was preaching.)

6:44 - Jesus said he would do what for people who believe in him?

6:45 - A prophecy in the Old Testament said some day people would be taught by who? Jesus was the ______ of God.

6:46-47 - Believers of all this will have what?

6:48-50 - People who ate bread that came out of heaven in Moses' day eventually died. Jesus said anyone who eats him (the Word of God) will never what?

6:51-56 - Relate this to the Lord's Supper that Christians keep every Sunday.

6:57-58 - How important is it to keep the Lord's Supper every Sunday?

Option 2 – Alone Among Enemies or Continue Worship in a Group

LORD'S SUPPER

Sing or whisper MARK 14:22

READ JOHN 18:12-14, 19-24 - Jesus' trial before the high priests, and his torture by the temple soldiers.

Take a bite of unleavened bread, representing Jesus body tortured on the cross for us.

Pray silently about Jesus' sacrifice, dying in your place for your sins.

Take a sip of grape juice, representing Jesus' blood

that dripped away on the cross for you,

Pray silently about your own sins and desire to live more as God wants you to.

Sing or whisper MARK 14:23-24

COLLECTION

Prayer: Thank God for your blessings.

Set the money aside to be used to buy a flash drive to put Bible study material on it, or help someone in need that you know.

CLOSING PRAYER

GOD BLESS AND KEEP YOU SAFE UNTIL NEXT SUNDAY

Sunday 31

Guilty Person Trapped & Light of the World (John 8)

Option 1 – Worship in a Small Group

READ ALOUD JOHN 8:1-11

8:1 - Jesus sometimes spent the night in an orchard overlooking Jerusalem called the _______ of _______.

8:2 - As soon as he returned to the temple, people recognized him and did what?

8:3 - The Pharisees and scribes who were leaders of the Jewish religion brought who to Jesus?

8:4 - Since they caught her in the act, why don't you think they brought the man to him?

8:5 - The Law of Moses was made 2000 years earlier and said they should do what to both men and women caught in the act of adultery?

8:6a - They wanted to _______ Jesus because they knew he was a man of peace.

8:6b - Do you think Jesus was writing the names of the other men who had committed adultery with this woman?

8:7 - What did Jesus answer her accusers?

8:8-9 - Why do you think the men slipped away?

8:10-11 - Jesus did not condemn her, but warned her to do

what?

READ ALOUD JOHN 6:15-30

      8:12 - Jesus said, "I am the _______ of the world." Was he talking about physical darkness or spiritual darkness?
      8:13 - The Pharisees who ruled the Jewish religion, said it wasn't legal to give a legal testimony about who?
      8:14 - Jesus replied that he knew where he had ___________ and where he was going, but they didn't know.
      8:15-16 - Jesus judges only according to his what?
      8:17 - According to the Law of Moses, the testimony of how many men makes it true?
      8:18 - Jesus said what two beings testified about him?
      8:19 - Even though the Pharisees knew the answer, they asked Jesus who his _______ was.
      8:20 - He kept making the Jewish leaders mad, but no one _______ him because his time of death had not arrived yet.
      8:21 - Jesus referred to going away to heaven. Did he say the Pharisees could go there too?
      8:22 - But the people thought he was referring to doing what to himself?
      8:23 - Jesus said being below was the same thing as being in the ___________.
      8:24 - He warned them that, unless they believed in Jesus, they would die how?
      8:25-27 - Even though Jesus kept telling them who he was, they didn't want to believe; so they didn't know he was speaking the world of who?
      8:28a - Jesus predicted that the Jews would ________ Jesus up onto a cross.
      8:28b - Jesus spoke only the words of who?
      8:29-30 - Who was always with Jesus?

READ ALOUD JOHN 8:31-59

      8:31 - We are Jesus followers only if we continue to do what?
      8:32 - Memorize this verse.
      8:33-34 - Everyone who commits _____ is a slave to ______.
      8:36-37 - If the master son sets slaves free, are they free?
      8:38 - Jesus only spoke the words he "heard" from who?

8:39 - They claimed Abraham was their father, but Jesus said they weren't because they didn't what?

8:40 - Jesus told them he knew they were trying to _______ him.

8:41-43 - So they changed from Abraham being their father to God being their father. Did Jesus agree? Why?

8:44a - Who did Jesus say was the father of the Jewish religious leaders?

8:44b - The murderer of mankind ~ both physical and spiritual ~ has always been who? Therefore, did God create death?

8:44c - The father of lies is who?

8:45-47 - A person who is a child of God will hear the _________ of God.

8:48 - So the Pharisees called Jesus a Samaritan (half breed) with a what?

8:49-51 - Jesus said whoever keeps his Word will never what?

8:52-53 - They called Jesus a liar because righteous Abraham and all the prophets were dead. But Jesus mean what kind of death?

8:54-56 - Abraham saw the day in the future when Jesus would come. Compare this with Hebrews 11:8-13.

8:57 - What did the Jewish leaders not understand when they said Jesus wasn't even 50 years old yet, but claimed to have seen Abraham?

8:58 - What was Jesus' reply?

8:59 - He had once again claimed he was God. So they picked up _________ to kill him for blasphemy. But he hid himself in the crowd and escaped.

Option 2 – Alone Among Enemies or Continue Worship in a Group

LORD'S SUPPER

Sing or whisper MARK 14:43-44

READ JOHN 18:28-40 - Jesus is interviewed by Governor Pilate who wanted to set him free.

Take a bite of unleavened bread, representing Jesus
body tortured on the cross for us.

Pray silently about Jesus' sacrifice, dying in your
place for your sins.

Take a sip of grape juice, representing Jesus' blood
that dripped away on the cross for you,

Pray silently about your own sins and desire to live
more as God wants you to.

Sing or whisper MARK 14:55-56

COLLECTION

Prayer: Thank God for your blessings.

Set the money aside to be used to buy a flash drive to put Bible
study material on it, or help someone in need that you know.

CLOSING PRAYER

GOD BLESS AND KEEP YOU SAFE UNTIL NEXT SUNDAY

Sunday 32

A Man Born Blind & "Kill Jesus!"
(John 9)

Option 1 – Worship in a Small Group

READ ALOUD JOHN 9:1-12

9:1-2 - Jesus' 12 disciples thought a man had been born
___________ as punishment because he or his parents sinned.

9:3 - Jesus said no one had sinned, but it happened so that
people might see a miracle from _______.

9:4 - Jesus said we must work God's works while it is
spiritually _______ for us.

9:5 - Jesus said that, as long as he was in the world, he was
the __________ of the world.

9:6-7 - Jesus put clay on the man's eyes and told him to
wash in the __________ of Siloam.

9:8 - The formerly blind man used to get a few coins to live
on how?

9:9 - Some said he wasn't the former beggar, but the man
kept saying what?

9:10-12 - His neighbors and friends asked the man what?

READ ALOUD JOHN 9:13-33

9:13-15 - The neighbors took the former blind man to the Pharisees to tell what?

9:16 - The self-righteous Pharisees declared Jesus had sinned by making mud and healing on what Jewish holy day?

9:17 - What did the former blind man call Jesus?

9:18a - Did the Jewish leaders believe the man had really been healed?

9:18b - They sent for the __________ of the former blind man.

9:19 - What did they ask them?

9:20-21 - What did they answer?

9:22-23 - Anyone who confessed Jesus was the Christ (Messiah, divine king), he would be put out of the Jewish __________.

9:24 - How many times did the Jewish leaders question the former blind man?

9:25 - Did the former blind man think Jesus was a sinner for healing him on the Sabbath day?

9:26-27 - They asked again how he was healed, and the man asked them if they wanted to become Jesus' __________.

9:28-29 - Who did the Jewish leaders declare was their leader who had died 2000 years earlier?

9:30-31 - The former blind man said "We know that god does not hear ______.

9:32-33 - Had the former blind man ever heard of another man like him being healed?

9:34 - The Jewish leaders declared that the former blind man was born in _____, then threw him out of the Jewish religion.

READ ALOUD JOHN 9:35-41

9:35 - When Jesus heard what happened, he found the man and asked him if he believed in the ______ of Mankind.

9:36-38 - Jesus told the man he was seeing him and talking to him. What, then did the man do before Jesus? This proves that Jesus meant for the term, ______ of Man to mean he was Godman.

9:39 - Jesus said he came into the world to prove which ones were spiritually ______.

9:40-41 - People who claimed they could see spiritually, but still didn't believe in Jesus still had their what?

Option 2 – Alone Among Enemies or

Continue Worship in a Group

LORD'S SUPPER

Sing or whisper MARK 15:9

READ JOHN 19:1-15 - The Roman governor Pilate hands Jesus over to be crucified.

Take a bite of unleavened bread, representing Jesus body tortured on the cross for us.

Pray silently about Jesus' sacrifice, dying in your place for your sins.

Take a sip of grape juice, representing Jesus' blood that dripped away on the cross for you,

Pray silently about your own sins and desire to live more as God wants you to.

Sing or whisper MARK 15:13

COLLECTION

Prayer: Thank God for your blessings.

Set the money aside to be used to buy a flash drive to put Bible study material on it, or help someone in need that you know.

CLOSING PRAYER

GOD BLESS AND KEEP YOU SAFE UNTIL NEXT SUNDAY

Sunday 33

Bad Shepherd & Good Shepherd
(John 10)

Option 1 – Worship in a Small Group

READ ALOUD JOHN 10:1-21

10:1a - The door to heaven in represented in this parable as a door to what?

10:1b - Some people try to get into heaven like a _______.

10:2 - The Good Shepherd enters by the ________.

10:3 - The Good Shepherd calls his sheep (followers) by their _________.

10:4 - The sheep know the ______ ov the Good Shepherd.

10:5 - The sheep will not follow who?

10:7 - Jesus said he is not only the Good Shepherd, but he is also the ______ into heaven (the sheep fold).

10:8 - He said that everyone who claimed to be the Good Shepherd or the door into heaven before him were what?

10:9-10a - The thief comes to the sheep to ________ and ________.

10:10b - Jesus said, "I have come that they may have ______, and have it ___________."

10:11 - Now Jesus is back to talking about him being the Good ________.

10:12-13 - A hired shepherd will flee when he sees ______ coming to snatch the sheep.

10:14-15 - Jesus said, as the Good Shepherd, he was

planning to _______ for his sheep.

10:16 - Some people believe the _______ sheep he mentioned were Gentiles (non-Jews).

10:17 - Why does God the Father love God the Son/Word?

10:18 - Jesus explained that no one could _________ without his permission.

10:19-20 - Some of the Jews thought Jesus had a ________ in him for talking like this.

10:21 - Others said Jesus was true because he was the only one who could do what?

READ ALOUD JOHN 10:22-42

10:22-23 - During the Feast of Dedication at the Temple in Jerusalem, it was what season? So Jesus went to teach in the _______ of Solomon.

10:24 - The Jews asked him once again if he was what?

10:25a - Jesus said once again that he had already told them but they wouldn't what?

10:25b - Jesus said his miracles ____________ about him.

10:26-27 - He told unbelievers they didn't believe because they didn't what?

10:28-29 - Jesus gives eternal _______.

10:30 - God the Son/Word is ______ with God the Father.

10:31 - So, once again the Jews picked up _______ to ______ him to death.

10:32 - Jesus asked which of his _______ words they wanted to kill him for.

10:33 - They said they were going to kill him because he was telling people he was ______.

10:36 - Jesus said, "I am the ______ of God."

10:37-38 - Jesus told them, if they didn't believe his words, to at least believe because of his ______.

10:39 - Then Jesus escaped their __________.

10:40-42 - He then went to the Jordan River where John the Baptist used to baptize, and many people did what there?

Option 2 – Alone Among Enemies or Continue Worship in a Group

LORD'S SUPPER

Sing or whisper MARK 15:16-17

READ JOHN 19:16-25 - Jesus is crucified.

Take a bite of unleavened bread, representing Jesus body tortured on the cross for us.

Pray silently about Jesus' sacrifice, dying in your place for your sins.

Take a sip of grape juice, representing Jesus' blood that dripped away on the cross for you,

Pray silently about your own sins and desire to live more as God wants you to.

Sing or whisper MARK 15:18-20

COLLECTION

Prayer: Thank God for your blessings.

Set the money aside to be used to buy a flash drive to put Bible study material on it, or help someone in need that you know.

CLOSING PRAYER

GOD BLESS AND KEEP YOU SAFE UNTIL NEXT SUNDAY

Sunday 34

Returns Man to Life, "Kill Jesus!"

Option 1 – Worship in a Small Group

READ ALOUD JOHN 11:1-45

11:1 - Lazarus of Bethany had two sisters name what?

11:2-3 - The sisters sent word to Jesus waying the one he loved is __________.

11:4 - Jesus said his death was so that who could be glorified?

11:5-6 - Even though Jesus loved this brother and his sisters, he stayed away from them how long?

11:7-8 - Bethany was just a few miles from Jerusalem where people had just tried to __________ him to death.

11:11 - Jesus told them Lazarus had fallen __________, and he wanted to __________ him up.

11:12 - Jesus' 12 disciples said it sounded like Lazarus was going to __________.

11:13 - But Jesus was really talking about Lazarus' __________.

11:14 - So Jesus explained plainly that Lazarus was __________.

11:15 - Jesus told his disciples he was glad he wasn't there so they would __________.

11:16 - Thomas was probably the bravest of the 12 disciples, because he said, "Let us go with Jesus so we may __________ with him."

11:17 - By the time they arrived, Lazarus had already been in the _________ for _________ days.

11:18 - How far away was Bethany from Jerusalem?

11:19 - Many Jews from Jerusalem came to the funeral to comfort ___________ and ___________.

11:20 - Which sister ran to meet Jesus when he drew near to their house?

11:21 - She had a lot of faith and said that, if Jesus had been there when they first sent for him, her brother would not have _________.

11:22 - She believed that whatever Jesus asked of _________ would be given to him.

11:23 - Jesus replied, "Your brother will ___________ again."

11:24 - She thought he was talking about the _______ day of the world.

11:25 - Memorize this verse.

11:26 - Jesus also said if someone was alive, but believed in him, s/he would never _______.

11:27 - What did the sister confess to Jesus?

11:28-29 - This sister went to get her sister to come meet Jesus. What was the other sister's name who was still at home?

11:30-31 - The people in the house thought she was going to the cemetery, so _________ her.

11:32 - This sister told Jesus the very same thing her sister had said earlier when she first saw Jesus. What did she say?

11:33 - When Jesus saw everyone _______, he was deeply troubled and angry at Satan's use of death.

11:34-35 - Verse 35 is the shortest verse in the Bible. What is it?

11:36-37 - The Jews gathered around knew he had healed people before, so asked each other why he didn't come and do what before Lazarus died?

11:38 - Lazarus was buried in a _________.

11:39a - Jesus commanded that some men do what?

11:39b - Sister Martha objected that by now his body would _________.

11:40-42 - After they moved the stone away from the entrance, Jesus thanked God that he had already _________ _________.

11:43 - After his prayer of thanksgiving, Jesus commanded that dead Lazarus do what?

11:44 - Lazarus was bound like a mummy, feet to head, but

he did what?

11:45 - After seeing this, many Jews _________ in Jesus.

READ ALOUD JOHN 11:46-57

11:46 - Some of the Jews reported to the Pharisees what?

11:47 - So the Pharisees and ________ priests met in council.

11:47 - Did they believe Jesus was performing those signs and wonders?

11:48 - They were afraid the _________ who controlled their country would take away their jobs and even their _______.

11:49-50 - But Caiaphas, the _______ _________ said one person should _________ for the people.

11:51 - Without knowing it, Caiaphas _________ what was going to happen to Jesus.

11:52 - Not only would Jesus die for the nation, but he would die for all the _________ of God worldwide.

11:53 - So the council met daily after that the figure out a way to ______ Jesus.

11:54 - So Jesus no longer traveled how?

11:55 - When the annual Feast of Passover drew near, many people went to _________ to prepare for it.

11:56-57 - Everyone wondered if Jesus would show up at the temple because the chief priests and Pharisees had ordered that, if Jesus did, what were people who saw him supposed to do?

Option 2 – Alone Among Enemies or Continue Worship in a Group

LORD'S SUPPER

Sing or whisper MARK 15:25

READ JOHN 19:16-25 - Jesus dies on the cross and is embalmed and buried.

Take a bite of unleavened bread, representing Jesus

body tortured on the cross for us.

Pray silently about Jesus' sacrifice, dying in your place for your sins.

Take a sip of grape juice, representing Jesus' blood that dripped away on the cross for you,

Pray silently about your own sins and desire to live more as God wants you to.

Sing or whisper MARK 15:26

COLLECTION

Prayer: Thank God for your blessings.

Set the money aside to be used to buy a flash drive to put Bible study material on it, or help someone in need that you know.

CLOSING PRAYER

GOD BLESS AND KEEP YOU SAFE UNTIL NEXT SUNDAY

Sunday 35

The Church Begins & 3000 Are Baptized (Acts 1-2)

Option 1 – Worship in a Group

READ ALOUD ACTS 1:1b-11

1:1b - The book, Acts of the Apostles, begins with the time Jesus was taken up to __________.

1:2 - First, Jesus gave orders to his __________ (formerly called disciples) how to begin the church.

1:3 - Jesus appeared alive after his crucifixion over a period of how many days before turning to heaven?

1:4 - Jesus told his apostles they were to wait in what city?

1:5 - At that time, the 12 apostles were going to be __________ with the Holy __________ of God.

1:6 - They were still confused, thinking Jesus was going to start an earthly __________.

1:7-8 - Jesus told them they would receive power to spread the gospel of Jesus to the farthest parts of the __________.

1:9 - Then, suddenly he began to rise, and went up through the __________.

1:10 - While his apostles were still gazing up into the sky, watching Jesus leave, who men wearing what suddenly appeared beside them?

1:11 - They explained that Jesus would return in the same way they saw him go into heaven. Compare this with I Thessalonians 4:17.

READ ALOUD ACTS 2:1-47

2:1 - The Day of Pentecost was 50 days after the Day of Passover at which time Jesus was crucified and came back to life.

2:2 - A rushing _________ filled the whole __________ where the 12 apostles were.

2:3 - Then fire in the shape of ________ rested on each of them.

2:4 - They were all filled with the Holy _______ of God and began to speak in ____________ they had not learned.

2:5-6 People from every nation were in Jerusalem and rushed to the house where the wind was. They were fused because they could hear the apostles speaking in their own ___________.

2:7-11 - How many different nationalities and tongues were present who heard the apostles speak and understood them?

2:12-13 & 15 - Some people, not wanting to admit the miracle, just said the men were just drunk with _______.

2:14 - How many preached the first sermon?

2:17 - Back at the firth of Jesus, Simeon and Anna both prophesied when they saw baby Jesus in the temple. Joseph was the young man who saw a vision. Zechariah and the wise men were the old men who dreamed dreams.

2:18 - God was planning to pour out his spirit on all who did what? (See verse 38)

2:19a - The star that appeared when Jesus was born was the great wonder in the sky. The sign on earth was the Holy Spiri5t descending like a dove when Jesus was baptized.

2:19b-20 - There was blood at the crucifixion, and the sun turned dark for three hours during the crucifixion.

2:22-24 - Jesus performed _______, was nailed to a ________, then was ________ up again from _________.

2:27 - This prophecy is from Isaiah 53:11. Look it up. The word hades here is translated from the word meaning hell. Jesus escaped hell.

2:29-31 - David prophesied that Jesus' soul would not be abandoned in hell, nor his flesh do what?

2:36 - Peter was brave when he accused the people of cring out for Jesus to be ___________.

2:37 - Feeling their guilt, the audience cried out what?

2:38 - Memorize this verse. It tells us how to have our sins forgiven and receive the Holy Spirit.

2:39 - This promise is good for everyone in the audience and their __________ many generations later.

2:41 - How many in the audience were baptized that day? If there were 12 apostles and six hours of daylight left, how many would each apostle have to baptize every hour? How many every minute? They wouldn't have the strength. Don't you think the new Christians baptized each other to help out?

2:42 - After that the new Christians devoted themselves to the apostles' teachings (the New Testament half of the Bible wasn't written yet), to _______, to the Lord's Supper, and the __________.

2:43 - Who performed miracles among them?

2:45 - Probably some began losing their jobs, because the new Christians began selling __________ and sharing with those in need.

2:47 - Who added them to the church? People or the Lord?

Option 2 – Alone Among Enemies or Continue Worship in a Group

LORD'S SUPPER

Sing or whisper ROMANS 6:3

READ JOHN 20:1-18 - Jesus raises from the dead and appears to some women.

> Take a bite of unleavened bread, representing Jesus body tortured on the cross for us.

> Pray silently about Jesus' sacrifice, dying in your place for your sins.

> Take a sip of grape juice, representing Jesus' blood that dripped away on the cross for you,

> Pray silently about your own sins and desire to live more as God wants you to.

Sing or whisper ROMANS 6:4

COLLECTION

Prayer: Thank God for your blessings.

Set the money aside to be used to buy a flash drive to put Bible study material on it, or help someone in need that you know.

CLOSING PRAYER

GOD BLESS AND KEEP YOU SAFE UNTIL NEXT SUNDAY

Sunday 36

5000 More Baptized, Apostles Arrested (Acts 3-4)

Option 1 – Worship in a Group

READ ALOUD ACTS 3:1-10

     3:1 - at 3:00 in the afternoon, _____ and ______ went to the temple

     3:2 - A beggar was at the gate who had been _______ from the time of his birth.

     3:3-6 - Peter and John told him "We don't have silver or gold, but what we have we give you: In the name of ______, stand up and ______."

     3:7-8 - What did the lamb man do?

READ ALOUD ACTS 3:9-26

     3:9-12 - While Peter and John had the attention of all the people, ________ preached the second recorded Christian sermon.

     3:13a - The God of Abraham, Isaac, and Jacob glorified who?

     3:13b - Peter accused his audience of __________ Jesus, even after Governor ______ had decided to release him.

     3:15 - So, they ended up putting to death the Prince of ______.

3:16 - But it was faith in who that strengthened the lame man so he could walk?

3:18 - The prophets had already prophesied centuries earlier that the Christ would do what?

3:19 - Peter told the Jews listening to him to do what?

3:20-22 - Jesus was the one prophesied by ___________ who said the Lord would raise up a prophet like him.

3:23 - All the Old Testament ________ spoke of the days of Jesus and the church.

READ ALOUD ACTS 4:1-12

4:1 - While Peter and John were speaking, The priests, Sadducees and captain of the temple _______ went to them.

4:2 - They were angry because Peter and John were telling people Jesus had __________ from the __________.

4:3 - What did the officials and captain do to Peter and John?

4:4 - How many in the crowd decided to become Christians anyway?

4:5-7 - The next day, they held court, and the officials asked them in what ______ and by whose power they had performed their miracle.

4:8-10 - Peter replied that it was in the name of Jesus whom they had cruely __________ that the man was healed.

4:11-12 - Under how many names can someone be saved then and today? Is there salvation in anyone else besides Jesus?

4:15-16 - The trial councilmen told each other that it was obvious that a __________ had actually taken place, so they couldn't ___________.

4:17-18 - So they told what to Peter and John?

4:19-20 - What did Peter and John reply to them?

4:21-22 - All the people were glorifying God because the lame man who had been healed was how old?

Option 2 – Alone Among Enemies or Continue Worship in a Group

LORD'S SUPPER

You Can Be A Hero Alone

Sing or whisper REVELATION 1:6

READ ALOUD JOHN 20:19-31 - Jesus appears to his apostles. Explanation why biography of Jesus written.

Take a bite of unleavened bread, representing Jesus body tortured on the cross for us.

Pray silently about Jesus' sacrifice, dying in your place for your sins.

Take a sip of grape juice, representing Jesus' blood that dripped away on the cross for you,

Pray silently about your own sins and desire to live more as God wants you to.

Sing or whisper ROMANS 12:1

COLLECTION

Prayer: Thank God for your blessings.

Set the money aside to be used to buy a flash drive to put Bible study material on it, or help someone in need that you know.

CLOSING PRAYER

GOD BLESS AND KEEP YOU SAFE UNTIL NEXT SUNDAY

Sunday 37

Church Grows, Apostles Imprisoned (Acts 5)

Option 1 – Worship in a Group

READ ALOUD ACTS 5:12-16

5:12a - Who performed miracles?

5:12b - They gathered daily in the temple on ___________ porch.

5:13 - None of the Jews associated with them, but the other Jews did think of them how?

5:14 - How many men and women were constantly added to the church?

5:15 - Many carried their ______ out into a street they thought _______ would walk down, hoping his shadow might fall on them and heal them.

5:16 - People from nearby cities did the same thing. Were part of them healed or all of them?

READ ALOUD ACTS 5:17-32

5:17 - The high priest and other Jewish leaders felt what toward the apostles and all the thousands of new Christians?

5:18 - So they arrested the twelve apostles and put them where?

5:19 - Who appeared to the apostles during the night? What

did he do?

5:20-21a - He also told the apostles to go back to the _____ and keep healing and preaching.

5:21b-23 - The next morning when the council requested the apostles be taken to them, what did the officers tell them?

5:24-25 - They wondered what to do until someone reported the apostles were back in the _______ preaching again.

5:26 - So they ordered that the apostles be taken back to the council for trial, but without what?

5:27 - Did the apostles go with them?

5:28 - The council scolded the apostles for preaching again and bringing the ______ of Jesus on their heads.

5:29 - Memorize Peter's reply.

5:30 - What did Peter accuse the council of doing?

5:31 - He said Jesus was now at the ______ of God, reigning as _______ and _______ of the world.

5:32 - Who does God give the Holy Spirit to?

READ ALOUD ACTS 5:33-42

5:33 - So the council decided to do what to the apostles?

5:34 - The council had a member named _________ who was respected by everyone.

5:35-36 - He reminded them that a man named Theudas with ______ followers was _______ and nothing more heard of his movement.

5:37- He also reminded from of a man named ______ in the province of Galilee rose up against the movement, but he too was _____ and his followers scattered.

5:38 - The old man told the council they should stay away from the apostles because, if their movement is __________, it will die to.

5:39 - But if the apostles' movement is of____, no one will be able to overthrow them.

5:40 - So the council ordered the apostles all __________ and told them to stop preaching about Jesus. Then they _________ them all.

5:41 - The apostles left rejoicing that they were counted worth to ______ for Jesus.

5:42 - So, what did they do every day after that?

Option 2 – Alone Among Enemies or Continue Worship in a Group

LORD'S SUPPER

Sing or whisper 1ST THESSALONIANS 4:16

READ JOHN 21:1-14 & 25 - Jesus shows himself some more to his apostles. Reasons given for writing this gospel.

Take a bite of unleavened bread, representing Jesus body tortured on the cross for us.

Pray silently about Jesus' sacrifice, dying in your place for your sins.

Take a sip of grape juice, representing Jesus' blood that dripped away on the cross for you,

Pray silently about your own sins and desire to live more as God wants you to.

Sing or whisper 1ST THESSALONIANS 4:17

COLLECTION

Prayer: Thank God for your blessings.

Set the money aside to be used to buy a flash drive to put Bible study material on it, or help someone in need that you know.

CLOSING PRAYER

GOD BLESS AND KEEP YOU SAFE UNTIL NEXT SUNDAY

Sunday 38

An Ethiopian & a Terrorist are Baptized (Acts 8-9)

Option 1 – Worship in a Group

READ ALOUD ACTS 8:26-40

8:26 - An ________ told __________ to go to the road between Jerusalem and _________.

8:27 - On the road was an Ethiopian who held the office of ________ in the queen's court.

8:28 - He was sitting in his ________ reading the prophet _________.

8:29 - Since Philip had special powers, the Holy Spirit told Philip to do what?

8:30 - When Philip heard the Ethiopian reading aloud, he asked him what?

8:31 - There must have been two seats in the chariot plus a driver because the Ethiopian invited Philip to do what?

8:32 - Who did John the Baptist call the Lamb of God? (See John 1:29)

8:33 - What happened in the end to the Lamb of God according to this prophecy?

8:34-35 - When the Ethiopian asked who this prophecy was about, Philip began preaching to him about who?

8:36-37 - The Ethiopian spotted _______ and asked if he could be _________.

8:38-39a - Was the Ethiopian baptized by having water sprinkling or poured on him? They went ______ into the water, then came _____ out of the water.

8:39b-40 - What was the Ethiopian doing when he left Philip?

READ ALOUD ACTS 9:1-31

9:1 - Saul (the future apostle Paul) was doing what to disciples of Jesus Christ (Christians)?

9:2a - He got letters from the high priest to go to the city of _________ in Syria to find Christians.

9:2b - At first they weren't called Christians. they were called members of the ______.

9:2c - What did Saul/Paul intend to do to men and women in Damascus?

9:3 - As he got near Damascus, a bright ______ flashed around him.

9:4 - He fell to the _____ and heard a voice saying, "Saul! Why are you ___________ me?".

9:5a - Shocked, Saul/Paul knew it was the ______ speaking, but he didn't understand who he was. Who was he?

9:6 - Jesus told him to go on into Damascus and will be told him what he must _____.

9:7 - The men traveling with Saul/Paul heard the _______ but did not see _______.

9:8 - When Saul/Paul got up, his eyes were ________.

9:9 - How long did Saul/Paul fast?

9:10 - There was a disciple in Damascus who Jesus spoke to. He had no title. He was just a disciple, a followers. What was the disciple's name?

9:11 - He told Ananias to go over to the street called __________ to a house where Saul/Paul was ________.

9:12 - Saul/Paul saw in a vision that Ananias would come and do what to him?

9:13-14 - Was Ananias afraid or anxious to go see him?

9:15 - But Jesus replied that he had chosen Saul/Paul to carry his name to non-Jews called _________ and to _________.

9:16 - Now it was Saul's/Paul's turn to ________ for Jesus.

9:17 - Even though Saul/Paul had seen a vision, did he have the Holy Spirit yet?

9:18 - According to Acts 2:38, Paul received the Holy Spirit when?

Option 2 – Alone Among Enemies or Continue Worship in a Group

LORD'S SUPPER

Sing or whisper MARK 16:6

READ 1st CORINTHIANS 11:23-33 - A review of how Jesus told us to keep the Lord's Supper.

Take a bite of unleavened bread, representing Jesus body tortured on the cross for us.

Pray silently about Jesus' sacrifice, dying in your place for your sins.

Take a sip of grape juice, representing Jesus' blood that dripped away on the cross for you,

Pray silently about your own sins and desire to live more as God wants you to.

Sing or whisper MARK 16:9-10

COLLECTION

Prayer: Thank God for your blessings.

Set the money aside to be used to buy a flash drive to put Bible study material on it, or help someone in need that you know.

CLOSING PRAYER

GOD BLESS AND KEEP YOU SAFE UNTIL NEXT SUNDAY

Sunday 39

Christians are Beloved Children of God (Romans 8)

Option 1 – Worship in a Group

READ ALOUD ROMANS 8:1-13

8:1 - Who is not condemned?

8:2 - Jesus sets us free from the law of _______ that requires _________.

8:3 - God sent his son in the form of ___________ as an offering for our _________.

8:5 - People whose minds are only _________ things all the time, repeat only fleshly rewards. Those whose minds are only on _________ things all the time, repeat spiritual rewards.

8:6 - The mind only thinking on fleshly things leads to ___________, but the mind only thinking on spiritual things leads to _________ and _________.

8:7 - The mind only thinking on fleshly things is against who?

8:8 - The mind only thinking on fleshly things cannot please who?

8:9 - This verse mentions the Spirit of _______ and the Spirit of _________. they are the same.

8:10 - If Christ is in us, our body is ______, but our soul is _______. Compare this with Romans 6:2-4.

8:11 - If the Spirit of God who raised ___________ from the dead is in you, He will also _________ your body to life.

 You Can Be A Hero Alone

8:12-13 - If you are living for fleshly things, you must put what to death? How do you do that? Look again at Romans 6:2-4.

READ ALOUD ROMANS 8:14-25

8:14-15 - If the Spirit is in, you, you are _______ of God by being _________ by God.

8:16-17 - If Jesus is the only begotten son of God, and we are adopted children of God, we are co-__________ with Jesus because we have the same Father.

8:18 - If we suffer for being Christians, it is not worthy to be compare to the _________ we receive from God.

8:19-22 - Such suffering is like going through the pains of ________ so we can receive blessings from God.

8:23 - Such suffering is also something we go through awaiting our being taken to heaven.

8:24-25 - In _________ we have been saved. Hope is based on what we have not yet _______.

READ ALOUD ROMANS 8:26-39

8:26 - The Holy Spirit helps us when we pray by doing what?

8:27 - God __________ our hearts when we pray.

8:28 - Memorize this verse.

8:29 - God only predestines people to be like Jesus who he knew ahead of time wanted to. Jesus was the _________ among many brothers (us by adoption).

8:30 - God only predestines people who answer his call to be Christians. Those who God justifies, he also _________.

8:31 - Memorize this verse.

8:32 - Memorize this verse.

8:33 - No one on earth can condemn Christians. Who is the only one who can if we fall?

8:34 - Who intercedes between God the Father and us?

8:35-36 - Name the seven bad things that can happen to Christians on earth?

8:37 - Memorize this verse.

8:38 - Death, nor life, nor angels, nor principalities, nor the past or present, nor powers, nor height or death can separate us from the ________ of _________ in Christ Jesus.

Option 2 –Alone Among Enemies or Continue Worship in a Group

LORD'S SUPPER

Sing or whisper MATTHEW 26:26

READ ROMANS 6:1-11 - We are buried with Christ in baptism, then raised to spiritual life with him.

Take a bite of unleavened bread, representing Jesus body tortured on the cross for us.

Pray silently about Jesus' sacrifice, dying in your place for your sins.

Take a sip of grape juice, representing Jesus' blood that dripped away on the cross for you,

Pray silently about your own sins and desire to live more as God wants you to.

Sing or whisper MATTHEW 26:27-28

COLLECTION

Prayer: Thank God for your blessings.

Set the money aside to be used to buy a flash drive to put Bible study material on it, or help someone in need that you know.

CLOSING PRAYER

GOD BLESS AND KEEP YOU SAFE UNTIL NEXT SUNDAY

Sunday 40

Love All & Obey Even Bad Rulers
(Romans 12-13)

Option 1 – Worship in a Group

READ ALOUD ROMANS 12:1-21

12:1a - We should give our bodies to God as living ______.

12:1b - We can be worshipping when we use our bodies in spiritual ________.

12:2 - We are not to be like people of the __________.

12:3 - We are not to think of ourselves how?

12:4 - The church is a like a body with many _______ doing different jobs.

12:5 - All members of the church are one body in who?

12:6 - Everyone of us has different ______.

12:6 - Prophecy is another way of saying we have a gift of being able to memorize and quote what is in God's Word, the ______.

12:7 - Some of us have the gift of ________, and others have the gift of _________.

12:8a - Some of us have the gift of convincing others to do what is right, and others have the gift of being able to _______ much to the church.

12:8b - Some of us have the lift of being a ______, and others have the gift of being ________ to people who need forgiving.

12: 9 - We are to love how?

12:10 - We are to be devoted to each other in the church with ___________ love. We are even to honor others over _______.

12:11-12 - We are to keep on keeping on when we are experiencing ________, and we are to be devoted to ________.

12:13 - We are to contribute to the needs of each other, and practice __________.

12:14 - How are we to treat people who persecute us?

12:15 - We are to be happy with those who are _______, and be sad with those who are _______.

12:16 - We are not to be proud, but to associate with what kind of people?

12:17 - We are never to pay back ________ for ________.

12:18 - As far as it is possible within us, we are to be at _________ with everyone.

12:19a - We are never to take _________ on people who do wrong to us.

12:19b - Who will take revenge for us?

12:20 - If our enemy is hungry or thirsty, what are we to do? What will this do to our enemy?

12:21 - We can only overcome evil how?

READ ALOUD ROMANS 13:1-14

13:1a - We are to obey who?

13:1b - All government, whether good or evil, are in power with whose permission?

13:2-3 - Bad rulers are not feared if our behavior is _______.

13:4 - Even bad rulers are in office for everyone's ________ in some way we may not understand.

13:5 - Bad rulers are in power as avengers to punish other ________ people.

13:6 - Therefore, we must pay ____ because, in some way, even bad rulers are _________ God.

13:8 - Are we to owe money to each other?

13:9-10 - Four of Moses' Ten Commandments are quoted here. But the whole law is summed up in this: Love your __________ as __________.

13:11 - In what way can a Christian be asleep spiritually?

13:12 - We are to wear the armor of ________.

13:13 - We are not to get drunk, be involved in things that lead to sexual sins, and not to express ___________.

13:13 - Instead, we are to wear _________ as a protective

cloak around us.

Option 2 –Alone Among Enemies or Continue Worship in a Group

LORD'S SUPPER

Sing or whisper HEBREWS 5:7

READ ISAIAH 53:1-12 - Prophesy made 700 years before Jesus that he would bear our sins, be beaten, pierced on the cross, killed like a lamb, killed among thieves, and buried by the rich.

Take a bite of unleavened bread, representing Jesus body tortured on the cross for us.

Pray silently about Jesus' sacrifice, dying in your place for your sins.

Take a sip of grape juice, representing Jesus' blood that dripped away on the cross for you,

Pray silently about your own sins and desire to live more as God wants you to.

Sing or whisper MATTHEW 26:37

COLLECTION

Prayer: Thank God for your blessings.

Set the money aside to be used to buy a flash drive to put Bible study material on it, or help someone in need that you know.

CLOSING PRAYER

GOD BLESS AND KEEP YOU SAFE UNTIL NEXT SUNDAY

Sunday 41

Love & Bodies Changed in Heaven (Corinthians)

Option 1 – Worship in a Group

READ ALOUD 1st CORINTHIANS 13:1-13

13:1 - Even if I speak in the language of all _______ and _______, but have not _______, my words are just like a _______ gong.

13:2 - If I prophecy, understand all mysteries and have more faith than anyone else in the world, if I do not have _______, I am _________.

13:3 - If I give everything I own to feed the ______, and even if I allow myself to be _________ to death, but do not have ______, it profits me _______.

13:4 - Name two things love is. Then name three things love is not.

13:5 - Name four more things love does not do.

13:6 - What does love rejoice over?

13:7 - Name four things love always does.

13:8 - Prophecy will be done away, speaking instantly in foreign _________ will cease, automatic _______ of God's will shall be done away with.

13:9 - At the time Paul wrote this, automatically knowing God's will, and being able to prophecy was done how?

13:10 - When the Perfect arrives, all those parts of divine

knowledge and prophecy will be done __________ with.

13:12 - At the time Paul wrote this, the New Testament scriptures had not all been written yet, so people just knew part of God's will. But some day soon he said all will be fully __________. (The New Testament was fully written with the death of the last apostle ~ John who wrote Revelation.)

13:13 - What three things will always prevail? Of those three, which is the greatest?

READ ALOUD 2nd CORINTHIANS 5:1-21

5:1 - We are souls who have a temporary body on earth to house our souls. In heaven we will have bodies not _______ by __________.

5:2 - On earth, we long to be clothed/housed with our house in __________.

5:3 - Our souls will never be _______.

5:4 - Our bodies which are mortal, will be swallowed up by what?

5:5 - God gave us his Holy Spirit as a __________ that we will get more in heaven.

5:6 - While we are living in our mortal bodies, we are away from who?

5:7 - Memorize this verse.

5:8 - If we are absent from our mortal bodies, we are at _______ with the Lord.

5:9 - But where ever God wants us, we want to __________ God.

5:10 - Even though Jesus paid the penalty for our sins, on the Day of Judgment, we must still give an account of the _____ we did in our mortal bodies.

5:14a - What and who controls us?

5:14b-15 - If Jesus died for all, then we too _______ with him. If we are dead, then our spirit lives because Jesus did what?

5:17 - Everyone in Christ is a new _______, and old ways of life have _______.

5:19 - After Jesus died and came back to life, God no longer counts our _______ against us.

READ ALOUD 2nd CORINTHIANS 6:1-10

6:1 - We are workers together with who?

6:2 - Today is the day of _________ for whoever believes.

6:3 - We must not give anyone cause to __________ us, so no one will resent the church.

6:4-6 - Name the 13 things our bodies go through on earth for Christ.

6:7 - We are to have weapons of __________.

6:8 - Our enemies may consider us deceivers, but we only tell the __________.

6:9 - Our enemies may try to kill us, but still we ________.

6:10 - Our enemies may think we are poor and having nothing, yet spiritually what do we have?

Option 2 – Alone Among Enemies or Continue Worship in a Group

LORD'S SUPPER

Sing or whisper MATTHEW 26:47

READ 1st CORINTHIANS 15:1-11 - Jesus' appearances to 500 people after his resurrection from the dead.

Take a bite of unleavened bread, representing Jesus body tortured on the cross for us.

Pray silently about Jesus' sacrifice, dying in your place for your sins.

Take a sip of grape juice, representing Jesus' blood that dripped away on the cross for you,

Pray silently about your own sins and desire to live more as God wants you to.

Sing or whisper MATTHEW 26:50

COLLECTION

Prayer: Thank God for your blessings.

Set the money aside to be used to buy a flash drive to put Bible study material on it, or help someone in need that you know.

CLOSING PRAYER

GOD BLESS AND KEEP YOU SAFE UNTIL NEXT SUNDAY

Sunday 42

How to Get Into Jesus & List Of Sins (Galatians)

Option 1 – Worship in a Group

READ ALOUD GALATIANS 3:24 - 29

3:24 - The Law of Moses in the Old Testament was a _______ to lead us to Christ who would help us be saved by ________, not works of a law.

3:25 - Now that we live under a simple law of _______, we not longer need the Old Testament _______.

3:26 - Through our faith, we have been made _________ of God.

3:27 - We are __________ into Christ. At that point, we are _________ with Christ.

3:28 - In Christ, there is neither ______ or Gentile (non-Jew), freeman or _______, female or _______.

3:29 - Because Abraham was the Father of all the Faithful, we with faith in Christ are Abraham's _________ through faith.

READ ALOUD GALATIANS 4:1-7

4:1-2 - Even though a child may own a house, the child has to _______ certain rules just like _______ in the house have to.

4:3 - In the same way, people keeping the old Law of Moses in the Old Testament were being treated like _________, having to obey a lot of rules.

4:4 - When the right time came, God did what?

4:5 - Because God did this, he _________ us and made us his _________.

4:6 - So now, whose Spirit is in us?

4: 7 - And we are co-heirs with Christ, being _______ of god.

READ ALOUD GALATIANS 5:1-26

5:1 - Once we are set free from the Old Testament Law of Moses, are we to go back and obey any of it?

5:2 - One of the main points of the Law of Moses was to be _________. If a man is _________ today to become a Jew, he no longer has who?

5:3 - Some people worship with musical instruments and candles, etc. like they did under the Law of Moses. If we do that, we must keep what part of the old Law of Moses?

5:9-10 - We are not to let someone introduce religious things from the old Law of Moses into our worship, because a little _______ leavens the _______ lump of dough.

5:13 - Our worship is not to be fleshly, but to express _______ for each other.

5:14 - Besides, the whole Law of Moses is summarized in one statement: You shall ______ your neighbor as _________.

5:15 - People in the church must not _________ each other over such things.

5:16 - If we walk in the ______, we will not be interested in worshiping in such a way that is worldly.

5:17-18 - We know we are no longer obeying the Law of Moses when we are led by ______ __________.

5:19-21a - This is a list of sins. How many of them are sins of attitude?

5:21b - Anyone who does these things regularly will not inherit what?

5:22-23 - What are the fruits of the Spirit? Are there any laws in any country of the world against these things?

5:24 - If we have died with Christ, we have crucified _______ desires in our personal, public and worship life.

5:25 - If we live by the Spirit, throughout our life we will _______ by the Spirit.

5:26 - One final warning on how to get along in the church.

What is it?

Option 2 –Alone Among Enemies or Continue Worship in a Group

LORDS SUPPER

Sing or whisper MATTHEW 26:59

READ 1st CORINTHIANS 15:12-28 - Importance of Jesus' resurrection. The order of our resurrection at the end of the world.

Take a bite of unleavened bread, representing Jesus body tortured on the cross for us.

Pray silently about Jesus' sacrifice, dying in your place for your sins.

Take a sip of grape juice, representing Jesus' blood that dripped away on the cross for you,

Pray silently about your own sins and desire to live more as God wants you to.

Sing or whisper MATTHEW 26:67

COLLECTION

Prayer: Thank God for your blessings.

Set the money aside to be used to buy a flash drive to put Bible study material on it, or help someone in need that you know.

CLOSING PRAYER

GOD BLESS AND KEEP YOU SAFE UNTIL NEXT SUNDAY

Sunday 43

Saved from Hell, Alive in Jesus (Ephesians)

Option 1 – Worship in a Group

READ ALOUD EPHESIANS 1:1-23

1:1-3 - The apostle Paul wrote this letter to the saints at Ephesus on today's west coast of Turkey. Was he writing and blessing just one or two special people in the congregation, or everyone in their congregation?

1:4 - The word "choose" in the original Greek means selecting the qualified. God selected Christians to be saved from what time period.

1:5 - God predestined that Christians would become _______ sons of God.

1:7 - Our sins are forgiven through the _______ of Jesus paying the penalty for us.

1:11 - We have obtained an ___________ from God.

1:13-14 - Our salvation is sealed by the _______ ___________. When do we receive this? (See Acts 2:38)

1:16 - Who did Paul, the writer, pray for?

1:18 - He prayed that the eyes of their _______ would be opened.

1:20 - Jesus Christ was raised from the _______ and _______ at the right hand of god in heaven.

1:21 - Jesus is now far above all rule, authority, power, and every _________ that is named on earth.

1:22 - Jesus is head of what?

1:23 - The church is also Jesus' _______. Therefore, who is the head of the church, the body?

READ ALOUD EPHESIANS 2:1-22

1:1 - When we sin our souls are ______.

1:2 - Sinners walk the path of the __________ of the power of the _______. Are they called the sons of God or sons of disobedience?

1:3 - Every sinner walks in the desires of their ______ and their _______, and makes us children of _______.

1:5 - But, while we were dead in sin, God made us ______ with __________.

1:6 - Jesus was raised from the dead and seated in _________. So, when we die in baptism and are raised out of the water, our souls are also seated in _______.

1:8-9 - Do we earn salvation by doing more good works than bad works?

1:10 - However, God created us to be His ___________.

1:13 - Jesus brought us ______ to God by his _______.

1:11, 14-15 - It is only through _______ that the dividing barrier between Jews and non-Jews will be broken down.

1:16 - Both Jews and non-Jews can be equal in the one ______ of Jesus, thus putting to death _______ for each other.

1:17 - Jesus came preaching ______

1:18 - We can be one in one Holy _______.

1:19 - Then, instead of being aliens, we are fellow _______ in the same kingdom and ______ of God.

1:20 - The church/kingdom/family of God was built on the foundations of the New Testament ______ and Old Testament _____, with Jesus being the corner ______.

1:21-22 - We are the stones, all being fitted together to become the living holy _______, which is the dwelling of God on earth.

Option 2 – Alone Among Enemies or

Continue Worship in a Group

LORD'S SUPPER

Sing or whisper MATTHEW 27:22

READ 1st CORINTHIANS 15:35-49 - How we will be raised from the dead, flesh body to spiritual body.

Take a bite of unleavened bread, representing Jesus body tortured on the cross for us.

Pray silently about Jesus' sacrifice, dying in your place for your sins.

Take a sip of grape juice, representing Jesus' blood that dripped away on the cross for you,

Pray silently about your own sins and desire to live more as God wants you to.

Sing or whisper MATTHEW 27:31

COLLECTION

Prayer: Thank God for your blessings.

Set the money aside to be used to buy a flash drive to put Bible study material on it, or help someone in need that you know.

CLOSING PRAYER

GOD BLESS AND KEEP YOU SAFE UNTIL NEXT SUNDAY

Sunday 44

In Prison for Jesus, Peace, Dying Now (Philippians)

Option 1 – Worship in a Group

READ ALOUD PHILIPPIANS 1:1-11

1:1a, 7 - Who was in jail with the apostle Paul?

1:1b - They wrote to all the Christians in Philippi including what two group of leaders?

1:3 - Who did Paul thank God for?

1:6 - God began a good _______ in the Christians in the congregation at Philippi.

1:9 - Paul prayed that the ______ in this congregation would abound _______ and ________.

1:11 - What is the fruit of righteousness? See Galatians 5:22-23.

READ ALOUD PHILIPPIANS 1:12-20

1:13a - Paul's imprisonment was for preaching who?

1:13b - As a result, who at the prison know about Christ?

1:14 - Since Paul was keeping up his courage while in prison, this was doing what for other Christians?

1:15-18 - Even though the enemies of Jesus were telling about Jesus out of anger, what good was coming from it?

1:19 - The Holy Spirit and the _______ of those he was writing would eventually lead to Paul's what?

1:20 - If not, Paul was certain that Christ would be exalted whether Paul's body was _______ or ______.

READ ALOUD PHILIPPIANS 1:21-30

1:21 - Memorize this verse

1:22-24 - Paul had a hard time choosing between life and death. Why?

1:26 - Still, he hoped to come to ______.

1:27 - Paul told them to conduct themselves in a manner worth of what and who?

1:28 - The Christians in Philippi were not to be alarmed by their enemy, because, even if they were killed, they were also _______.

1:29 - The Christians in this congregation had been assigned to go through something for Christ's sake. What was it?

READ ALOUD PHILIPPIANS 2:1-11

2:1 - What are the four IF's in this verse?

2:2 - No matter what, they were to be of the same ______ with the same _____, united in one _______.

2:3 - Memorize this verse.

2:4 - Don't look out for your own interests, but the interests of ______.

2:6 - In heaven, Jesus exists in the form of who?

2:7 - But he came to earth and ______ himself, taking on the form of _________.

2:8 - He obeyed God the Father (Mind) because he was God the Son (Body)) and example to everyone of us to ________ God.

2:9 - Whose name is above every other name on earth?

2:10 - Some day, every ______ of every person in heaven and on earth will do what before Jesus?

2:11 - Some day, every ______ will confess that _______ is the _______.

2:12 - Working out our salvation doesn't mean we earn it, but that we are letting who work in us?

2:14 - Do everything without what?

2:15a - Instead, we are to be _________ and _________

children of God above reproach.

2:15b - We are to like ___________ in a world of darkness.

2:16 - Hold right to the word of ______.

2:17 - Even if Paul was sacrificed by being killed for Jesus, he will ______ and wanted the Christians in Philippi also to _______.

READ ALOUD PHILIPPIANS 3:1-17

3:1 Where is Christ seated?

3:2 - Therefore, we are to think about things _______ and not below on earth.

3:3 - When did we die? See Romans 6:2-4.

3:4 - If our earthly body is dead, we no longer have what kind of desires?

3:8 - What are some kinds of sins we should no longer commit?

3:9-10 - Why?

3:11 - In Christ, there is no difference between what kinds of people?

3:12 - We are to express what with our heart?

3:13 - If we have a complaint about someone, what should we do?

3:14 - How are we to act toward each other within the body of Christ?

3:16 - What is one special way we are to encourage one another?

3:17 - Throughout our life, whatever we do, we are to do it in whose name?

Option 2 – Alone Among Enemies or Continue Worship in a Group

LORD'S SUPPER

Sing or whisper MATTHEW 27:40

READ 1st CORINTHIANS 15:50-58 - How we will be changed at the last trumpet call of the angels to live forever in heaven.

Take a bite of unleavened bread, representing Jesus body tortured on the cross for us.

Pray silently about Jesus' sacrifice, dying in your place for your sins.

Take a sip of grape juice, representing Jesus' blood that dripped away on the cross for you,

Pray silently about your own sins and desire to live more as God wants you to.

Sing or whisper MATTHEW 27:42

COLLECTION

Prayer: Thank God for your blessings.

Set the money aside to be used to buy a flash drive to put Bible study material on it, or help someone in need that you know.

CLOSING PRAYER

GOD BLESS AND KEEP YOU SAFE UNTIL NEXT SUNDAY

Sunday 45

All are Saints, Jesus Emptied into a Body (Colossians)

Option 1 – Worship in a Group

READ ALOUD COLOSSIANS 1:13-29

1:12 - God the Father made us __________ to be a saint, a saved one.

1:13 - He rescued us from the _______ of _______ to the kingdom of His _______.

1:14 - God's Son saved us by _________ our sins.

1:15 - Jesus is the _____ of the invisible God.

1:16 - By Jesus, the Word, all things were _______.

1:17 - Jesus existed _______ all things.

1:18a - Jesus is the head of his ______, also called the church.

1:15, 18b - Jesus was the first one to be ______ from the dead.

1:19 - All the fullness of God dwelled in who?

1:20 - Jesus made peace between God the Father and us through his what?

1:21-22 - Jesus made peace for us by taking on a fleshly ______, and ______ in our place to make us blameless.

1:23 - By the time this book of the Bible was written, the gospel had been preached where?

1:24 - Jesus body is also called the what?

1:25-27 - The mystery of the ages is that Christ now __________ in Christians.

1:28-29 - The power Paul used to preach to peo9ple actually came from who?

READ ALOUD COLOSSIANS 2:1-23

2:2-3 - The mystery of Jesus Christ is the treasure of ______ and _______.

2:6 - We are to walk in who?

2:7 - We are to be rooted in who?

2:8 - We are not to be taken captive (fooled) by empty __________ of men.

2:9 - In Jesus dwells all the __________ of God bodily.

2:11-12a - Instead of circumcision to make one a Jew, we are to be ______ to make us a Christian.

2:12b - If we are raised up in baptism like Jesus was raised from the dead, is baptism pouring or sprinkling water?

2:13 - We are dead when we have what in our life?

2:14 - Jesus took the written law of Moses and did what to it on the cross?

2:15 - Rulers and authorities here partly refers to Satan's demons. What did Jesus do to them? Therefore, they cannot harm us today.

2:18 - Some people think they're spiritual if they worship ______ and having _______.

2:19 - People who do this are not holding on to the head. Who is the head?

2:20-21 - It is a waste to refuse to ______, _______, or _______ certain things because it is Jesus who makes us holy, not ourselves?

2:23 - Such type of false spirituality is really _______ made religion.

Option 2 –Alone Among Enemies or Continue Worship in a Group

LORD'S SUPPER

Sing or whisper MATTHEW 27:45

READ HEBREWS 2:9-18 - Jesus was made a little lower than the angels, but now is crowned and over all things.

Take a bite of unleavened bread, representing Jesus body tortured on the cross for us.

Pray silently about Jesus' sacrifice, dying in your place for your sins.

Take a sip of grape juice, representing Jesus' blood that dripped away on the cross for you,

Pray silently about your own sins and desire to live more as God wants you to.

Sing or whisper MATTHEW 27:50

COLLECTION

Prayer: Thank God for your blessings.

Set the money aside to be used to buy a flash drive to put Bible study material on it, or help someone in need that you know.

CLOSING PRAYER

GOD BLESS AND KEEP YOU SAFE UNTIL NEXT SUNDAY

Sunday 46

Chirstian Death & End of the World (Thessalonians)

Option 1 – Worship in a Group

READ ALOUD 1st THESSALONIANS 4:1-12

4:1-4 - We who are saved must abstain from what?

4:5 - People who commit such sins do not know who?

4:6a - We should never _______ our brother in Christ.

4:6b - If we willfully sin and don't try to change, God will do what?

4:7-8 - People who commit such sins are really rejecting who?

4:9 - We have been taught to love each other by who?

4:10-12 - We should lead a ______ life and mind our own ______, working with our ______, and behave properly toward people who are not in the church.

READ ALOUD 1st THESSALONIANS 4:13-18

3:13 - Who do you think are people who are "asleep"? We should not mourn for them as do who?

3:14 - If we believe Jesus died and came back to life, then we fall asleep in who?

3:14-15 - When Jesus returns on the last day, those who have fallen asleep in ______ will be with him.

3:16a - On the last day, an ___________ will shout and the ________ of God will blast forth.

3:16b - Then the _______ in Christ will rise ________.

2:17-18 - Next, those of us who are alive when Christ comes will meet Jesus where? Does this mean Jesus will never set foot on earth again>

READ ALOUD 1st THESSALONIANS 5:1-18

5:1 - The last day of the world will come upon us as what in the night?

5:2 - People declaring peace and safety with God will suddenly face what?

5:3-5 - We will escape that because Christians are sons of the ________.

5:6 - What is another way of being asleep besides being dead?

5:7 - Most people who get drunk do so when?

5:8 - So we must be sober thinking and put on the breastplate of _________, and the helmet of _________.

5:9-10 - So, whether we are alive or dead when Christ comes for us, we know what?

5:12-13a - We are to treat the elders over our congregation how?

5:13b - We are to live in peace with who?

5:14 - We are to do what with the unruly among us? The fainthearted and weak? Who are we to be patient with who?

5:15 - We are not to repay evil with what?

5:16 - Memorize this verse

5:17 - Memorize this verse.

5:18 - What are we to do every day?

Option 2 – Alone Among Enemies or Continue Worship in a Group

LORD'S SUPPER

Sing or whisper MATTHEW 28:2

READ REVELATION 4:1-11 - God's throne room in heaven.

Take a bite of unleavened bread, representing Jesus body tortured on the cross for us.

Pray silently about Jesus' sacrifice, dying in your place for your sins.

Take a sip of grape juice, representing Jesus' blood that dripped away on the cross for you,

Pray silently about your own sins and desire to live more as God wants you to.

Sing or whisper MATTHEW 28:3

COLLECTION

Prayer: Thank God for your blessings.

Set the money aside to be used to buy a flash drive to put Bible study material on it, or help someone in need that you know.

CLOSING PRAYER

GOD BLESS AND KEEP YOU SAFE UNTIL NEXT SUNDAY

Sunday 47

Only Church Officers Allowed by God & Warnings (Timothy, Titus, Philemon)

Option 1 – Worship in a Group

READ ALOUD 1ˢᵗ TIMOTHY 3:1-16 (& Titus 1:5-9 as background)

3:1 - The words overseer, shepherd, and elder are the same _________ in the church.

3:2a - He must be male because he must have one what?

3:2b-3a - What five things must this man have in his character?

3:3b - What two things must this man not be, and what three things must he be?

3:4-5 - If he cannot manage his own household, he will not be able to manage the household of who?

3:6 - He must not be a new convert so he does not become what?

3:7 - He must have a good reputation with who?

3:8 - Who must not be addicted to wine, or run after making money illegally?

3:9-10 - Before appointed a man an elder or deacon, they must be what?

3:11 - What is a Christian woman not to be?

3:12 - Deacons must be men because they are to have one

_____ and be able to manage their _____.

3:15 - What is another name for the household of God?

3:16 - What six things did Jesus do when he came to earth?

READ ALOUD 1st TIMOTHY 4:13-18 (& Titus 1:10-16 as background)

4:1a - The Holy Spirit says things. The Holy Spirit does not give just a good feeling, but makes statements. Compare this with John 14:17 and 17:17. What does it say the Holy Spirit of Truth is?

4:1b - A false doctrine introduced into the church is also called a doctrine of who?

4:2a - False doctrines are introduced into the church by hypocrites who pretend to be holy and are not, and who also do what?

4:2b - People who introduce false doctrines into the church have had their consciences what?

4:3 - What are two false doctrines that the writer of this book say would be introduced into the church?

4:4-5 - We are not to turn down any food. Why?

NOTE: While in prison, Paul converted a run-away slave of Philemon, Paul's friend, so returned him to his Christian master. Between 1st Timothy and 2nd Timothy, Paul was temporarily released from prison and visited this friend, Philemon. Then he was rearrested and executed.

READ ALOUD 2nd TIMOTHY 3:1-17

3:1 - Paul warned that in the church in later years, times will sometimes become _____.

3:2-4 - Name the 18 bad traits some Christians will become, leading to their downfall.

3:5 - What are we to do with such people who look so holy but aren't?

3:6 - They will even lead weak-minded _____ to follow them.

3:7 - They will always be learning and teaching some new thing, but never teaching what?

3:12 - Memorize this verse.

3:13 - Deceivers in the church will just get what?

3:14 - From Timothy's childhood, he learned what? And

what did they lead to?

    3:15-16 - Memorize these two verses.

READ ALOUD 2nd TIMOTHY 4:1-8

    4:2 - In what ways was Timothy to preach the Word of God?

    4:3-4 - Paul warned Timothy once again that the time was coming when people will turn aside from the truth to what?

    4:5 - What four things did Paul tell Timothy to do?

    4:6 - What do you think Paul meant when he said he was being poured out as a drink offering to God?

    4:7-8 - Memorize Paul's last words about himself before he was executed for being a Christian?

Option 2 – Alone Among Enemies or Continue Worship in a Group

LORD'S SUPPER

Sing or whisper ROMANS 6:23

READ 1st PETER 4:12-19 - We must share in the sufferings of Christ.

        Take a bite of unleavened bread, representing Jesus body tortured on the cross for us.

        Pray silently about Jesus' sacrifice, dying in your place for your sins.

        Take a sip of grape juice, representing Jesus' blood that dripped away on the cross for you,

        Pray silently about your own sins and desire to live more as God wants you to.

    Sing or whisper 1ST PETER 2:24

COLLECTION

Prayer: Thank God for your blessings.

Set the money aside to be used to buy a flash drive to put Bible study material on it, or help someone in need that you know.

CLOSING PRAYER

GOD BLESS AND KEEP YOU SAFE UNTIL NEXT SUNDAY

Sunday 48

God Changes his Old Last Will & Testament to a New Testament. (Hebrews)

Option 1 – Worship in a Group

NOTE: The Jews were originally called Hebrews. This was written to Jews who had become Christians but also wanted to keep their old traditional Laws of Moses (all 600+ of them!). The writer explains the difference in the Old (Last Will and) Testament of God and the new (Last Will and) Testament of God. The author quotes the Old Testament of God many times to show why the New is much better.

READ ALOUD HEBREWS 1:2 – 2:14

    1:2 & 5 – Compare this with Genesis 1:1-3 and John 1:1-3 and 14. Who was the Word of God?

    1:5 – If Jesus is the Word and there is only one Word of God, does that make Jesus the "only begotten" Son of God?

    1:10 & 14 – If the ministering spirits are angels, does that people who will "inherit salvation" have guardian angels?

    2:9-10 – Jesus dying for the world made it possible for God

to have many sons. How can that be since Jesus is the only Son of God? Find your answer in Ephesians 1:5)

____

     2:14 – Jesus made death powerless when he died and came back to life. Whose power did he destroy? _______________

READ ALOUD HEBREWS 3:12 – 4:16

     3:12-15 – Is it possible to fall away from our faith?

____

     4:12 – How does the Word of God (Bible) judge us?_______________________________________

     4:15-16 – How are temptation and sin different?____ Did Jesus ever sin? ______

READ ALOUD HEBREWS 7:23 – 8:13

     7:23-24 – High priests in the Old Testament died and had to be replaced. God made Jesus his High Priest in his New Testament. How long will Jesus be our new high priest?

____

     7:25 – When we pray, who is our intercessor? (Some people say Mary is.) ___________________

     8:5 – The Tabernacle/Temple in the Old Testament was just a copy/shadow of the Tabernacle/Temple where?

____

     8:13 – The covenant was God's first Last Will and Testament. What happened to the old one?

____

READ ALOUD HEBREWS 9:1 – 10:9

     9:7 – Under the Old Testament, how often did the high priest have to enter the inner Holiest Place of the Tabernacle/Temple?

____

     9:14 – At that time, the high priest took the blood of an animal with him into the Holiest Place which he offered for forgiveness for the sins of himself and all the worshipers. But when Jesus became our high priest, he offered whose blood for forgiveness? _______________________ Did he have to do it every

year?____
So was

9:15 – Did Jesus' sacrifice on the cross forgive only those who live under Covenant, God's New Last Will and Testament today? Or both? ________________

9:16 & 28 – There has to be a death in order to put a testament into effect. Animals died to keep the old Last Will and Testament into effect who died to put the New Last Will and Testament into effect ? _________

10:9 – What happened to the first/Old Last Will and Testament? ______ Why?

READ ALOUD HEBREWS 12-13

12:2 – Who should we keep our eyes on? _____________________. He did not let the shame of the _____________________ stop him.

12:5-6 – Sometimes we suffer because God is disciplining us and making us life heavy weights so our spiritual muscles will grow. Why? What does God consider us?_______________________________

13:1-2 – We should show hospitality because some have entertained ________________ without realizing it.

QUESTION: Read Leviticus, which is where most of Old Last Will and Testament is laid out – animals sacrifices, priests with special clothing, burning incense and candles, great choirs and orchestras, etc. Are those things repeated in the New Last Will and Testament? Search it. Do you think that, if they are, we must do them all in today's church organization and worship? Or, if they are not, should we eliminate them in today's church organization and worship?

Option 2 – Alone Among Enemies or Continue Worship in a Group

LORD'S SUPPER

Sing or whisper 1ST JOHN 1:7

READ REVELATION 22:1-21 - Description of heaven, and Jesus' final message to Christians until the last day of the world.

Take a bite of unleavened bread, representing Jesus body tortured on the cross for us.

Pray silently about Jesus' sacrifice, dying in your place for your sins.

Take a sip of grape juice, representing Jesus' blood that dripped away on the cross for you,

Pray silently about your own sins and desire to live more as God wants you to.

Sing or whisper ACTS 20:28

COLLECTION

Prayer: Thank God for your blessings.

Set the money aside to be used to buy a flash drive to put Bible study material on it, or help someone in need that you know.

CLOSING PRAYER

GOD BLESS AND KEEP YOU SAFE UNTIL NEXT SUNDAY

Sunday 49

The "Royal Law" & Treating Others Better Than Yourselves (James)

Option 1 – Worship in a Group

NOTE: It is thought that James and Jude were Jesus's half-brothers. Matthew 13:55 says his brothers were James, Joseph, Simon, and Jude. We know the apostle James was martyred just a few years after the church began (Acts 12:2). James says the word "brother" 17 times in his writing.

READ ALOUD JAMES 1:1-27

1:2 – Why in the world would any Christian be cheerful amidst problems resulting from his faith?

____

1:5-8 – Asking for wisdom is attached to our need to be happy when persecuted. (It takes great wisdom to know how to handle persecution.) So, when he says we should not doubt when we pray, are we praying for just anything? _________________
What are we praying for? _______________________

1:12 – If you are miserable because of persecution, just keep on keep on. Why? _____________

____

1:19 – Is having a quick temper a bad habit or a sinful habit? _________________

1:22-24 – People who read the Bible and agree with it, but don't obey are like what?_________

____

READ ALOUD JAMES 2:1-26

2-4 – When we are friendly to people who are clean and dress well, but not to people who are dirty with holes in their clothes, what are we like? _____________________________________

2:8 – Quote the Royal Law:

____

____

2:10 – If someone keeps every part of the Law of Moses with its 600 rules, but breaks just one of those rules, he is guilty of what?____

2:14-17 – Having faith without regularly doing good works is what kind of faith? _____________

2:19 – Is just having faith enough to save us? Who else has faith?_____________________
Does it help them? _______________

READ ALOUD JAMES 3:1-18

3:6 – Our tongue is small, but can cause a person to go where? _________________

3:9 – What does God think of people who praise him in private prayers, but curse in public?

READ ALOUD JAMES 4:1-17

4:13-14 – Instead of announcing what we are going to accomplish tomorrow, we should add "If it is the Lord's
_________________."

4:17 – It is a sin to not do ________________ that you know needs to be done.

READ ALOUD JAMES 5:1-20

5:1-6 – People who get rich by take advantage of poor

people think they are getting by with it. Are they?

____

     5:10-11 – When things are bad, instead of complaining, we should be what? ________________

     5:16b – The prayer of a righteous person is powerful and

____________________.

     5:19 – What should the faithful do to a person falls away by wandering from the truth? -__________ ____________________

Option 2 –Alone Among Enemies or Continue Worship in a Group

LORD'S SUPPER:

Sing or whisper 2ND CORINTHIANS 5:21

Read MATTHEW 26:26-30, about Jesus and the very first "Lord's Supper"

    Take a bite of unleavened bread, representing Jesus body tortured on the cross for us.

    Pray silently about Jesus' sacrifice, dying in your place for your sins.

    Take a sip of grape juice, representing Jesus' blood that dripped away on the cross for you,

    Pray silently about your own sins and desire to live more as God wants you to.

    Sing or whisper 1ST THESSALONIANS 2:15

COLLECTION:

Prayer: Thank God for your blessings.

Set aside a little money to be used to buy a flash drive to put Bible study material on it, or help someone in need that you know.

CLOSING PRAYER

GOD BLESS AND KEEP YOU SAFE UNTIL NEXT SUNDAY

Sunday 50

You're Going To Be Persecuted & The World Will Burn Up Some Day (2 Letters of Peter)

Option 1 – Worship in a Group

READ ALOUD 1st PETER 1:1-13

 1:1 - Did Peter introduce himself as the pope? _______________

 1:11 – The Holy Sprit is the Spirit of who? ________Compare this with John 1:1-2.

 1:13 – If we have true faith, we will prepare our minds for what? ___________________

READ ALOUD 1st PETER 2:1-25

2:1-2 – What five things must we stop in our lives to act reborn into Christ? ____________

____

____

2:5 – Christians are _________________who offer up spiritual sacrifices to God.

2:9 – All Christians belong to a royal

____________________________.

2:13 & 17 – Does God expect us obey evil kings/prime minister/presidents? ______________

2:14 – God allowed evil rulers so they will ______________ bad people in that country. Then, when they are done, God destroys the destroyers.

2:22 – Who never sinned? __________________

2:24 – What did Jesus bear on his body when crucified?

____

READ ALOUD 1ST PETER 3:1-22

3:1 – Wives are to submit to even unbelieving _________________ so they might become believers because of her behavior.

3:7 – Husbands are to be gentle with their _________________ . Otherwise, God will stop hearing their

_________________.

3:9 – Do not do evil to people who have been _________________ to you.

3:15 – Be prepared. Always be ready to explain to _________________ why you are a Christian,

3:21 – We know that faith in Jesus saves us. What else saves us? _________________

READ ALOUD 1st PETER 4:1-19

4:1 – Since Jesus ___________________________ in his flesh, you will too

4:8 – What covers a multitude of sins?

____

4:16 – If you are persecuted for being a Christian, don't be _____________. Instead you need to ____________________________.
Why?

READ ALOUD 1ST PETER 5 1-11

5:1-2 – Elders in the church are also called overseers and
______________________.

5:4 – Did Peter call the Chief Shepherd the pope?
____

5:8-9 – Always be alert because the devil prowls around like a roaring _______________ looking for people to
_____________________.

READ ALOUD 2ND PETER 1:1-21

1:5-7 – We are not saved by faith alone. What seven things should we have besides faith? ______
____
____

1:12-15 - Peter believes he will soon do what?
____

1:16 – Peter said he was an eye ______________ to what Jesus did.

1:18 – Peter even heard the voice of ____________________.

1:19 – Peter calls Jesus the "Morning Star". In Latan that term is "Lucifer". So, do you think that is Satan's name?
____

READ ALOUD 2ND PETER 2:4-22

2:4 - When God punished rebellious ______________, he kept the good ones.

2:5 – When God punished all the evil doers in a flood, what preacher did he save? ______________

2:6 – When God destroyed two entire cities because of their homosexuality what preacher did he save? __________________

2:20 – But those who follow God and then leave him, their punishment will be _______________.

READ ALOUD 2nd PETER 3:

3:7 & 10 & 12 – When the world ends, it will be destroyed by
__________________.

3:9 – Does God choose which ones he plans to save? Who does he want to be saved? __________

Option 2 – Alone Among Enemies or Continue Worship in a Group

LORD'S SUPPER

Memorize, then sing or whisper 1st Peter 1:8

Read MATTHEW 27:27-37 about soldiers beating Jesus, mocking him, then nailing him to a cross.

Take a bite of unleavened bread, representing Jesus body tortured on the cross for us.

Pray silently about Jesus' sacrifice, dying in your place for your sins.

Take a sip of grape juice, representing Jesus' blood that dripped away on the cross for you,

Pray silently about your own sins and desire to live more as God wants you to.

Memorize, then sing or whisper JOHN 14:6

COLLECTION

Prayer: Thank God for your blessings.

Set the money aside to be used to buy a flash drive to put Bible study material on it, or help someone in need that you know.

CLOSING PRAYER

GOD BLESS AND KEEP YOU SAFE UNTIL NEXT SUNDAY

Sunday 51

Loving & Not Loving. (3 Letters of John + Jude)

Option 1 – Worship in a Group

NOTE: There are 3 kinds of sins: (1) doing bad, (2), not doing good, (3) attitudes.

READ ALOUD 1st JOHN 1:1-10

  1:1 – John said he had ____________, ________________. ________________. and ________________ the ________________ of Life. Compare this with John's biography and teachings of Jesus near the beginning of the New Testament – John 1:1-3 & 14.

  1:10 – If we say we do not sin, who are we making a liar? ____________

READ ALOUD 1ST JOHN 2:1-18

  2:3 – How do we know we are saved/know Jesus?

____

________________ (This is the 1st of 25 times John says "know" in this letter.

2:4 – THOUGHT QUESTION: How do we know we are keeping his commandments?

2:15-16 – Lists 3 kinds of sins of dong bad: (1) Elevating our flesh [being beautiful, handsome, buying expensive clothes] is first in our lives. (2) Elevating what we see [pornography, etc.] above everything else. (3) Give an example of elevating pride above everything else. ------------------------

----

2:18 – Is there just one anti-Christ or many anti-Christs?

____

READ ALOUOD 1ST JOHN 3:1-24

3:1 – In most world religions, God has no personality (like Nirvana and Brahman) or is distant (like Islam). The God of the Bible considers us his _______________________. Why?

____

____

3:2 – When Jesus returns for us on the last day, our bodies will be transformed to be like who? _____________________

3:5 – Did Jesus ever sin? _____________

3:9a – Who has always sinned? _______________

3:9b – Who has destroyed the effectiveness of Satan?

____

2:14 – How do we know we have eternal life?

____

READ ALOUD 1ST JOHN 4:1-21

4:8 – God is _______________.

4:13 – What is one way to know God's Holy Spirit is in us?

____

4:18 – Christians do not fear bad things being done to them because perfect ___________ casts out fear.

4:19 – Who loved us while we were still sinners?

___________________________]

READ ALOUD 1ST JOHN 5:1-15

5:4 – Our faith is the ___________________________ that overcomes the world.

5:14 – Does God grant our prayers all the time? _______________

READING ALOUD 2ND JOHN 1:1-13

READ ALOUD 2ND JOHN 1:1-13

1:10 – If a traveling preacher needs a place to stay, but does not teach everything Jesus taught, should we allow that person to stay with us anyway? _______________

READ ALOUD 3RD JOHN 1:1-15

1:7-8 – What should we do with faithful traveling preachers?_______________________

READ ALOUD JUDE 1-25

1:4 – False teachers slip into a congregation and gradually start teaching something that is not in the Bible. No matter how holy they look and act, they are _______________________________ people.
1:5 – Even though God helped the Jewish people escape _______________ after 400 years of slavery, he still condemned those who disobeyed him. Even _______________ God is not tolerated. He sent them out of heaven and they are now in _______________,
1:15-16 – Grumblers, fault finders, lustful, arrogant people are actually against who? _______________
1:24 – Who is the only one who can keep you from stumbling? _______________

Option 2 – Alone Among Enemies or Continue Worship in a Group

LORD'S SUPPER

Sing or whisper GENEIS 3:24

Read MATTHEW 27:27-37 about soldiers beating Jesus, mocking

him, then nailing him to a cross.

Take a bite of unleavened bread, representing Jesus body tortured on the cross for us.

Pray silently about Jesus' sacrifice, dying in your place for your sins.

Take a sip of grape juice, representing Jesus' blood that dripped away on the cross for you,

Pray silently about your own sins and desire to live more as God wants you to.

Sing or whisper REVELATION 22:1-2

COLLECTION

Prayer: Thank God for your blessings.

Set the money aside to be used to buy a flash drive to put Bible study material on it, or help someone in need that you know.

CLOSING PRAYER

GOD BLESS AND KEEP YOU SAFE UNTIL NEXT SUNDAY

Sunday 52

Visions of Heaven Seen by old John (Revelation))

Option 1 – Worship in a Group

READ ALOUD REVELATION 4:1-11

4:1 – Where was the door? ______________________

4:2-3 – There was a beautiful ______________________
of the ______________________ of God.

4:5 – What two things could be seen and heard coming out
of the throne? ______________________

____

____

4:6 – In front of the throne of God was a sea made of

______________________.

4:11 – The worshipers says God deserved glory, honor, and
power. Why______________________

____

____

READ ALOUD REVELATION 5:1 – 6:17

5:12 – Who did the angels praise with loud voices?
______________________ Compare this with John 1:29. Who
did John the Baptist say was the Lamb of God?

____

6:9 – Beneath the altar in heaven were the souls of who?____________________________________

6:10 – They were crying out to God "How long will you refrain from ____________________ ______ those who killed us on earth?

READ ALOUD REVELATION 7

7:9 – A great multitude in heaven from every nation and tribe on earth was wearing_______________ clothing.

7:10 – They declared they had bee saved because of God and the ___________________.

7:12 – Then everyone bowed to the floor and declared what seven things belong to God forever?

____

____

____

____________________________________   7:14b – How did their robes get to be so white? They had been washed in what?

____

____

7:15 – Out of gratitude, they worship God when?

____

7:16 – In heaven they will never ___________________________ or

____

7:17a – Who is on the throne of God? ___________________________ Compare this was John 1:1-3 & 14.

7:17b – What will God wipe away?

____

READ ALOUD REVELATION 12:1-17

12:7-9 – Who was thrown down from heaven?

____

12:10-11 – When did it happen? (Hint: Look in v. 11) When ___________________ was ___________________________ (Many people claim Satan was thrown down before the world was created. Was Jesus did Jesus lose his blood? Before or after the world was created?)

READ ALOUD REVELATION 19:1-21

19:1-2 – On the Day of Judgment, God will
_____________________ the _____________________ of Christian
martyrs.

19:7-8 – Then will come the marriage of
the_____________________ to his bride Who is the bride of Christ?
(Ephesians 5:24-27)

____

19:11—13 – Who is symbolically depicted as riding a white
horse and wearing a robe of blood?

____

19:16 – And what other name does he have?

____

____

READ ALOUD REVELATION 20:1-15

20:10 – On the Day of Judgment, what will happen to the
devil and for how long?_____________

____

–

20:12 – On the Day of Judgment, God will open the book
of_____________________. There will be other books and they will
contain the good an bad _____________________ of everyone in
the world.

READ ALOUD REVELATION 21:1 - 27

21: 8 – List the 8 kinds of sins that will cause people to cast
into hell. _____________________

____

____

____

____

21:18 – Heaven is described as a city of ________________.
21:19-20 lists 12 kinds of precious stones that will be the
foundation. Compare this with Ephesians 2:20. How many
apostles were there (see Matthew 10)? _____________

READ ALOUD REVELATION 22:1-21

22:1 – What is coming out of the throne of God?

____

22:2 – After God made Adam and Eve leave the Garden of Eden so they would not eat of the Tree of Life, where did he transfer the tree? _______________________________

22:4 – In heaven we will see God face to _____________.

22:4 – In heaven there will be no night because who will always shine on them? _______________

22:16 – Again, Jesus calls him the Morning Star (Lucifer). Don't let anyone tell you that is Satan's name!

22:19 – One last warning to never add to the Bible anything you wish God had said, nor take out of the Bible things you don't want in the Bible. Anyone who does this will not be allowed in the ___________ city.

Option 2 – Alone Among Enemies or Continue Worship in a Group

LORD'S SUPPER

Sing or whisper REVELATION 1:7-8

Read MATTHEW 27:27-37 about soldiers beating Jesus, mocking him, then nailing him to a cross.

Take a bite of unleavened bread, representing Jesus body tortured on the cross for us.

Pray silently about Jesus' sacrifice, dying in your place for your sins.

Take a sip of grape juice, representing Jesus' blood that dripped away on the cross for you,

Pray silently about your own sins and desire to live more as God wants you to.

Sing or whisper REVELATION 21:22

COLLECTION

Prayer: Thank God for your blessings.

Set the money aside to be used to buy a flash drive to put Bible study material on it, or help someone in need that you know.

CLOSING PRAYER

GOD BLESS AND KEEP YOU SAFE UNTIL NEXT SUNDAY

THANK YOU

Thanks for reading my book! I'm so honored that you chose to spend your precious time with my research. You are appreciated. I'm an author who relies on my readers to help spread the word about stories you enjoy and facts you discover. Would you take a few minutes to let your friends know on Facebook, Pinterest... wherever you go online?

Also, each honest review on bookseller websites means a lot to me and helps other readers know if this is a book they might enjoy.

CONNECT WITH THE AUTHOR

I welcome contact from readers which you can do here:

WEBSITE

Pictorial INDEX to all books & categories
https://NorthernLightsPublishingHouse.com
Come read a sample chapter of each book

FACEBOOK

Facebook JUST ME Profile:
https://www.facebook.com/ReadsForAllAges/
Daily inspiration, poster, & prayer

Facebook BOOKS Page
https://www.facebook.com/katheryn.maddox.haddad/
Get in on discounts only known by you

PINTEREST
https://www.pinterest.com/haddad1940/

YOUTUBE
https://www.youtube.com/@KH-bi3fr

email: khaddad1940@gmail.com

ABOUT THE AUTHOR

Katheryn Maddox Haddad grew up in northern USA with its ice and snow, and now lives in India where she doesn't have to shovel sunshine. She basks in 100-degree weather with banana trees, monkeys, and a computer with most of the letters worn off.

Besides the US and India, she has lived in four other countries ~ Korea, Canada, Afghanistan, and Abu Dahbi, and has made short visits to Tokyo and Sri Lanka.

With a bachelor's degree in English, Bible and social science from Harding University and part of a master's degree in Bible from the Harding Graduate School of Theology (including Greek), she also has a master's degree in human relations from Abilene Christian University.

She spends half her day writing and the other half teaching English over the internet worldwide using the Bible as a text book. She has taught nearly 10,000 Muslims over 15 years in the Middle East. Students she has converted to Christianity are in hiding in Afghanistan, Iran, Iraq, Yemen, Jordan, Uzbekistan, Tajikistan, and Palestine. "They are my heroes," she declares.

Currently, she also teaches History of the Hebrews at the MH School of Theology in Punadipadu, Krishna, Andhra Pradesh, India.

She is a member of American Christian Fiction Writers, the American Historical Association, World History Association, World Archaeological College, Association of Ancient Historians, and Archaeological Research Institute.

Oh, and for her next birthday, she plans to ride an elephant.

The best way to thank an author
Is to write a review.

HOW TO WRITE A BOOK REVIEW

...OF A HISTORICAL NOVEL

1) One or two words of your overall impression of the book.
2) A sentence or two of what or who the book is about (main plot).
3) How accurate do you think it was? Why?
4) Was logic or facts used to fill in what is known and not known?
5) What extras were included – maps, drawings, questions, etc.
6) What parts of the book made you think or rethink?
7) What do you think of the author's writing style?
8) Did it have a surprise ending that surprised you?
9) What do you recommend potential readers do about the book?

...OF A NON-FICTION BOOK

1) One or two words of your overall impression of the book.
2) A sentence or two of what or who the book is about.
3) Is it logical?
4) Is it disorganized, jumping from one point to another and back?
5) Were other experts quoted as backups to the point of the book?
6) Did you learn anything new from the book?
7) How did you feel at the end of the book?
8) What do you recommend potential readers do about the book?

POSSIBLE WORDS TO DESCRIBE ANY BOOK OU LOVED

1. Captivating – Holding interest or attention.
2. Challenging – Difficult in an interesting or stimulating way.
3. Compelling – Evoking interest or admiration in a powerful way.

4. Dynamic – Characterized by the unexpected
5. Eloquent – Fluent or persuasive in writing.
6. Engrossing – Absorbing all one's attention or interest.
7. Enlightening – Providing greater knowledge or understanding.
8. Entertaining – Providing enjoyment or amusement.
9. Fascinating – Extremely interesting or attractive.
10. Gripping – Holding one's attention intensely. A page turner
11. Insightful –Showing a deep understanding or awareness.
12. Intriguing – Arousing one's curiosity or interest.
13. Moving – Stirring deep emotions - sadness or sympathy.
14. Profound – Having deep insight or understanding.
15. Revealing – Insight or information not previously known.
16. Suspenseful – Involving anticipation, and anxiety.
17. Thought-provoking – Stimulating careful consideration
18. Unforgettable – Impossible to forget; very memorable.

POSSIBLE WORDS TO DESCRIBE ANY BOOK
YOU HATED (well....)

1. Ambiguous - Unclear or inexact.
2. Clichéd – Lacking originality or freshness; overused.
3. Confusing – Difficult to understand; unclear.
4. Dry – Dull and uninteresting.
5. Dull – Boring; lacking interest or excitement.
6. Overwhelming –Overpowering.
7. Predictable – Able to be foreseen or anticipated.
8. Superficial – Lacking depth or substance; shallow.
9. Underwhelming – Failing to impress or excite.
10. Wordy – Using or expressing in more words than are needed.

(...I'll love you anyway)

BUY YOUR NEXT BOOK NOW

HISTORICAL NOVELS & STORY BOOKS
Series of 8: They Met Jesus
Ongoing Series of 8: Intrepid Men of God
Mysteries of the Empire with Klaudius & Hektor
Series of 10: A Child's Life of Christ
Series of 10: A Child's Bible Heroes
Series of 8: A Child's Bible Kids

WORLDWIDE HISTORICAL RESEARCH FOR
DOCUMENTARY, THESIS, NOVEL & SCREENPLAY WRITERS

TOPICAL
Applied Christianity: Handbook 500 Good Works
Christianity or Islam? The Contrast
The Holy Spirit: 592 Verses Examined
Inside the Hearts of Bible Women-Reader+Audio+Leader
Revelation: A Love Letter From God
Worship Changes Since 1st Century + Worship 1sr Century Way
Was Jesus God? (Why Evil)
365 Life-Changing Scriptures Day by Date
The Road to Heaven
The Lord's Supper: 52 Readings with Prayers

RESTORATION REPRINT LIBRARY
Instrumental Music in the Public Worship of the [Presbyterian] Church, 1880
Best of Alexander Campbell's Millennial Harbinger, 1830-1839
Writings of and About Churches of Christ 14th to 17th Centuries England

FUN BOOKS
Bible Puzzles, Bible Song Book, Bible Numbers

TOUCHING GOD SERIES
365 Golden Bible Thoughts: God's Heart to Yours
365 Pearls of Wisdom: God's Soul to Yours
365 Silver-Winged Prayers: Your Spirit to God's

SURVEY SERIES: EASY BIBLE WORKBOOKS
→Old Testament & New Testament Surveys,
→Questions You Have Asked

GENEALOGY: CLIMB YOUR FAMILY TREE WITHOUT FALLING OUT
Volume I & 2: Beginner-Intermediate & Colonial-Medieval